Routledge Revivals

Helping Young Children with Behaviour Difficulties

First published in 1983, *Helping Young Children with Behaviour Difficulties* aims to help all teachers involved with groups of young children to deal constructively with any behaviour problems they may encounter in their daily work. The book provides guidance on—selecting children in need of special help; finding out comprehensive information about the child's difficulties; and planning and carrying out measures which will lead to the better adjustment of the child in the group or classroom.

Illustrative case studies are used to show the value of the guidance offered in this book. All approaches emphasise the value of a positive, consistent, and sustained teacher-child relationship, both on a one-to-one basis and in group activities. The handbook also emphasises the desirability of using the child's strengths as a basis from which their difficulties can be tackled. It highlights the need for clear aims and objectives in planning intervention, the importance of flexibility and careful record-keeping, and the value of working closely with parents. The book adopts a systematic approach throughout and includes several detailed assessment schedules, recording charts, and a behaviour checklist developed by the authors.

Helping Young Children with Behaviour Difficulties

A Handbook

M. Chazan, A.F. Laing, J. Jones, G.C. Harper and J. Bolton

Routledge
Taylor & Francis Group
Routledge Revivals

First published in 1983
by Croom Helm Ltd

This edition first published in 2025 by Routledge
4 Park Square, Milton Park, Abingdon, Oxon, OX14 4RN

and by Routledge
605 Third Avenue, New York, NY 10158

Routledge is an imprint of the Taylor & Francis Group, an informa business

A Library of Congress record exists under LCCN:

ISBN: 978-1-041-16466-1 (hbk)
ISBN: 978-1-003-68505-0 (ebk)
ISBN: 978-1-041-16528-6 (pbk)

Book DOI 10.4324/9781003685050

Helping Young Children with Behaviour Difficulties

A HANDBOOK

M. Chazan, A.F. Laing, J. Jones, G.C. Harper
and J.Bolton

CROOM HELM London & Canberra
UNIVERSITY PARK PRESS Baltimore

Croom Helm Ltd, Provident House, Burrell Row,
Beckenham, Kent BR3 1AT

British Library Cataloguing in Publication in Data

Helping young children with behaviour difficulties.
1. Child psychopathology
I. Chazan, M.
618.92'89 RJ499

ISBN 0-7099-0777-X

Published in North America by
UNIVERSITY PARK PRESS
300 North Charles Street,
Baltimore, Maryland 21201

ISBN 0-8391-1914-3

Library of Congress Card Number: 83-080750

Printed and bound in Great Britain

CONTENTS

List of Tables and Figures
Preface

INTRODUCTION

1. USING THIS HANDBOOK

(a) Aim of handbook 3
(b) Plan of handbook 3
(c) How to use this handbook 4

PART ONE

LOOKING AT CHILDREN'S DIFFICULTIES

2. RECOGNISING BEHAVIOUR DIFFICULTIES

(a) What behaviour should we expect of children of this age? 8
(b) Which children are likely to need special attention because of their behaviour? 10
(c) Using the Swansea Behaviour Checklist (Schedule 1) 14

3. UNDERSTANDING THE PROBLEM

A. Background

(a) What does assessment involve? 16
(b) Factors associated with behaviour problems in young children 17
(c) A cautionary note 29
(d) Keeping records 29

B. Practical Steps

(e) Behaviour Assessment (Schedule 2) 33
(f) General Assessment (Schedule 3) 37
(g) Talking to Parents (Schedule 4) 39
(h) Help from Others (Schedule 5) 49

PART TWO

DECIDING WHAT TO DO

4. USING CREATIVE AND LANGUAGE ACTIVITIES

(a) Creative Activities 60
(b) Language Activities 67

5. SPECIAL HELP IN THE CLASSROOM

Introduction 81

(1) Play Activities 92
(2) Behaviour Modification 128
(3) Problem-solving Approaches 177

6. MAKING A PLAN OF ACTION 203

APPENDICES

A. Schedules 1 - 5 257
B. Record Book 290
C. Explanatory Notes 303

GENERAL INDEX 307

CHILD STUDIES INDEX 311

TABLES AND FIGURES

Tables

3.1 Help for children with special needs 53

5.1 Stages of imaginative play 111

Figures

5.1(a) and 5.1(b) Graphing changes resulting from intervention 143

5.2 The frequency of Anna's isolated play 156

5.3(a) Malcolm's whining behaviour 158

5.3(b) Malcolm's clinging behaviour 158

5.4 Lucy's constructive activity before and after interventions 160

6.1 Frequency of Jane's isolated behaviour (first intervention) 228

6.2 Frequency of Jane's isolated behaviour (second intervention) 231

PREFACE

In our research work in a wide range of nursery schools and classes, we have found that many of the staff feel a need for help and advice in the management of children presenting problems of behaviour. This Handbook is intended as a response to this need, and its preparation was made possible through a grant from the Department of Education and Science, which funded a two year project, beginning on 1st January 1980 and located in the Department of Education of the University College of Swansea, on 'The Management of Behaviour Problems in Young Children' (the Welsh Office gave a supplementary grant to enable a Welsh version of the Handbook to be produced).

In compiling the Handbook, our main aim has been to provide nursery staff with material that will be of practical use and will encourage them to think positively and constructively about ways of handling children with behaviour problems. We have tried to avoid a 'cook-book' approach or suggesting that there is one right way of solving any child's difficulties. As far as possible, we have used non-technical language. We hope that the Handbook will be useful to teachers and others in nursery schools and classes, reception classes in infant schools, and playgroups, as well as in relevant training courses. As we emphasise in the Handbook, the principles underlying the management of behaviour problems are not very different from those which should guide staff in dealing with children in general. We would hope, therefore, that the Handbook will not only be found of value in the handling of individual children needing special help, but will also provide guidelines for nursery staff in their daily work, whether or not they have a serious behaviour problem in their group.

Explanations have been provided in Appendix III (Explanatory Notes) of terms specific to the British scene.

The preliminary draft of the Handbook was used experimentally in a number of nursery groups, and the final version owes a great deal to the perceptive feed-back given by the staff involved. We should like to express our thanks to them for their help and also to the Department of Education and Science, the Welsh Office and the members of Liaison Committee D for their support throughout the project. The research team also gratefully acknowledges the generous help given, in the areas concerned, by the Chief Education Officers and members of their staffs; the playgroup advisers and organisers in the region; the children and parents involved; and Mrs. Sheila Morgan and Mrs. Ann White, the secretaries attached to the project.

It should be noted that the names of the children mentioned in the Handbook are fictitious code-names and not their actual names, and that all views expressed (other than those attributed to specific sources) are those of the writers alone.

Maurice Chazan
Alice F. Laing

INTRODUCTION

Chapter 1

USING THIS HANDBOOK

(a) Aim of Handbook

The aim of this Handbook is to help nursery school teachers and others responsible for looking after groups of young children to deal constructively with any behaviour problems they may meet in their daily work. The Handbook provides guidance on (1) picking out the children who are especially in need of help; (2) finding out as much as possible about the nature of the child's behaviour difficulties; and (3) planning and carrying out measures which are likely to lead to the better adjustment of the child in the group or classroom.

While we do not want to put undue emphasis on the problems of young children, we believe that it is very important to prevent, through early action, the development of behaviour and attitudes which may interfere with a child's adequate social functioning. Although in some cases outside assistance may be needed, in all cases the adult in regular contact with the child has a vital role to play in fostering harmonious emotional and social development. In preparing this book, we have tried to put ourselves in the place of nursery staff who are anxious to give special help to an individual child while attending to the needs of all members of a sizeable group. Throughout, we put a great deal of stress on the desirability of maintaining a positive attitude towards children who are difficult or unresponsive, and we underline the value of a systematic approach towards helping these children.

(b) Plan of Book

Incorporated in the handbook are several assessment schedules (Appendix A) and a Record Book (Appendix B). Their relationship with the various sections of the Handbook and instructions for using the book are to be found below.

Sufficient numbers of assessment schedules and record books for your class may be duplicated by any method you find convenient.

(c) How to use this Book

The handbook is designed to guide you through the steps of assessing a particular child's behaviour difficulties and planning and implementing an individual programme which you hope will lead to better adjustment in the future.

We suggest that you might begin by quickly skimming through the book, more to get an idea of its aims and basic layout than to grasp all the detail. Once you understand something of its nature and structure then it will be helpful for you to look at each section again more thoroughly. You may find it makes more sense if you have a particular child in mind while you are doing this preliminary reading.

Set out below are step-by-step instructions on how to use this book to tackle the behavioural difficulties of a child in your care.

1. (a) Read the section "Recognising Behaviour Difficulties" (pp. 8-15).

(b) Fill in Schedule 1 : Swansea Behaviour Checklist (Appendix A, pp. 257-261) for class or group and select child/ren needing further assessment.

Omit this identification stage if you already have a child in mind.

2. (a) Read the section "Understanding the Problem" (pp. 16-57).

(b) Complete Assessment Schedules 2-5 (Appendix A, pp. 262-289).

(c) Complete the appropriate section in the Record Book (Appendix B, pp. 290-302).

3. (a) Read the section "Deciding What To Do" (pp.58-254).

(b) Select most suitable approach/es from

Play Activities (pp. 92-128)
Behaviour Modification (pp. 128-177)
Problem-Solving Approaches (pp. 177-202).

You may also like to consider some of the ideas contained in Creative Activities (pp. 60-67) and Language Activities (pp. 67-80).

4. (a) Read section "Making a Plan of Action" (pp.203-254).

(b) Work out a programme of activities and write down details of your plan in the Record Book.

(c) Implement your plan of action.

5. (a) Monitor the child/ren's progress in appropriate pages of the Record Book.

(b) Review progress periodically and alter your programme if necessary.

PART ONE

LOOKING AT CHILDREN'S DIFFICULTIES

Chapter 2

RECOGNIZING BEHAVIOUR DIFFICULTIES

(a) What behaviour should we expect of children of this age?

Children of nursery school age have already come a long way in their emotional and social development. By the age of 3 or 4, most children will be able to accept a limited amount of separation from their parents without undue anxiety. They will be well on the road to gaining some measure of independence and self-control. They wll respond to friendly adults other than those with whom they have close and intimate bonds, and show great pleasure in conversing with them. Most will be reasonably easy to manage both at home and in a group outside. On the whole they will enjoy opportunities for mixing with other children, some being happy in any gathering of young children, but many preferring a small group of familiar companions. They will be wide-awake and alert, seeking to engage in activities and enjoying play of various kinds - individual and social, constructive and messy, reality and make-believe. To some extent, they will share with others and be prepared to take turns; many children of this age group will show a surprising degree of consideration for others. They will take some pride in their personal possessions and show persistence at tasks that arouse their interest. The 'typical' nursery school child will be bright, happy and cheerful, generally free from excessive anger and fear.

However, we would be unwise to expect too much conformity, co-operation and tranquillity from three to four-year-olds, who still have much to learn about self-control and many social skills yet to acquire. Children at this stage will often be frustrated by their inability to do everything they wish to do, or to get everything that they want, so that they may now and then resort to temper tantrums or to the destruction of objects lying to hand. Sometimes, when they realise that their mother is not around, they will show some anxiety and want to cling to the nearest familiar adult. Unexpected events, strangers, loud noises or unfriendly animals may show that they are capable of 'unreasonable' fears. They will not always be as tolerant as they usually are, or be prepared to wait their turn as patiently as their elders. When tired or bored, their behaviour may be very troublesome, and when really upset, they may wet the bed or have a nightmare. In short, almost all young children present some behaviour problems, and tears are never far away even in the case of the happiest child.

You should bear in mind, too, that children's behaviour varies greatly according to the person they are with and the situation they are in. Everyone will have difficulty with some children at one time or another. A child's relationships tend to be very person-specific, that is, they will react positively to some adults but less so to others. It is quite normal for nursery staff to get on better with some children than others, and you should not feel a sense of failure if you are unable to deal with a child.

We should not, therefore, rush into calling children 'real problems' merely because they do not consistently maintain an adult-like standard of 'good' behaviour, or because they do not always conform. It is difficult to know precisely what patterns of behaviour we should consider to be of significance in a child's development. Some behaviour problems will disappear with time, others may eventually become serious. It would be useful to be able to distinguish between transitory and more permanent problems, but this is usually impossible in the age group with which we are concerned. However, it would seem that children who present <u>many</u> or <u>more extreme</u> behaviour problems at the pre-school stage are 'at risk' of having later difficulties if they do not receive appropriate help. It is all too easy, also, for any behaviour which interferes with effective functioning or normal social interaction to become fixed. So even if we are unable to <u>predict</u> the consequences of young children's behaviour, it is important to help children in their <u>current</u> functioning and adjustment. Such help must be given in the context of understanding the child's development as a whole, and in a manner which preserves the child's dignity.

The first step is to recognise those children who show more than the usual problems characteristic of their age group, not for the sake of picking them out but to gain better insight into the nature of their difficulties and to give them the attention they need.

(b) Which children are likely to need special attention because of their behaviour?
The number of children in any nursery class or playgroup in need of special attention because of their behaviour will vary greatly from group to group. Some classes and groups give priority to children who have developmental difficulties of many kinds, including physical and mental handicap, and the adults in charge will, accordingly, be prepared to cope with a fairly high proportion of behaviour problems. Classes or playgroups serving areas where social disadvantage is common may well have a higher than usual proportion of children presenting problems of adjustment.

It is not possible, therefore, to give you any precise indication of how many children in your class or group are likely to require help because of their behaviour. All one can say is that, on the basis of surveys which have been carried out so far, about 1 child in 10 is likely to need some attention because of poor social or emotional adjustment at the nursery school stage. Not every class or group will contain children who show behaviour difficulties, but if you have a class of 16 to 20 children, you may well find that at least one or two of them come into this category, though their problems will mostly be moderate rather than severe.

Types of problem
It is not desirable, and rarely useful, to think of children's problems in terms of distinct types or categories. Most children show a wide range of behaviour, at times being quiet and inhibited, at others lively and outgoing. But the children likely to be in need of help will, in the main, be those who are:

(i) shy/withdrawn/timid
(ii) immature/dependent
(iii) restless/overactive
(iv) aggressive/anti-social/destructive

Recognizing Behaviour Difficulties

(i) Shy/withdrawn children

> Richard (aged 4) tends to be passive, withdrawn and dreamy, over-anxious and timid. Occasionally he is difficult to make contact with. He watches others play but makes no attempt to join in; he rarely talks to others. He lacks confidence, and has difficulty in coping with new situations. He will follow his teacher around for a while, not saying a word; often he is content to play on his own for long periods. His teachers consider that this is not an extreme problem, 'for Richard does not actively shun other children's company but seems not to need it'. He has good hand-eye co-ordination and good self-help skills, enjoying puzzles of various kinds.

Shy, withdrawn children like Richard do not cause any trouble to others in the group, and so they may easily escape notice, or at least fail to receive much attention. However, some of them are already adopting ways of responding to their environment which are unhelpful to their general development and which will prevent them from making the most of their school experiences. Such children tend to keep very much to themselves and to say little or nothing to others, either adults or peers; they are unwilling to take part in the usual activities of the group, and may not be making a relationship with anyone. They may lack confidence, being timid and fearful, especially in new situations, and they frequently show anxiety and tension. Some, though not by any means all, will appear unhappy and miserable much of the time.

Many shy, withdrawn children will, however, come out of their shells, perhaps only very gradually, if they are not rushed and if they are encouraged gently but systematically. Most, in fact, want to join in with others and to be like them, but cannot bring themselves to do so because of their lack of self-confidence; all will need more than the usual amount of adult attention.

A very small number of children (about 4 or 5 in 10,000) show extreme withdrawal and an almost total unwillingness to communicate with others, as well as exhibiting a variety of strange mannerisms. These children, referred to as 'autistic', will certainly need a full medical and psychological assessment.

(ii) Immature/dependent children

Jonathan (aged 3) frequently clings to adults for assurance and does not attempt to attend to his own needs. He tries to join in group activities but finds it very difficult because of his inability to communicate adequately. He is also prone to temper tantrums, and is extremely restless, nearly always on the move. He rarely perseveres long enough to make the most of any activity. He can be destructive and disruptive. He has been observed to crawl around the classroom during 'Play School' making babyish noises. He enjoys water play with one other child, and being alone in the home corner.

Children such as Jonathan tend not to be as independent and self-reliant as most of their contemporaries. They look for adult support and re-assurance far more than others of their age, particularly when faced by anything new or unfamiliar. Often, they are not happy to let mother go when they come into the group, and seem to be worrying all the time about her absence. They frequently cling to the nearest adult, and require an excessive amount of comforting physical contact. You will certainly be aware of any very immature children in your group.

(iii) Restless/overactive children

William (aged 4) is highly restless and over-active. His concentration is fleeting, and he disrupts group play continuously. He is always on the move, boisterous and wearing to others. He is over-excitable and often disobedient. He is very demanding in nearly all situations, and is generally shunned and disliked by others. He has no understanding of the need to be careful with delicate objects and tends to suck and chew toys baby fashion. He does respond to adult attention and likes water and dough play as well as riding a tricycle, but his language is poor, he walks and runs awkwardly and he is unable to cater for his basic self-needs.

You will not have much difficulty, either, in identifying restless, overactive children like William in your group, though you will need to distinguish between those who are restless because they are bored and those who cannot settle to anything and move around a great deal most of the time. Most young children show a lot of restlessness and mobility, but those who are overactive in an aimless way are a particular cause for concern, because this kind of behaviour is likely to interfere with their learning. Such children will lack concentration, be very easily distracted and be unable to work towards a definite goal. In the more extreme cases, the child will not sit still for a moment, run about without purpose, and handle toys and other things in a random manner. Sometimes restlessness and overactivity are combined with anti-social and destructive behaviour, to which we now turn.

(iv) Aggressive/anti-social/destructive children

> Eric (aged 4) is aggressive, anti-social, disobedient and generally demanding. He is frequently rude, and offers verbal aggression if thwarted or frustrated. He hits other children, and indulges in frequent temper tantrums. He is unable to share toys, and over-reacts if his demands are not met. He seeks to be the centre of attention, but tends to dislike physical contact. He functions well in a number of areas, including language and self-help skills, and has good mobility and co-ordination.

Most children of nursery school age have occasional temper tantrums, especially when they are tired or frustrated, though they tend to indulge in bad temper more at home than in the school or playgroup. Most young children, too, will at times be anti-social and even destructive, seeming to enjoy damaging their own or other people's things. Some of the children in your care, however, will behave like Eric, seeming to go out of their way to be aggressive or destructive. Their general way of behaving will be to grab toys from others, to seek to annoy them in a variety of ways, often hitting and banging them. They will readily scream and shout at the slightest provocation, or with none. No play materials will be safe with them for long.

They will be a very disturbing influence in a group, and be unpopular with the other children.

Look for Strengths

We have given a generalised picture of various types of behaviour problem you are likely to have to deal with in your group. Because this picture has been so negative, we would again stress that every child has strengths and good points and that you should always keep these in mind when you are seeking to identify children with behaviour problems in your group.

(c) Using the Swansea Behaviour Checklist

Provided that you feel that you have got to know the children in your class or group well enough (e.g. you have had them in your care for at least a month) we suggest that you should complete the Swansea Behaviour Checklist (Schedule 1) for each child (see Appendix A, pp.257-261).

The Behaviour Checklist is intended to help you to identify those children in your class/group who seem to need special attention. It is meant as a brief screening device, not to provide a detailed record of the child. However, the checklist does give you scope for recording the child's strengths as well as any problems which he may be presenting. This is because, as we have already pointed out, it is important that, from the outset, you should adopt and maintain a positive attitude towards the child - something which is not always easy to do. You will also find that the child's strengths will be a good starting point for any procedures you adopt to help the child towards better adjustment.

You should find that completing the checklist will help you in clarifying your thoughts about the children in your charge. But if you think that filling in the checklist would not add greatly to your recognition of any behaviour problems in your group, you may omit this step and proceed to the assessment and action stages without this formal preliminary screening.

If you decide to complete the Behaviour Checklist, this should not take up a great deal of your time. All you have to do at this stage is (1) to tick the ten descriptions which most closely approximate to the child's current behaviour, (2) to record your ratings to give a mini-profile of behaviour and (3) to answer two questions about the child. You may find that the descriptions given do not fit a particular child exactly, but mark those which give the best description. In order to keep the checklist a reasonable length, we have used categories which are narrower than would be possible in a longer schedule.

Most children of nursery school age will score a number of b's, and no scoring system will precisely identify those children who need help. But, on the basis of our experience with the checklist to date, we suggest that you should think carefully about any children who record 2 or more 'c's or 6 or more 'b's. It is very likely that such children would benefit from further assessment. Consider also any children who score 4 'b's in the aggressive or withdrawn categories.

Chapter 3

UNDERSTANDING THE PROBLEM

BACKGROUND

(a) What Does Assessment Involve?

The identification of children with emotional or behaviour problems in your nursery group is the first step in gaining insight into the needs of these children. The next step is to make a careful assessment of the problem. A comprehensive assessment involves (a) describing in precise terms both the nature of the difficulties presented and the context in which these occur; (b) getting to know something of the child's home background; (c) drawing up a profile of the many aspects of the child's development; (d) highlighting those factors which seem to be associated with the child's behaviour; and (e) trying, from what is known about the child and the background, to make inferences about the child's needs and to draw up a programme of action which will lead to better adjustment.

The Warnock Report stresses that there are four main requirements of effective assessment. These are:

1. parents must be closely involved;
2. assessment should aim to discover how a child learns and responds over a period, and not merely record performance on one occasion;
3. assessment must include the investigation of any aspects of a child's performance that is causing concern;
4. the family circumstances as a whole must be taken into account in any assessment of a child's needs.

It can be added that all too often lengthy assessment procedures are carried out without any further specific action following, but unless identification, assessment and intervention are regarded as closely linked in every case, much of the effort put into the first two stages may be wasted.

A full assessment of a child's special needs is a complex matter, and in many cases requires the expertise of professionals outside the nursery group, for example, those working in the school psychological service. However, those in daily contact with the child - parents and nursery staff - can always contribute a great deal to assessment. Even when outside help is called in, the professionals involved will spend only a limited amount of time with a child and his or her family and will rely on parents and nursery staff for much of the information on which they will base their assessment of a case. They need to do this, since children behave very differently in different situations. Many children who are aggressive or destructive in the nursery group are perfectly well-behaved and fully controlled in the one-to-one situation, for example when tested or observed at play by a psychologist in an office or clinic. Some children, too, who are happy and co-operative in the nursery group present serious problems at home, and some who are no trouble at home present difficulties outside. Whoever is involved, assessment is always a matter for team-work, with each one concerned taking a broad view of the situation while making a particular contribution. It is necessary, too, to exercise caution in reaching conclusions about the causes of behaviour, as there are many factors associated with behaviour problems in young children. These will now be discussed.

(b) Factors Associated with Behaviour Problems in Young Children

It is rarely possible to state with precision what has caused a child to behave in a particular way at any time. Even in cases which seem, on the surface, to be straightforward, careful assessment often shows a combination of factors to be at work rather than one definite factor. The 'precipitating' factor which appears to have been directly responsible for an outburst may be less important than other 'predisposing' factors which have helped to bring about an explosive situation. For example, a mild reproof by an adult may provoke a violent temper tantrum in a child, but it may well be the case that the child is reacting to a prolonged experience of stress at home rather than to being told off in the nursery group. Further, it is often difficult to sort out cause and effect, whether, for instance, a speech difficulty is causing emotional disturbance, or is caused by it. Nor should we always look for extreme or 'abnormal' circumstances in the life of the child who is a problem. Children have to face 'normal' stresses of many kinds, e.g. when they have to start something new, such as going to a nursery group for the first time, or when there are changes in the structure of the family, perhaps as a result of illness or bereavement.

Temperamental differences. We tend to emphasise the environmental factors related to disturbance in childhood, probably because they are easier to pinpoint than other factors. But we should not forget that children are temperamentally different, and that temperament or emotional disposition seems to be genetically determined to quite an extent, that is, it has a major 'innate' component. Individuals, even within the same family, vary widely in their susceptibility to emotional disturbance, and considerable differences in temperament have been found in very young children. Some are very placid and rarely cause any trouble, others are easily excited and over-react to quite ordinary occurrences; some are nearly always happy and cheerful, others are often miserable or moody; and while some are easily 'put off' and readily distracted from the activities in which they are engaged- others show much persistence, even in the face of difficulties. The interaction between adult and child is certainly affected by temperamental make-up on both sides: most adults find that they get on better with some children than with others. We now tend to think in terms of interaction - a two-way process - rather than of the child merely responding to his environment. Children help to shape their own environment in many ways - for example, a difficult child may cause a mother's attitude, which was positive to begin with, to become rejecting.

At this stage, you may like to consider whether there are any kinds of behaviour in children which you find hard to tolerate, or any children with particular temperaments whom you cannot bring yourself to like. If this is the case, think about possible reasons for your reactions. Understanding one's own response to individual differences tends to help in dealing effectively with children.

Physical factors. Physical factors, especially handicap or ill-health, may also play a part in the causation of behaviour disturbance. An association is sometimes found between brain-damage and hyperactivity, and although 'brain-damage' is perhaps too readily used as an explanation for behaviour problems, it is desirable that a medical opinion should be sought in cases of extreme restlessness and mobility (as it should be in any case where physical factors are involved and the child is not already under medical supervision). Physically handicapped or delicate children will often be frustrated at not being able to do what others are capable of doing, and while most of this frustruation is unavoidable, adults can help greatly by making sure that such children are given tasks at which they can succeed.

Delayed general development. Frustration and feelings of inadequacy are also the frequent experience of children who are mentally handicapped or slow in their general development. These children often have difficulty in controlling their impulses and in assessing the demands of the external world; and they take longer than others to achieve some measure of independence. Slow learners are likely to have more behavioural difficulties than normal children, and these difficulties tend to persist over a much longer period of time. They are also likely to be retarded in speech and language, and as a result their ability to communicate with and relate to others will be impaired, and they will have less idea of themselves as individuals. Indeed, delayed language development is bound to have generally adverse effects on the child's emotional and social growth (pp.68-70). Often the key to the management of behaviour problems in slow-learning children is providing them with plenty of well-graded activities, carefully planned to promote their motor, sensory, linguistic and cognitive development.

Brian (aged 4 years) appears to be extremely immature in all aspects of development, more like a two-year-old than a four-year-old. He did not walk until he was 2+ and had no speech at all until 3+; his language development continues to be slow. At home he has many temper tantrums; in school, although being kept occupied reduces the occurrence of such tantrums, he becomes frustrated when he cannot communicate his wishes and needs. He is lethargic, frequently clings to adults for assurance, and rarely plays with other children.

Factors in the nursery group. As the Warnock Report points out, behaviour problems may be brought about or accentuated by factors relating to the school, such as its premises, organisation or staff. It is always worthwhile for nursery staff, without becoming over-introspective, to consider whether attitudes, classroom practices or other factors connected with the nature of the nursery group have anything to do with a child's behaviour problems. It is even possible that factors relating to the nursery group itself may be of major importance in the causation of disturbed behaviour. Children in nursery groups are, for the most part, handled with great sensitivity by the adults in whose care they are placed. Nevertheless, they may react badly to uncomfortable conditions in the nursery setting or to the way they are treated by adults or peers in the nursery group. To illustrate, children may be upset by

(a) over-criticism by adults when any misdemeanour occurs, especially if the emphasis is put on blaming the child's intrinsic nature - 'I've never come across such a terrible child in all my life!' rather than specific actions, thus contributing to the building up of a negative self-image. It is all too easy for a whole staff to label a child as 'naughty' and a 'nuisance' to include only a catalogue of misdemeanours in any records kept, and to have little time for such a child, who will soon feel rejected;

(b) carelessly expressed remarks or even covertly-held attitudes relating to children from particular social backgrounds or ethnic groups;

(c) receiving much less attention from adults than others in the group, which may well happen if a child does not demand attention in some way;

(d) adults making excessive fuss when a child is clumsy, is incontinent or has some other accident, causing embarrassment and undue guilt-feelings;

(e) listening to very frightening stories - while most three to five-year-olds take these in their stride, some children, particularly those from highly disturbed backgrounds, may find them anxiety-provoking;

(f) excessive demands made on them resulting in frustration at failure to perform a task;

(g) being in a highly authoritarian and inflexibly-organised group, which allows little freedom or choice of activity.

As the child matures, acceptance by other children in the group becomes increasingly important. Young children are not as conscious of individual differences, and in the nursery group, social rejection rarely results from being handicapped or a member of an ethnic minority group. However, some children may be the victims of aggression, or, being somewhat aggressive themselves, have retaliatory action directed at them. It is not always possible to prevent a child from being upset by other children or from becoming socially isolated or rejected, but timely and tactful intervention by an adult may help in potentially explosive situations.

Even without any of the upsetting experiences outlined above, some children find it difficult to accept the initial separation from the mother and may take a long time to adjust to the physical, cognitive and social demands of the nursery group. Putting pressure on these children may exacerbate or prolong their difficulties in adjusting to being with other children.

It is, of course, undesirable to overprotect children within the nursery group or to encourage them to avoid meeting normal challenges. It is also important not to exaggerate the potential sources of upset, but incidents that seem trivial to the adult may cause considerable distress to a child and even result in unwillingness to attend a nursery group. In the main, however, disturbance in young children is likely to be related to factors in the home, where influences have the greatest impact. The extent to which the young child's basic needs are met depend a great deal on family background, and some of the many situations at home which may adversely affect the child's emotional development will be outlined below.

Factors in the Home. Clearly, if children are not given enough to eat, or if they are otherwise neglected or physically abused at home, their emotional growth will be affected, but there are many other family situations which have a bearing on a child's behaviour. Increasingly, children are growing up in homes where the even tenor of family life is disturbed by unemployment, or in homes upset by divorce. All too often, one family problem leads to another, so that a variety of adverse factors is frequently found rather than a single one, as the following cases illustrate:

> The family background of Jonathan (aged 3), an immature, over-dependent child with speech and language problems and frequent temper tantrums, has several adverse features. He was premature, and because of his very low birth weight (3 lbs.) was kept in hospital for several weeks. He was re-admitted to hospital at 10 months, for reasons not entirely clear, and suffered separation from his parents for over a month. His mother finds it difficult to cope, and Jonathan sometimes arrives at school unkempt and unwashed, although at other times he will be well clad and spotless. His father recently had a heart attack, a cause of great worry to the family, as there is the possibility that

> he may lose both his job and his home (attached to his job) as a result of his ill-health. Appointments at clinics for speech therapy are rarely kept.
>
> William (aged 4), who is disruptive, over-active and unsociable, is the middle child of three, having a brother of 5½ and a younger sister (18 months) with cystic fibrosis. His father, a semi-invalid, is considerably older than his mother, both parents coming from poor back-grounds themselves. The house is materially and hygienically of a very low standard, and is kept under super-vision by health visitors as well as social workers. William has had little intellectual stimulus, routine or dis-cipline at home, and according to his teacher, he over-reacts to the attention given to him by adults in the nursery. He is emotionally, linguistically, socially and cognitively immature as a result of his poor home background and lack of training.

It is not possible here to discuss all the factors in the home which may affect social and emotional development, but most nursery groups will contain some children feeling strain or pressure as a result of one or more of the following:

1. Unsatisfactory housing conditions. In addition to poverty, housing conditions can be regarded as a major factor in the break-up of families and the causation of ill-health, strain and disharmony in the home, with consequent adverse effects on children's emotional adjustment. The social development of young children will be es-pecially impaired by a lack of space and opportunity for play and other activities both within and out-side the home. Living in high-rise, and even low-rise, flats is a particular disadvantage for under-fives. Their activities are severly restricted; they are often isolated, with few opportunities to mix with other children; and their mothers tend to suffer from frustration, loneliness and depression. Where there is overcrowding, with children perhaps having to share the same bed, fatigue and

irritability in the family circle may well be the result. Children coming to the nursery group from disadvantageous social conditions may well have little idea of how to play; they will tend to be destructive rather than constructive in their activities. Other possible effects of social disadvantage include inadequate language skills and restless or anti-social behaviour, though it must be emphasised that such adverse effects do not inevitably result from adverse living conditions.

2. A lack of routine at home. Some children are given plenty of warmth and affection at home, but are brought up in an atmosphere of chaos, with little routine or regularity in times of meals or of going to bed. Young children need a coherent framework of routine, if one tempered by occasional flexibility, and those who frequently stay up late at night may come to the nursery group over-tired, irritable and restless (see William).

3. Prolonged separation from the mother. If the normal bonds of attachment linking mother and child are broken, perhaps because the mother has to go into hospital or for other reasons, the child may show signs of acute distress, sometimes followed by a period of apathy. In some cases, developmental progress, especially in language and social responsiveness, is slowed down. These effects are not necessarily long-lasting, but are likely to be manifest in the child's behaviour outside the home at least for a time. Children suffering a fairly lengthy separation from the mother will need understanding and sensitive handling in the nursery group (see Jonathan).

4. Domestic crises. Even the very young child can be disturbed by open rows or a general atmosphere of tension at home. Parental disharmony has been found to be highly associated with behaviour problems presented by young children at home, and may also result in a child showing considerable anxiety and tension in the nursery group (see Jonathan).

> Nicola, aged 4, is restless, lacks concentration and deliberately destroys her own and other children's property. She is the youngest of a second family. Both families have been closely-knit, although the eldest daughter had left home to live with her natural father because she could not get

on with her mother. Nicola very much misses this sister. Although mother only works part-time, Nicola reacts badly to her going out to work. Nicola generally seems happy and carefree, and comes to school well-dressed. However, she often shows signs of insecurity and immaturity. That her insecurity was not unwarranted was demonstrated by her parents splitting up during the course of the project.

5. Parental illness. Parental ill-health, physical or mental, may contribute to the causation of behaviour problems in young children (see Jonathan and William). It is easy to see how, for example, the relationship between mother and child can be damaged if ill-health prevents the mother from giving the child adequate care, or makes her irritable or moody. Mental illness in the parents, in particular, has been found to be strongly linked with the presence of behaviour problems in pre-school children. As a consequence of mental ill-health, parents may not only be erratic in their handling of the child, but may present a model of anxiety, tension, aggression or even bizarre behaviour which the child will be ready to copy. Not infrequently, a child's behaviour in the nursery group is a reflection of parental behaviour.

6. Unsatisfactory parental attitudes and practices. It is not possible to state with certainty what the association is between parental attitudes and practices and the child's emotional development, and it is important not to make over-simplified interpretations of the relationship between parental behaviour and children's behaviour. However, there is no doubt that most children react sensitively to the way in which they are treated by their parents. Many parents show a wide range of feelings and practices in relation even to a single child rather than go to extremes, but certain attitudes and practices are highly likely to result in problem behaviour in the child. In particular, three main patterns can be highlighted - (a) rejection; (b) over-protection; and (c) inconsistency.

(a) Rejection
There are many possible reasons for parental rejection of a child. For instance, the child may be unwanted, being seen as adding to financial difficulties or preventing the pursuit of a career, or because the child is mentally or physically handicapped; the mother may be on her own, without support; the parents may be very young and not ready for the responsibility of bringing up children; or the parents may not understand the child's fundamental need for acceptance and love. Parental rejection, too, takes a variety of forms. In many cases, rejecting parents tend to be unaffectionate, disapproving and hostile to the child, harsh in their methods of control and destructive of the child's confidence and self-image; but in some instances, parents may pamper and indulge a child to conceal their rejecting attitude from others and perhaps also from themselves. Or they may vacillate between harshness and indulgence as the mood takes them.

The effects of parental rejection on children are likely to be devastating, although not always immediate. Sooner or later, most children who experience rejection will come to be antagonistic to adults and perhaps also to other children; and they will often be lacking in self-confidence, either withdrawing from challenges or seeking to assert themselves by means of aggression and anti-social behaviour. Rejected children at the nursery group stage will tend to demand a lot of attention and affection which they will often try to obtain by unacceptable means, from nursery staff, who have a difficult task in meeting some of their needs while not being in a position to take over the parental role in these cases.

> Eric (aged 4) is aggressive, overactive and disobedient. He has an older brother (6 years) and a new baby sister. His mother, while not neglecting him materially, has given him little attention, and the new arrival has tended to make the situation worse in this respect. Eric lacks positive attention, particularly from his mother, and is bound to feel rejected to a considerable extent.

(b) Over-protection

Over-protective parents prolong infantile care and are reluctant gradually to diminish physical contact with the child. They encourage the child to turn to them immediately for help in the face of any difficulty, however mild. The child is discouraged from becoming less dependent on parental assistance with growing maturity. Over-protective parents may be permissive and indulgent, satisfying every whim the child has; or else they may be dominating, interfering and restrictive. Reasons for over-protective parental attitudes include the child being delicate or handicapped; the parents trying to compensate for affection missing from the marriage or in their own lives; psychological disturbance in the parents; or ignorance of children's needs.

Over-protected children tend to be slow to adapt to new situations, to cling to adults, and to be passive and submissive. They will need considerable time to adjust to school or playgroup, and will benefit from carefully graded social training, which encourages independence and greater participation in activity with others.

> Howard (aged 4) is an over-protected, dependent, timid and tearful child. He is the older son of young parents, his brother being nearly 2 years old. The husband's mother tries to exert a great deal of influence on the young parents, and Howard's mother resents this very much. She is a gentle person, rather shy and very protective towards her children. In the past, she has not allowed the boy to go out to play with other children - she considered them too rough and ill-mannered. Howard has spent his early years with a number of adults constantly at his beck and call. He has great difficulty in mixing with other children and in standing up for himself.

(c) Inconsistency

Few parents are entirely consistent in their behaviour towards their children, and indeed a certain amount of flexibility is to be preferred to rigidity in child-rearing practices. However, grossly inconsistent attitudes and behaviour on the part of the parents are likely to be damaging to children.

If the standards set by either parent are fluctuating and unpredictable, or if the parents do not have a reasonably common policy, children will not know where they stand and so will find themselves in an impossible position. They will not be able to learn which of their actions will meet with approval or condemnation, and may as a result develop into indecisive, conflict-ridden individuals. Nursery staff, if they are consistent, can help to provide children with a more coherent framework to their lives, though this will not necessarily help a child's relationship with his parents.

> Ian (aged 4) is overactive, demanding and aggressive. Mother is reluctant to discipline the child in any way and is fearful of the father's disapproval of her actions; father is strict, and resents any interference or attempts by others to help Ian. He appears to ignore the mother's attempts to deal with the boy, who hits his younger sister (aged 3) if she has anything he wants.

Jealousy and sibling rivalry (see Ian). By the age of three, the child may have made great strides in learning to relate to and play with brothers or sisters, and will usually get much satisfaction and pleasure from their company. However, it is very common for a certain amount of rivalry to exist among children in the same family, who will vie for their parents' love and attention. Nearly every child, too, under five or six will experience fairly intense feelings of jealousy when a new baby arrives on the scene and demands a lot of parents' time. Rivalry and jealousy will be exacerbated when parents have not prepared their child for the new arrival, particularly when this event coincides with entry into the nursery group. Difficulties may also be created when the parents (consciously or unconsciously) give markedly preferential treatment to one of their children.

A child who feels displaced or inferior in the family circle may compensate by seeking a lot of attention from nursery staff, and may be very demanding and difficult to handle, at least for a period. It is helpful to nursery staff to know something about the child's relationships with siblings and to find out when there is an addition to the family.

(c) <u>A Cautionary Note</u>
In concluding this section on factors associated with behaviour problems in young children, it is perhaps necessary to stress that the above discussion of possible causative factors is not meant to be comprehensive. Much more could be said about each of the factors listed, and it should also be emphasised once again that conclusions about the causation of behaviour problems should not be arrived at too readily. The total picture may take a long time to emerge, and in most cases you are likely to have only a hazy idea of what the parents are really like. Remember that a child coming from a poverty-stricken home may have plenty of loving care, and that some children from affluent backgrounds may be rejected or over-protected, or subjected to pressures of varying kinds. Be mindful, too, that some parents may be experiencing a great deal of stress and strain in their own lives and need understanding and support rather than criticism or blame.

(d) <u>Keeping Records</u>
Once you have embarked upon the process of assessing and planning a programme for a child, it is essential for a variety of reasons, that you keep accurate records of what you are doing:

1. gathering and collating a written record will help clarify your thoughts and enable you to gain a more coherent picture of a child. This will be of use when you are deciding upon a plan of action;
2. some system or record keeping is important when observing and assessing a child as you cannot rely upon your memory to retain the information over a period of time, much less recall it accurately months later;
3. records will indicate whether your chosen approach is being successful and if not, where alterations need to be made;
4. with records you will notice small but significant changes in behaviour which might otherwise be over-looked and perhaps result in a successful approach being abandoned prematurely.

To simplify your record keeping we have designed a Record Booklet (see Appendix B), further copies of which can be reproduced by any means convenient to you. The booklet comprises four sections; the purpose of each will be described below.

Section I

This first section is for you to make an orderly summary of the information you have gained about a child in the assessment phase. Taking each of the assessment schedules in turn, the relevant information is condensed and transferred to the appropriate pages of the record book.

Section II

Once the assessment phase has been completed and recorded you should then write down the aims and objectives of your plan of action and select the most suitable approach(es)for yourself and the child. In this section you are required to note the most worrying aspects of the child's behaviour and the order in which they will be tackled together with the changes you hope to achieve and the approaches that will be employed. It is important to write the plan in some detail, specifying when, where and how much time will be devoted to a particular approach, which activities (in what order) will be tried and who will be responsible for carrying out the programme and keeping the records. If you are at all unsure about how to go about designing and writing a plan of action then please refer to Chapter 6, Making a Plan of Action (pp.203-254), which includes examples of plans designed and used successfully by adults working in nursery groups.

Section III

This section consists of a series of blank sheets on which to monitor your progress at weekly intervals. During the week you may find it useful to carry around a small notebook in which to jot down quickly any important observations as they occur and then it is an easy matter to summarise these more neatly in the Record Book at the end of the week. Careful record keeping will indicate whether or not you are succeeding in your aims and should it appear that the child is not making progress then you will have to re-appraise both your methods and your application of them. You should, however, be careful to give your chosen approach sufficient time to have some effect as long standing difficulties will not vanish overnight. It is sometimes helpful to involve another adult in monitoring as well as yourself, as it is difficult to retain a sense of objectivity when closely involved with a child.

Section IV Re-assessment

At the end of each term it is useful to re-assess the child using Schedules 1 and 2, as comparison with the results of previous assessments will provide another valuable yardstick with which to measure the child's progress. Space has also been left for you to note down your impressions of the term's progress.

If the child should leave your care whilst you are still working with him/her, please pass on the Record Book and materials to his/her new teacher or group leader so that she understands what you are trying to accomplish and will be able to take over where you left off.

FURTHER READING

Bower, E.M. (1969) Early Identification of Emotionally Handicapped Children in School. Springfield, Ill. : C.C. Thomas.

Chazan, M. (1976) The early identification of children with adjustment problems. Chapter 5 in Wedell,K. and Raybould, E.C. (eds., 1976) The Early Identification of Educationally 'at risk' Children. Educational Review Occasional Publication, Number Six, School of Education, University of Birmingham.

Lee, C. (1977, 2nd ed.) The Growth and Development of Children. London : Longman.

Mussen, P.H., Conger, J.J. and Kagan, J. (latest edition) Child Development and Personality (especially Parts 1 to 4). New York : Harper and Row.

Richman, N., Stevenson, J. and Graham, P.J. (1982) Pre-School to School : a behavioural study. London : Academic Press.
Rutter, M. (1975) Helping Troubled Children. Harmondsworth : Penguin Books.

B. PRACTICAL STEPS

(e) Behaviour Assessment (Schedule 2)
Schedule 2 (Behaviour Assessment) is designed to enable you to describe and record in some detail the behaviour shown by a child whom you wish to help. Too often, we are satisfied with a somewhat vague description of a behaviour problem, for example referring to a child as 'aggressive', 'destructive' or 'withdrawn' without further elaboration. Such labels are not much help to you when it comes to planning action. What one person means by 'aggressive' is different from someone else's opinion, and the word 'aggressive' is not so much a description of behaviour but more the meaning that someone attaches to a behaviour. Also, it is all too easy to label a child on the basis of first impressions which may be totally erroneous, as can be demonstrated by Mrs. S. She was concerned about a child in her group who she felt was not getting the most from his nursery experience.

Although James enjoyed outside activities and boisterous games Mrs. S. thought he should be encouraged to try out some of the quieter pursuits on offer such as painting, small constructional toys and jigsaws. She perceived him as a somewhat shy child with few friends, who was easily led and bossed about. After a period of observing him Mrs. S. was forced to revise her opinion of James. Contrary to her immediate impressions he did, in fact, show interest in a wide variety of activities and was observed participating in almost the entire range provided by the nursery. His social contacts were much broader than at first thought and he was seen to join several different groups, sometimes as a leader and sometimes as a follower. Without this period of close observation James would have been labelled by his teacher as shy and lacking in confidence when, in fact, he proved to be an average four-year-old, no different from his peers.

Before you can deal constructively with a problem you need to know as much as possible about the behaviour you want to change and this can only be achieved by close observation of the child in question. You may then find, like Mrs. S., that the problem is not as serious as you first thought. Observation without record keeping is a waste of time, as it is simply not possible for anyone to remember the information observed over a period of time and recall it accurately at a later date. Without making some sort of record of what is going on it will be difficult for you to get to know enough about a child and his behaviour to reorganise and manage the situation successfully in future. Observation and recording will also be important later on when you are trying to see what effect your intervention is having on the child. To aid and simplify your record keeping we have produced Behaviour Recording Sheets.

Part I. Behaviour Recording Sheets. These provide a means of ensuring that the same kinds of information are always collected, as haphazard and casual observations will be of little use when it comes to devising strategies to help the child. Using the sheets you should observe the child systematically for at least a week, noting down as exactly as you can how he behaves. (Generally speaking, the longer the period over which observations are made the more reliable the information you gather is likely to be.) It is insufficient, for instance, to record "Freddy was aggressive all morning". You need to know whether he kicks, scratches, bites, pinches. What or whom does he do it to? What happens beforehand? In what circumstances does he quieten down? Similarly "all morning" is unlikely to mean the entire morning. You will need to know how often and for how long the behaviour occurs and whether there is a regular pattern. Is it worse in the mornings or afternoons for instance? Does it happen more often outdoors than in? It is also important to make a note of the times when Freddy is behaving normally and positively. What activities, for instance, hold his attention? Which children does he play co-operatively with? Does he enjoy adult-directed activities?

Set out overleaf is a sample recording sheet which represents a morning's observations of Howard who, unlike Freddy, is a shy, withdrawn, dependent little boy. As you can see the date and time of each observation are carefully recorded, as are the settings (play house, block corner, milk table) where Howard was playing, together with the names of any adults or other children in the immediate vicinity. The recordings are not continuous but are made at varying intervals during the morning until five separate observations have been gathered. You may find it easier to take notes if you devise for yourself some form of personal shorthand or coding, which will allow you to record large amounts of information more rapidly. Such a personal brand of shorthand, providing it is not too complicated, can greatly increase the efficiency of your observations. At the end of the week you should have collected twenty-five observations for a child attending part-time such as Howard (fifty for a child attending full-time) and be ready to move onto the second part of behaviour assessment, which is a checklist.

Part II. Behaviour Assessment Checklist. This is a checklist which describes in some detail the kind of problem behaviour which you have identified. The descriptions should be read carefully and those which apply to the child in question should be ticked. The descriptions may not fit exactly, but you should find it possible to tick an item which seems to match fairly closely the typical behaviour of the child. Make any additional notes which seem called for at the time you are completing the checklist. It is not easy to say what is 'normal' behaviour, and in completing this Schedule you will need to use your knowledge of the ways in which children usually behave in the nursery group. You should also bear in mind the actual age of the child.

BEHAVIOUR RECORDING SHEET

NAME: HOWARD DATE: 28.1.81 MONDAY A.M.

TIME	SETTING	ADULTS CHILDREN PRESENT	DESCRIPTION OF BEHAVIOUR
9.30	Block Play	NNEB Gareth James Steven	NNEB and children are building a motorway. Howard is watching with great interest but when NNEB tries to include him he covers his face with his arm and walks away.
9.45	Home Corner	Cathy Bethan Sarah	The girls are playing birthday parties. Howard peeps around the corner; they want him to sit down and join in but he runs away and sits in the Quiet Room on his own.
10.00	Milk Table	NNEB Paul Daniel Gareth	Howard is standing at side of table sucking his thumb. Mrs. A. offers him a mug of milk, he gets under the table and will not come out - cries bitterly.
10.30	Music and Movement	Mrs.G. and large group	The group are playing 'The Farmer's in his Den'. Anthony chooses Howard who turns away and hides his face for the rest of the session.
11.15	Story Time	Mrs.L. and group of younger children	Howard cannot be found. NNEB locates him in the cloak-room where he is hiding behind the coats. He comes in and buries his head in the chair throughout story time.

contd...

MONDAY P.M.

TIME	SETTING	ADULTS CHILDREN PRESENT	DESCRIPTION OF BEHAVIOUR

(f) General Assessment (Schedule 3)
Schedule 3 will enable you to systematise your impressions and observations of the child in the nursery group. Behaviour problems need to be viewed in the context of the child's general development, and Schedule 3 will help you to pin-point the child's strengths and weaknesses, and to take appropriate action. For example, if the child shows weaknesses in areas such as self-help or language skills, you need to consider what help may be given to develop such skills. Specific help of this kind, although not necessarily directed at the behaviour problem, is likely to contribute to the child's better adjustment in the group. Schedule 3 will also help you to decide whether the child needs a more detailed assessment, e.g. for defects in vision or hearing, or perhaps to confirm your view that the child is well below the norm in general learning ability.

Read through Schedule 3 carefully and, before completing any section, try to observe the child in as many different situations as possible and at various times of the day. It is suprising how differently children can react in different contexts. See what happens when the child is attempting a task or playing independently, and also when with another child or in a group. But do not assume that children are unable to succeed at a task because they are not actually doing it - they may not have had the chance to try. So experiment with all sorts of games and activities, at a level that will present children with something of a challenge without being too difficult for them. The Schedule itself gives you some idea of what kinds of activities to engage in. Make careful notes of the child's response both to others and in carrying out a variety of activities.

You may find it difficult to assess what is 'normal' functioning. As far as possible, the Schedule requires you to record whether the child performs specific skills successfully, partially or not at all. Your own experience with children of nursery age will help you to judge what can be expected of any child but remember, when comparing the child with others, that a few months of chronological age can make a lot of difference in the case of young children. If you can, discuss your own observations with a colleague who also knows the child well.

It is far from easy to make detailed and accurate observations of children, especially as in the nursery group they tend to flit from one activity to another and also you yourself will be perpetually busy with other things. But you will find that you become a better observer as you practise making a record of behaviour as required by Schedule 3. This Schedule asks you to observe the way in which the child moves around (Section I Mobility) and hand-eye co-ordination (Section 2). Neither of these sections should present you with much difficulty. It is more difficult to assess children's vision and hearing (Sections 3 and 4), and to judge whether their functioning in the group is impaired by a sensory defect; if you are in the slightest doubt whether this is the case, do not hesitate to seek a specialist opinion.

Self-help skills (Section 5) are reasonably easy to assess, though you will need to ensure that children are given ample opportunity to demonstrate how independent they are in carrying out the tasks listed in this section. The assessment of a child's language development (Sections 6 and 7) may prove less easy, and usually requires extensive periods of observation. Most young children have rather better receptive than expressive language skills, and some will need considerable encouragement before they will talk readily to adults, even when they are able to express themselves adequately. Some will talk only or mainly when they are on their own with one adult whom they know well, but say little or nothing in the group. So it is necessary to give children varied opportunities in which to show their language ability, but, of course, trying too hard to elicit a response may put off a child reluctant to talk.

The final two sections provide for a record of children's responses in various play situations (Section 8) and also their general response to the opportunities for learning that they are provided with in the nursery group (Section 9 - Response to Learning/Adaptability). In most (though not all) groups one or two children will stand out as being slow to learn as compared to the others, and these may well be retarded in their general development. But in a number of cases, it will not be clear whether the children are less capable of learning than other children, or whether they need extra attention and encouragement from adults before showing what they can do. Quite a few children are prematurely judged to be below the norm in ability, when all they need is time to adjust and appropriate stimulation. Do not, therefore, hesitate to suspend judgement and to make only a tentative assessment when you are in any doubt. Refrain, also, from putting too much emphasis on the things the child cannot do. As noted at the end of Schedule 3, "Now that you are aware of the child's strong points it may be possible to use them as a basis for tackling his problem behaviour".

(g) Talking to Parents

Introduction

It is difficult, often, to know where to begin your discussion of a child with the parents (or other caretakers) and to know how far to go in your talks with them. A discussion can easily become too wide-ranging or involve you more deeply than is necessary or desirable.

It is important that you start off with a clear idea of what you want to achieve in talking to the parents about their child's behaviour. A useful first step is to try and form in your mind a picture of the total problem area to be covered. For example, one child may show a particular pattern of problem behaviour in the nursery and you may want to know whether this pattern holds true for the home as well. Additionally, contact with the parents will be an opportunity to ask for specific details of any physical illnesses, injuries or other problems that cannot be obtained from the school records.

Aims

The main aims of talking to parents are:

(a) to seek and to give information about the child's development, so as to promote a better understanding of the child on both sides;

(b) to find out whether the family has had, or needs, contact with support services;

(c) to see to what extent and in what ways you can work with the parents in the management of the problem.

If you are a good listener and avoid rushing to give advice about family problems that may be the proper concern, say, of a health visitor, the discussion could prove to be constructive and useful.

A Delicate Relationship

After what has been said already about the importance of the home in meeting the young child's basic needs and about the extent to which the child's problem behaviour may stem from the family situation, the desirability of full parental involvement in dealing with the problem cannot be over-emphasised. In the case of playgroups, the parents are often very much involved already but getting the parents involved in nursery schools or classes may be a much lengthier process. Although parents nowadays are spending more time in nursery schools, teachers and parents do not always find it easy to relate to one another. Teachers may be unsure how far they should go in asking questions of the parents, and some may start off the relationship badly by implying, even if very indirectly, that the parents are to blame for a child's difficulties.

Again, some parents may be over-sensitive about their child and resent any questions about their family life. Take, for example, the case of Ian's parents:

> Ian is an aggressive, demanding child who frequently attacks the other children in the nursery, sometimes for no particular reason and on other occasions when he is thwarted in his attempts to obtain a favourite toy or to indulge in a particular activity. Ian's teacher is very concerned about his behaviour and has sought the advice of the headmistress about what she should do. They decide to approach Ian's mother about his behaviour to try and establish whether he behaves similarly at home, and what can be done to help him.
>
> The mother appears to be a rather timid, ineffectual person who rarely rebukes Ian, even when he is misbehaving on school premises at collecting time. The father, on the other hand, is a very dominant character who will brook no interference with his child. A health visitor who visited the home was dealt with in a very peremptory fashion by the father who demanded to know exactly what she was 'up to' with Ian. The mother is grateful for the concern shown by Ian's teachers and is glad to accept any help, but she is terrified that the father will learn of this and blame her for going behind his back.
>
> In this situation it is very difficult for a teacher to know what to do. She may well cause considerable problems for Ian's mother and create greater tensions in the home by seeking to involve the father even though it appears that the home situation is critical to the understanding of Ian's behaviour. He has a sister a year younger than himself whom he completely dominates at home. He will hit her or bully her to obtain a toy or to get his own way. The mother does not attempt to interfere because of the father's attitude.

> The father was approached by the teachers in this case and eventually agreed that they should try to change Ian's behaviour. The nursery staff planned a programme of help for Ian, with some success, but the long-term effect was not a happy one, as we shall find out later.

In the example given above the father's attitude was extreme. In fact, most parents are happy to cooperate with the teacher as they realise that it is for the child's benefit that the nursery staff are paying attention to their child. If the nursery staff are careful and diplomatic in the way that they approach parents, then considerable mutual benefit can be gained from the relationship.

Great care should be exercised to avoid making parents feel guilty about their child's behaviour. Most parents want to do their best for their children, but many live under very difficult conditions which are not of their own choosing. The father might be unemployed and unable to look after his family's needs as he would like, and a sensitive approach by the teacher would be needed to avoid further tensions in the home. Again, mothers with pre-school children are particularly vulnerable to stress, and a high incidence of depression has been found amongst those with several young children who have also to face severe financial and social constraints.

On the parents' side they may feel uncomfortable about talking to teachers, perhaps because they, themselves, have had mainly negative experiences of school in the past. They may be on the defensive when discussing their child's difficult behaviour, and not a few will give the rosiest possible picture of their child's behaviour at home, even when this is blatantly untrue. Again, individuals differ in the extent to which they are willing to part with any information about themselves that they regard as personal or private, even though this information maybe of crucial importance in understanding their child's behaviour.

Some of the questions you ask may deal with matters that the mother and father are deeply concerned about. It will be necessary to phrase questions in such a way as to avoid upsetting the parents unduly, but which will enable them to speak freely about their child's problems. You may well find that the parents will be only too happy to unburden themselves, and that both you and they will gain relief from talking. Of course, their initial response may be complete denial that the child has any problem at all, but a little probing may uncover a source of worry.

There again, care should be exercised to avoid putting ideas in the parents' minds. It is only too easy to start people worrying that there may be something wrong with their child by phrasing a question badly or by being too formal in your approach. You should aim to help the parents feel relaxed and get them chatting in a free, informal manner. Getting someone to talk openly is a definite skill that can be learned and improved with practice. We will give some hints later on as to how this skill may be improved.

It is important for you to realise that you have a unique perspective of the child's behaviour. Obviously, you see the child for longer periods than other professionals and you may have closer and more frequent contact with the parents. Often it is to you that parents will unburden themselves, although some may view you as a high status 'authority-figure' and may be reluctant to approach you initially. Again, some individual staff may wish to preserve their position and find it difficult to talk easily to parents. It may not be easy to achieve the desired relationship with parents but improved communication is always possible.

You may have strong feelings about the child - or even the parents - but it is important that these feelings should not obtrude or prevent you from being reasonably objective. Some parents will come from a social background which is different from yours, and you will need to have a sympathetic understanding of this background. Even without saying anything, it is very easy to convey to parents that you are reacting negatively to their appearance or speech. Parents living in very poor circumstances often provide their children with ample warmth and affection, while parents who are advantaged in terms of wealth and education sometimes fail to satisfy the basic emotional needs of their children.

To sum up, trying to make a relationship with parents and to work constructively with them to solve a problem is not a simple task, but one often fraught with difficulties. You should not, however, be put off by these difficulties but regard them as almost inevitable in the kind of relationship you are attempting to create and deal with them in a positive manner as they arise.

Direct and Indirect Information

There will be some items of information about the child's home background and behaviour away from the nursery that you will feel able to ask the parents about directly. Details relating to the child's health or position in the family,for example, may be asked without incurring hostility. However, there will be some items, such as emotional difficulties between parents or between the child and siblings, that may have to be approached very delicately or not at all, depending on how you gauge the situation and the likely response of the parents in question.

Considerable judgement will have to be exercised on your part when talking to individual parents, but very often you may be surprised and pleased by their frankness once you have broken the ice and got them talking freely about the child and family. Where you encounter open hostility or feel that you may exacerbate a problem by raising it, it may well be best to avoid putting the question in the first place. In order to sustain a good relationship with the parents you may have to do without certain information which you would like to have. Information about the home situation may be available from other professionals (see 'Help from Others', pp. 49-57).

The First Meeting with the Parents

The first meeting with the parents will be particularly important as the first impressions gained by them will often dictate their subsequent attitudes to you. On this occasion, the parents might be invited to the school at a time convenient for them and you.

Opportunites for a Continuing Relationship

Think about other likely occasions when you will be able to have a relaxed chat with the parents, though you may well be able to ask a few questions of them in a very brief meeting. Opportunities for a proper talk may present themselves as follows:

(a) when a child is brought to or taken home from school;

(b) when the child has to be taken home for some reason such as illness, an act for which the parent will probably be grateful and therefore more amenable to questioning;

(c) when there may be another reason for calling in the child's home area and you have some time to spare;

(d) when you meet casually on the street or in other circumstances. In many cases the parents will be more forthcoming when they meet you socially or on another occasion which is not seen as official or formal.

<u>Ways of Approaching Parents</u>
Your talks with parents should aim to be relaxed and informal, but should also ensure that you are able to obtain the information that you are seeking. There is no set of formal rules that should be rigidly adhered to but the following points may help to guide you:

(i) decide beforehand the areas of the child's behaviour or family background that you are going to ask about on this particular occasion. Make a note of these and decide how each question should be put;

(ii) ask fairly straightforward questions initially, so that the parents do not develop a resistance to being questioned early on in your talk;

(iii) when you feel that the moment is right, put any questions to the parents about more delicate matters, such as the child's relations with brothers or sisters, or enquire in a general way whether there are any aspects of behaviour that the parents find worrying;

(iv) allow the parents to expand upon the information they give you and probe very gently about any details that may be of specific interest to you. It may transpire that the parents will talk very frankly to you once a subject has been broached and be glad to unburden themselves of certain worries about their child. You should allow them to do this by listening sympathetically to what they have to say and maybe offering some support by making the occasional understanding remark such as ...... "quite a few children of his age are like that of course ..." or ... "that is not all that unusual". Thus you may assuage some of their anxiety and convey that you share their concern for the child. Occasionally fairly neutral comments will help to keep the conversation flowing and dispel any impression that the parents might have that they are talking in a vacuum. Essentially, what we are saying here is that you should remember that the act of talking to parents is an <u>interaction</u> between them and yourself. Try to be both a good listener and to offer advice sympathetically;

(v) avoid letting the talk become too chatty and irrelevant. It is only too easy to get side-tracked by some fairly trivial detail and spend a great deal of time talking about something which has little to do with the child's difficulties. Avoid making too many comments on your own, but try to guide the conversation into more relevant paths;

(vi) do not be unduly surprised if on subsequent occasions the parents contradict what they have said to you earlier. It is easy to give a wrong impression unintentionally and virtually impossible to be totally objective about one's own child. Thus parents commonly overrate their child's abilities and underplay shortcomings. A few may underestimate their child's good points and be over-critical. Try to keep a sense of balance and be as objective as you possibly can. Note what you consider to be over-exaggeration on the parents' part, or an undue emphasis on attainments that may be unrealistic for their child. Remember that contradictions in information may be merely due to poor recall. Distant events in particular can become distorted. Thus always balance what the parents said during one talk against what they said on subsequent occasions;

(vii) be careful how you actually phrase a question. It is only too easy to ask a 'loaded' question - that is, to predetermine the likely response. This may often be due to certain key words being included or excluded from the question. Thus the question "Does your child often have temper tantrums?" is likely to evoke a rather different response from the parents than the question "Some children often have temper tantrums, does your child?". The first question may trigger off a denial, whilst the second question is less likely to cause resentment because it acknowledges that other children have temper tantrums. Try to make it clear by your phrasing of the question that a particular difficulty is not something which applies just to them and their child alone but may be a fairly common occurrence among children of this age group;

(viii) whenever possible, try to be positive and offer concrete suggestions about how to help the child. Praise good points as well as pointing out shortcomings. When you have decided upon a plan of action discuss this with the parents and describe what you would like to do to try to help their child.

Try to get the parents on your side, and view the intervention as a cooperative venture where you keep them informed and seek their approval for any course of action that you propose to take.

<u>A Summary of Points to Remember when Talking with Parents</u>

1. Have a clear idea about what information you want.
2. Prepare some questions beforehand and phrase these carefully.
3. Establish a free, relaxed atmosphere - get rapport.
4. Try to avoid spending too much time on irrelevant matters.
5. Probe deeper when the parents are receptive and obviously willing to talk about a particular problem.

6. Do not press on matters of delicacy when the parents clearly do not want the matter pursued.
7. Be prepared to talk with parents on several occasions and in different situations; balance what is said on one occasion against the total picture.
8. Show your concern for and interest in the child, and seek approval for your intended course of action.
9. Be positive, praise good points as well as describing difficulties.
10. Be specific - talk in concrete terms about what the child actually does and what might be practical courses of helpful action.
11. At all times be sympathetic and prepared to listen closely to what the parents have to say, and encourage them to express their ideas and help in concrete ways with the child.

The Swansea Assessment Schedule No. 4 : Talking to Parents

To help you when talking to parents, a schedule entitled 'Talking to Parents' (see Appendix A) has been drawn up. This is divided into three parts.

Part I denotes some general areas of interest and lists some items under each of these that you may wish to ask the parents about. Most of these items refer to fairly innocuous matters about which you should feel able to ask the parents a direct question. However, bear in mind what has been said about phrasing questions so as to avoid bias.

Part II consists of a list of items which refer to more delicate matters about the family and home background. You should exercise great care in how you approach the parents on these points, and should choose a time when they are being frank and obviously prepared to discuss matters openly.

Part III of the Schedule requires you to give a brief description of the child's home and family background. You will, of course, be repeating some information that will have been given in Parts I and II but this does not matter. It will be an asset to have a total picture of the home situation to act as a summary of the various bits of information noted elsewhere.

To re-emphasise an important point - all the items in the Schedule are merely suggestions as to what information should be sought. There may be other items that will occur to you. The way that you phrase the questions and the order in which you ask them are left to your judgement.

Talking to parents should not be thought of as a formal interview situation but some valuable tips may be gained from reading one or two of the references given below.

REFERENCES

Cannell, C.F. and Kahn, R.L. (1968) Interviewing. In Lindsey, G. and Aronson, E. (eds.) The Handbook of Social Psychology, vol.2, Research Methods. New York : Addison Wesley.

Cohen, L. and Manion, L. (1980) The Interview. In Research Methods in Education. London : Croom Helm.

Price Williams, P.R. (1962) Interviews. In Humphrey, G. and Argyle, M. (eds.) Social Psychology through Experiment. London: Methuen.

(h) Help from Others

If help is needed from others outside the classroom or group, you are particularly well positioned to seek out and co-ordinate this help. Fitzherbert (1977) says, "I would see the teacher's (or leader's) role as that of the conductor of the orchestra who brings in various instruments at the appropriate time". This co-ordinating role derives from the close and continuing contact you have with the children in your group, from the possibility of involving parents because you know them well and from the fact that you can speak to other professionals as equals. It is true, of course, that children's difficulties may not only be evident in the group setting. They may well be the source of worry and concern at home and children and their families may need help of a more continuous kind than it is possible for you to give. It is, therefore, very wise to work closely with the health visitor/school nurse and, through her, with the family health visitor who will probably have known the family over a number of years. Other people may also be able to offer support, and the purpose of this section is to discuss what help is available and how staff can gain access to it. An explanation of some of the terms used is given in Appendix C (pp.303-306).

Why Refer Children?

It is a mistake to wait until a problem is well established before doing something about it. The more long-standing the difficulty, the harder it is to alter it. What you should aim for is to have the kind of relationship with other professionals which enables you (or the head teacher/ group leader) to discuss with them your concern about any child, whether or not that concern proves to be justified in the long run. Such discussions when the problem is first noticed are better than waiting for a crisis to develop.

The reasons for referring children can be categorised as follows:

(a) when you feel that help is needed in an area in which you are not an expert. For example, a withdrawn child may never speak to you. Discussion with the mother indicates that the child has some speech at home but you suspect from what you are told that it is very immature and babyish. Referral to a speech therapist would be the right move in this case, either directly or through the health visitor or school nurse.

(b) when difficulties in the home are affecting the child. You may know through a visit to the home or talking to the parents or observation of the child that there is hardship in the family or very poor living conditions or parental ill-health or even possible abuse. These problems are not really for you to deal with but you have a responsibility to contact (or to encourage the parents to contact) those who can help, e.g. the health visitor, the family doctor, or the social worker if appropriate.

(c) when you are unable to meet the parents. It may be that, despite all your efforts to see the mother of a child who is presenting a problem, you fail to make contact with her. The health visitor/school nurse would be a very useful ally here as a source of information and possible action.

(d) <u>when the child fails to progress in the same way as others in the group</u>. For example, a child may seem to you to be very slow to pick up new skills or to be unduly clumsy, aggressive, over-active, un-co-operative or lacking in interest. The best person to contact in such cases is the educational psychologist, who can help you to find out exactly where the main problem lies and perhaps in conjunction with the school doctor or paediatrician give advice as to how to tackle it.

Who Can Help?

A number of professionals concerned with young children have already been mentioned and completion of Swansea Assessment Schedule 5 (see Appendix A, pp. 284-289)might indicate others from whom help is available. Some of these professionals, for example the school nurse, make regular visits to the school. Others may have to be contacted specially (see next sub-section). Remember that the problem may not be a new one, although sometimes difficulties arise for the first time with entry to a group. You may find that others, especially the health visitor, are already working with the family and your concern and co-operation would be useful.

The kind of information which can be obtained from various professionals is indicated in Table 3.1. This diagram gives an outline of the help available and the information which can be 'fed in' about children and their behaviour and development. It does not show the interlinking, which is considerable, within the various groups of professionals. Co-operation between the groups could often, it is true, be improved (see Court Report) and if you want to work with others you must be prepared for set-backs and difficulties. With perseverance, these may gradually disappear as people get to know one another.

How to Refer a Child

Usually a child is referred through the headteacher/group leader after the difficulty has been fully discussed with the member of staff most closely involved. It is helpful for everyone concerned if a written report is drawn up giving specific details of the child (full name, age, position in family, adress etc.) and of the problem (how long has the behaviour been going on, how often does it happen, what has been done about it, what effect it is having on the child's development and on other children etc.). The Behaviour Assessment Schedule 2 (see pp.262-268) would help here as it involves a careful breakdown of the problem. Be precise rather than vague (e.g. do not just say, "Richard is withdrawn" but say what he does and does not do), as this impresses on other agencies that you have really thought about the difficulty and believe them able to help. A telephone call giving the details may be acceptable but it is better to put everything down in writing. If you get no response from the outside agency, get in touch again. You may have to be persistent for the sake of the child. But do remember that often these professionals are considerably overworked and lack of response does not always mean lack of interest.

Following up Referrals

Bringing children to the notice of outside agencies is a beginning but your responsibility does not end there. Reports should be sent to you on the children and the information they contain has to be acted upon. Some information may be confidential and the headteacher may decide that it should not be passed on, but at least the outlines of the situation should be available to those working with the children. You have to know if things are difficult at home even if you do not necessarily need to know the exact details of any illness or the marital relationship or the family's income. Ask the headteacher for the results of the referral if you are given no information, as this may serve as a reminder to get in touch with the outside professional again.

It may be necessary to work out and implement a special programme. Nursery staff should be involved in planning any such programme as only they know whether they have the opportunity to carry it out. Ask to see the therapist or the psychologist so that you can talk over the programme. Often it is easy enough to say what the problem is but a great deal of ingenuity and imagination may be necessary to see what can be done about it.

Confidentiality

If information comes your way which is of a private nature, then you should make sure that you are not going to be the one to gossip about it. Try to be

Table 3.1 Help for Children with Special Needs

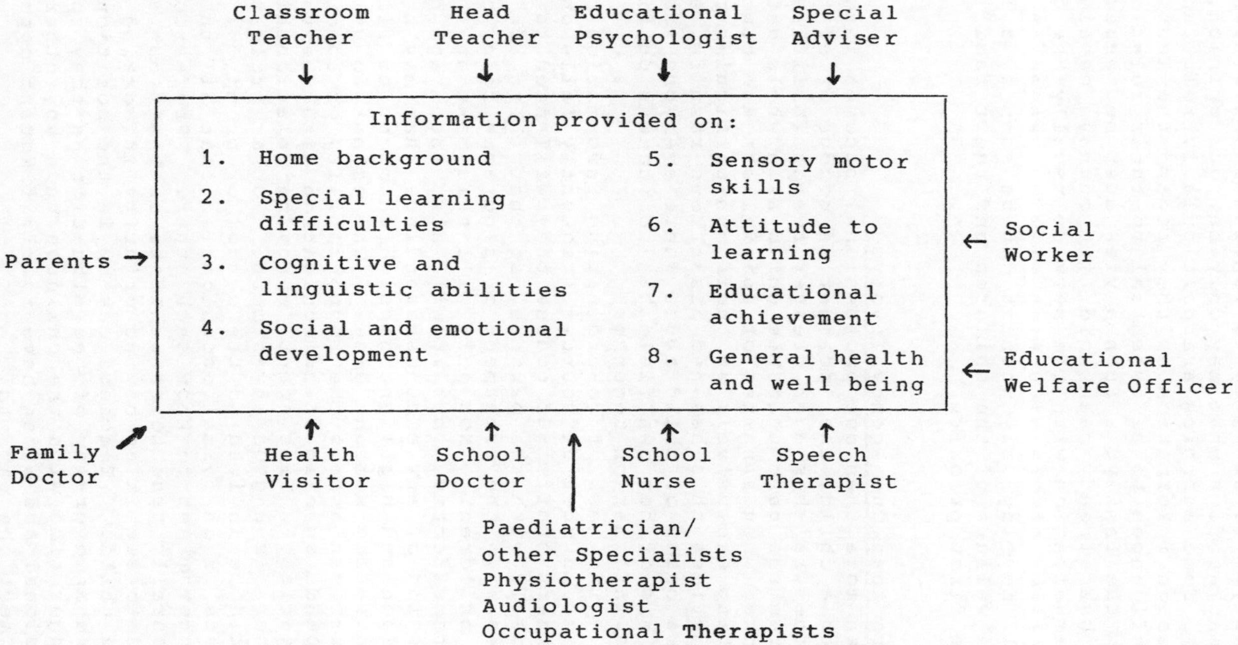

objective, too, about any information you receive so that you do not jump to conclusions too soon and treat as fact what may only be your opinion.

Some agencies are particularly reluctant to pass on information as they regard the keeping of confidences to be essential to their relationship with the family. Such a view must be respected but, as has already been said, if you have developed good communication with the service usually the general outlines of the situation will be passed on. Trust will develop only when it can be seen by all that the welfare of the children and their families is the first priority.

More than One Agency Involved?

When more than one professional becomes involved with a child, the 'teacher as conductor of the orchestra' has even greater responsibilities. It is often the case that the child as a whole gets overlooked when a number of specialists are concentrating exclusively on their own particular concern. Sometimes this has had disastrous results, as in some cases of child abuse where everyone was working in his or her own field but no one was putting all the information together.

The task of co-ordinating information or help from a number of sources frequently falls on the nursery staff. Of course they will need to work closely with the parents, so that there are no breaks in the treatment or programme being offered to children. Not only will this make any help more effective, but it will also encourage discussion of any misunderstandings that may have arisen and highlight gaps which might be filled by contacting someone else. The extent to which staff can assume the responsibility of co-ordination depends on ease of communication with the various agencies. Time spent improving relationships with others is a good investment. Other professionals could be invited to the school or group for informal chats or on formal occasions so that all the adults concerned get to know each other. Professionals naturally tend to concentrate on their own service and to see it as having priority in working with the child. Teachers may be in the position to take an overview of the situation as they spend longer time with the children than any other professional and often have fairly frequent opportunities to meet the parents.

The School and the Health Services

What is normally provided for all pupils is a routine medical examination on entry to school and subsequent examinations if need arises. There should be continuous health surveillance of children at home and in clinics, health centres etc., and the pre-school assessment of nursery school or class children is part of this. Any child with a handicap can be seen by the school health service from the age of two years onwards and children whose special needs are in the area of emotional development can be included in this category.

As far as advice on health problems goes, the key person is the health visitor/school nurse. She may be instrumental in contacting outside agencies in the first place and can carry out 'follow-up' visits to the home as considered necessary. The latter give her access to information helpful in the day-to-day handling of the child. She can also obtain information from the family's own health visitor and family doctor who should know about the child's general development since birth.

The School and the Social Services Department

Social workers are often not so involved with nursery staff or with young, handicapped children as they would like to be. Their role is to help families who are faced with considerable stress, whatever the nature of that stress, and a child with behavioural problems or emotional difficulties is in practically every case stressful. It may be your job, therefore, to realise that help could be given from this quarter and to alert the Social Services Department. Links with the social worker are also invaluable in promoting co-operation between the home and the group the child attends.

Young children are particulary vulnerable to child abuse or neglect. If you have any reason from your observation of children or their behaviour to suspect that their well-being may be at risk in this way, the Social Services Department must be contacted. If you find it difficult to tolerate certain behaviour during the fairly brief time the children are in the group, then you should consider that parents may be much more stressed or less able to cope with such stresses. Children with behavioural disturbance may be especially likely to become the victims of abuse; indeed, their difficult or withdrawn behaviour in the group may be a reaction to adverse handling at home.

The School and the Educational Services

No nursery school or class should have difficulty in obtaining help from specialists within the educational service itself. In some areas, for example, there are advisory teachers with special responsibility for the nursery and infant age ranges. They may well prove helpful in discussing behaviour problems and can act as a liaison between schools and outside agencies.

Educational welfare officers also perform a useful liaison service. Their responsibilities include not only problems of attendance in older children but, in addition, other aspects of family welfare, such as negotiating material assistance, advising parents on educational matters and bringing together the home, the community and the school. In some areas the service is less well developed than in others but it is worth while making contact with your EWO (or the one attached to the primary school which you feed) to find out what help he can offer.

The School and the Psychological Services

Children may be referred to an educational/clinical psychologist by their parents, their teachers, their doctors or any member of another profession concerned with them. Clearly it is simpler to refer children who are in school but the fact that children are not at school does not prevent referral. They can always be referred by their parents or their name can be put forward by any play group leader through the Social Services Department.

The educational psychologist is able to offer advice on the management of children, on the type of programmes which might prove helpful in individual cases and on developmental objectives. Recent research has emphasised the vital importance of the early years in children's development and in many areas the educational psychologists are becoming increasingly anxious to work with young children before problem behaviour has become firly established. The skills which they possess are very much in tune with the needs of young children and there is a growing interest in the profession in working with those who are involved daily with the problem. Clinical psychologists, who work within the Health Service, also offer help, mostly in a hospital setting, to children with behaviour problems.

It has to be said that the demand for psychological services from the schools is high and it is also true that very young children are not the easiest of clients, especially if their language development is retarded. There may, therefore, be a tendency to postpone seeing children until after they reach compulsory school age. But if you feel that a child requires the kind of help which psychologists can give, then you should not hesitate to make contact with the School Psychological Service.

With young children, it is always difficult to know whether their developmental difficulties are temporary or indicative of a long-lasting problem. It is tempting, therefore, to postpone action in order to allow the condition either to disappear or to develop. While some passage of time may be necessary on occasion before firm decisions can be taken about the need for special action, it is unwise for nursery staff to regard time as the 'great healer' in every case. Delay in offering help and in contacting the relevant agencies where necessary may allow the problem to establish itself and become increasingly difficult to alleviate.

FURTHER READING

Bryant, B., Harris, M. and Newton, D. (1980) Children and Minders. London : Grant McIntyre.

Chazan, M., Laing, A.F., Shackleton Bailey, M. and Jones, G. (1980) Some of Our Children. London: Open Books.

Family Welfare Association (501-503 Kingsland Road, Dalston, London E8 4AU) Guide to the Social Services. London: MacDonald and Evans (published annually).

Fitzherbert, K. (1977) Child Care Services and the Teacher. London:Temple Smith.

Garland, C. and White, S. (1980) Children and Day Nurseries. London : Grant McIntyre.

National Council of Social Services (1978) Voluntary Social Services - a Directory of National Organisations.

Pringle, M.L. Kellmer, Davie, R. and Hancock, L.E. (1969) Directory of Voluntary Organisations Concerned with Children. London : Longman (in association with National Children's Bureau).

Sainsbury, E. (1977) The Personal Social Services. London : Pitman Publishing Co.

Stroud, J. (1975) Where to get Help : a guide to the support services. London:Ward Lock Educational.

PART TWO

DECIDING WHAT TO DO

Chapter 3

USING CREATIVE AND LANGUAGE ACTIVITIES

The normal programme offered in nursery classes and play groups does much to help young children develop social and emotional control. It might be worthwhile for you to consider how fairly slight changes to your ordinary pattern of work could help children cope with behavioural difficulties, especially when these difficulties are not very pronounced. By changing the emphasis or extending the time allocated to certain activities, you might find that difficulties can be overcome before they have a chance to grow into problems. Two aspects in particular can do much in this respect:

(a) creative activities

(b) language activities

(a) CREATIVE ACTIVITIES

Introduction

By being given the freedom to manipulate a variety of materials, children can express their feelings one moment and erase them the next; for example, a child may spend a considerable amount of time and energy pummelling and shaping a piece of clay,only to squash it and flatten it out of recognition the next. This can be frustrating to a teacher wishing to 'save' the end product, but if the child has received some satisfaction from the task, this in itself is a worthwhile 'end product'. This kind of activity is particularly helpful for a child who is suffering from tension or stress, but there are other children who need a more powerful energetic outlet. For this type of child some sessions of expressive movement would be particularly helpful.

In flinging their bodies around, they release pent-up energies which may act as a safety valve for their emotions. Sometimes children who are experiencing difficulties at home and are under strain, can lose themselves in an imaginative situation.

> Nicola is a generally happy carefree child, but tends to show some signs of insecurity, e.g. thumb sucking and chewing toys. This insecurity was aggravated by the break-up of her parents' marriage and Nicola became restless and lacking in concentration. Included in some of the activities in the nursery were many sessions of imaginative play. The teacher would suggest a theme e.g. a visit to the seaside or a picnic and then the children would act out all the imaginary actions. A visit to the seaside might involve running to catch the train, travelling, arriving and seeing the sea - undressing and running into the water, splashing, swimming and so on. Nicola appeared to enjoy these activities very much. For a while afterwards she would be "smiling and happy with a look of wonderment on her face". Through these activities this little girl was able to transport herself to an imaginary world. This was satisfying to her if only offering a few minutes'respite from the stresses of her real world.

> Howard is a shy, withdrawn little boy. He clings to his mother, is passive and lacks confidence. Having observed Howard's behaviour over a period of time, the teacher sees that the quality of his play is poor, he is an 'onlooker' and does not stand up for himself in confrontations with other children. He cannot relate to his peers, and his lack of language would seem to aggravate this. On the other hand, he has good mobility, being quite agile. He enjoys listening to stories and understands most of what is being said.

It would seem that Howard needs an outlet for self-expression. A conversation with father reveals that Howard is his constant companion in his D.I.Y. activities. This being so, the teacher could arrange opportunities for him to work at a woodwork bench, which should be satisfying for him. If he has any expertise in the matter, he would achieve some standing amongst his peers. The teacher can also capitalise on an interest shown in sand and water play and allow him free rein in those areas. Being agile and well co-ordinated, Howard should enjoy some sessions of energetic music and movement if he can be persuaded to join in. He would inevitably be an 'onlooker' for the first few sessions, but if they are lively and fun he might be drawn to them in spite of himself. In movement sessions no individual is singled out for attention, and this would suit Howard.

Sometimes the novelty of using percussion instruments will break down the barriers of shyness in a child. The desire to touch and to play can be stronger than the anti-social feelings. Whilst a boy like Howard might not open his mouth to sing he can play his chosen instrument safe in the knowledge that no-one else is listening - all the other children are too absorbed in their own music making!

Difficult Children or Creative Children?

Sometimes nursery teachers place undue emphasis on the need for children to conform, and when they find them reluctant to do this they label them 'difficult'. This is not necessarily a correct description; it may be that these children have a highly creative nature and will seldom conform or be identified with the majority.

> Rachel is one such child. After a short period in the nursery, she would stay at an activity heedless of adults urging her to hurry up and finish. When the others would be putting on their coats for outdoor play she could be found playing a game by herself in the cloakroom. During some collage work she would not be content with any piece of material provided, but would stipulate the colour and texture of the piece required for her use.

This type of behaviour can sometimes lead to head-on collisions with nursery staff, unless time is spent observing the child and perhaps realising that her creativity cannot be confined within the normal routine. This does not necessarily mean that the 'rules' of the nursery must be changed solely for her benefit. Rather it calls for an understanding attitude on the teacher's part, and perhaps more thought given to the creative content of the nursery day.

Stimulating Creative Behaviour

It is possible for parents and adults to stimulate behaviour, and allow children to release whatever creative ability they may possess. Children need to express their feelings, but at this stage of development, verbal communication is limited, and they will need to find other means of communicating. Some will revel in artistic expression, others will find fulfilment in music and rhythm. Yet others will enjoy shaping and moulding clay, or sorting out pleasurable pictures and patterns to their satisfaction.

For most people the completion of a creative act provides a thrill. It is a pleasurable experience, and if the completed act gives someone else pleasure, then the impact on the creator is strong.

> A teacher ...."should act as a catalyst in bringing about children's growth in creativity. Her catalyctic potential may lie in part in her understanding of children, and her warm honest acceptance of their products" (Helen Merritt, 1967).

Care must be taken not to hurry the process of assimilation. Children need time to explore and discover, handle and experiment with materials and then repeat the performance many times over. When embarking on creative projects, they will need time to complete their creative activity to their own satisfaction. When children have made important discoveries about the materials and are given freedom of expression, they will then be in a position to handle the materials in a truly creative manner.

A. Creativity through the Medium of Art and Crafts

Painting and drawing offer children, whether they are having behaviour problems or not, a satisfying outlet for expression. The opportunity to indulge in messy activities without fear of reprisal is a new experience, and a necessary stage in their creative development. Finger painting in particular is satisfying inasmuch that it allows children to have direct control over the flow of movement, and the feel and touch of the paint substance is a very direct experience. For aggressive and over-active children, where painting at an easel with brushes may be too much of a temptation to act wildly, finger painting could prove to be immensely satisfying as they can see visible traces of their actions. They will easily create patterns, erase them and change direction continuously.

Working with clay. This is a medium helpful to all children. For the aggressive child it is something to pound and pummel, flatten and squeeze, thereby allowing acceptable release of any hostilities the child may be feeling. Shy, withdrawn children may not be using the medium in this energetic manner, but may be more gentle and probing and they may discover that clay responds to even the most gentle imprint of finger or clay tool.

Working with wood. Although most nurseries have a woodwork bench as part of their basic equipment, many teachers are reluctant to make full use of it. It may be that the noise level around the woodwork table disrupts other activities, or perhaps the teacher is unsure of the safety of the activities.

B. Creativity through the Medium of Music

For children and adults, musical sounds and experiences can be thoroughly satisfying as well as therapeutic. Music affords children many opportunities for self-expression; for some, music may generate a feeling of well-being and satisfaction, for others it will provide a release for pent-up or disagreeable emotions.

As many children may have had little experience of music before starting in the nursery playgroup, there is much that can be done to remedy this. Even non-musical teachers can provide the right environment and stimulus to make children aware of music. The ability to re-create music composed by others and to create music themselves develops later. The prime concern is to allow children to enjoy music, the emphasis being on the enjoyment rather than on any particular skills, and on the experience, not any end product.

> Margaret (4½ years) was a little girl who caused her nursery teacher some concern, as she would not communicate verbally with either adults or peers. This was not a

> case of language delay, as the teacher knew that the child spoke fluently at home. She was advanced in all other aspects of her development, and responded well to instructions in a non-verbal manner. During a singing together session, the teacher noticed Margaret's lips move, but was unable to perceive actual sounds. By halving the group she was able to hear the child's voice, and praised her for her singing. Gradually she decreased the numbers of children singing together at one time until Margaret was singing with one other child. Knowing by this stage that Margaret shied away from too much attention she did not ask her to sing alone, but on the next occasion asked for a volunteer and Margaret came forward and sang by herself. After this, Margaret showed a willingness to respond verbally on other occasions and situations.

This example shows how important some singing activities can be in encouraging the shy child to make a contribution. Another child, Christopher (aged 4), who was immature and had language problems also benefited from singing in a group. In this instance the teacher used a tape recorder to record the children's voices individually. When it was his turn Christopher was prepared to record his voice and immature speech. These sessions helped him to make an effort to communicate with others, thus in turn reducing the temper tantrums he had previously been exhibiting.

Percussion instruments. Because of their enthusiasm children often become excitable and difficult to control in a music-making session. This often results in the nursery staff being reluctant to allow the children to use the instruments. When they do, the unfamiliarity produces excitability and so it becomes a vicious circle. Good organisation is the key to enjoyable music making, and good provision of instruments. Sometimes a child will sulk if not given a favourite instrument, but if the children exchange instruments during the session, they will learn to be patient, and gain experience of a variety of instruments.

No music table ever has sufficient instruments, and it is sometimes necessary to make some. This can be a satisfying task if the children participate.

Most teachers are familiar with making these, from paper plates with bottle tops attached, or dowelling rods with bottle tops, to simple plastic containers filled with peas, rice, etc. The instruments should not be confined solely to the music area. They can be useful in story telling, e.g. the story of the Elves and the Shoemaker calls for a number of tapping noises, or the noise of the clock striking. Used in this way the children can see the imaginative potential of the instruments.

A timid child may be reluctant at first to hold a percussion instrument, let alone produce any sounds with it. Usually, however, any reservations will be overcome by the novelty and appeal of the music making. Children soon realise that they have freedom to experiment with their instruments and that no special expertise is needed in order to achieve some satisfying sounds.

C. Creativity through the Medium of Movement

Movement is at its most creative when children are able to interpret music in a highly individual way. But before reaching this advanced stage of expressive movement, children must be made aware of the infinite variety of body movements. In this way they will begin to understand themselves and realise that certain moods and feelings are bound up with expressive movement. The movements of a happy child contrast strongly with those of a child who is fearful and worried. It may be that children who are not receiving satisfaction from other media will find that this is the medium to which they can respond.

For some children, participating in a session of movement with an imaginative theme can allow for a release of energy that is unacceptable in other spheres. Boisterous aggressive children will delight in being fearsome giants or brave explorers hacking their way through the jungle. At the same time, shy withdrawn children, while reluctant to join in the activities, may enjoy watching the others, and sometimes will re-enact the themes or movements when playing elsewhere. This was true of Howard (aged 4), a timid, over-protected little boy. After a long period in the nursery he became attached to a boy who was the exact opposite of himself, extroverted and boisterous. Both boys had been engaged on some constructive block play which led to a space rocket theme. The nursery teacher then continued this theme later in music and movement, where they all participated in flying to the moon. Howard did not join in any of these movement sessions, merely observing the others. However, later that day, when the children played outdoors, the nursery staff saw that they were continuing the space theme, and that Howard was joining in enthusiastically.

Conclusion

Nurseries have the resources to facilitate creative ideas, and many teachers possess an artistic ability or preference for a certain aspect of creativity which will inevitably be passed on to the children. It has not been possible to describe creative activities in great detail, but listed below are some books which may extend your knowledge if you decide to use a creative approach to help a child with behaviour difficulties.

REFERENCES AND FURTHER READING

Chazan, M. (ed.) (1973) Education in the Early Years. Swansea : Faculty of Education, University College of Swansea.

Eliason, C.F. and Jenkins, L.T., (1977) A Practical Guide to Early Childhood Curriculum. St. Louis: C.V. Mosby.

Merritt, H. (1964) Guiding Free Expression in Children's Art. New York; Holt, Rinehart and Winston Inc.

Pickering, D. and M. (1974) Pre-School Activities. London: Batsford Books.

Yardley, A. (1970) Senses and Sensitivity. London: Evans Bros.

(b) LANGUAGE ACTIVITIES

Introduction

The role of language in early childhood education is currently receiving a good deal of attention (Cazden, 1979). We still do not fully understand the complex relationship between language and learning, and we must be careful not to over-estimate the role of language in early development: Piaget has warned us that lanugage can be used without real understanding, especially if sensory and motor experience is lacking. However, it is clear that many aspects of children's thinking are dependent on the acquisition of basic language skills. Language, in its oral and written forms, is the main medium of teaching in schools, and children need linguistic competence if they are to derive full benefit from their school years. Early childhood is characterised by very rapid language development, and it is desirable that children should get off to a good start (Woodhead, 1976a). Although the family has a major role in fostering language growth, nursery groups can contribute much to linguistic development in young children, and most nursery staff would place the encouragement of expressive and receptive language skills high on their list of goals.

How Language helps Emotional and Social Development

Up till now it is the role of language in cognitive development and school achievement which has received most attention. We tend to overlook the place of language in emotional and social development, and relatively little work has been carried out on this topic. Yet children's feelings and social skills are closely linked with their language development, and although interaction with others is not entirely dependent on verbal communication, it does not greatly progress without language. Smiles and gestures, whether from child or adult, make quite a lot of impact, but communication is on a different level once the child has some language. The child who says little or nothing soon ceases to obtain the fullest positive feedback even from loving parents; probably the same sort of thing happens in the nursery group. The acquisition, development and use of language are related to emotional and social development in a number of ways (Herriot, 1971; Tough, 1977). These are outlined below.

1. Language helps children to regulate their own behaviour and that of others. It enables children to direct their attention to their own actions, bringing them under their control, as well as to wield some sort of power over others, e.g. by expressing their needs or by issuing commands.
2. Language facilitates the development of a concept of self. Being involved in

verbal exchange, whether adult-child or child-child, helps children to be aware of their importance and value as individuals. Further, both the extent to which children understand descriptive and evaluative words such as 'good', 'bad', 'naughty' or 'nice' and the ways in which these words are applied to them will affect their perception of themselves as separate individuals.

3. Language influences the development of attitudes. The context in which words indicating values (e.g. 'right', 'wrong', 'wicked', 'lovely') are used by parents, nursery staff and others will, over time, contribute to the formation of the child's attitudes. Particularly in the early years, children are likely to imitate and internalise the behaviour and values of others.
4. Language helps the child to an increasing understanding of the feelings and reactions of other adults and children. This understanding comes slowly, but it is an important component of emotional and social development. Lewis has suggested that deficiencies in children's vocabularies relating to personal characteristics (e.g. 'happy','glad', 'sad') may retard personality development.
5. Language enables children to express themselves emotionally and socially in play to a fuller extent than is possible without it. Language helps the development of complex and imaginative forms of play, which might otherwise remain at a low level. Some kinds of play, accompanied by verbal expression (especially role playing) may be a means of working through conflicts. Ways of using language in play are suggested in the section on 'Play Activities'(pp.92-128).
6. Language assists the child to become aware that there is more than one possible response to most situations, and is an essential tool in the problem-solving strategies discussed in the Handbook. It can help the child to learn how to substitute more socially acceptable responses for physical aggression. On the

whole in our society, verbal attacks incur less displeasure from others than physical assault.

The Role of the Nursery Group in Fostering Language

There has been much discussion lately about the contribution which can be made by the nursery group to fostering language development. We cannot assume that participation in nursery school or playgroup necessarily provides adequate opportunities for young children to advance their language. In a small-scale study in South-East England, Valerie Thomas (1973) found that many of the questions put to children by the adults in a nursery class were not answered - the children either did not listen at all, tuned out before the completion of the question, considered a one-word answer sufficient or did not think the question worth an answer. As there was no pressure to reply, they probably did not think anyone cared whether they answered or not. A considerable proportion of the adults' speech was in the form of commands, or emotionally-toned remarks such as 'Naughty' or 'I am surprised at you!' or phrases such as 'Jolly good!' and 'Oh, pretty!'. Minimum verbalisation was accepted by the staff, and no child was expected to repeat, clarify or extend a statement; few remarks from the child developed into a conversation.

The results of this limited study cannot be generalised to all nursery groups, and the situation is always changing, with an increasing emphasis on planned adult-child verbal interactions. However, Barbara Tizard (1976), in looking at staff behaviour in pre-school centres, found that while the adults talked a great deal to the children, often the talk was at a lower level than it might have been. The Oxford Pre-school Research Project (Sylva et al., 1980), too, found that although the pre-schools involved in the study appeared to be alive with talk, conversations between adults and children were very fleeting. Real exchanges about a single topic were rarely conducted. Further, the children engaged in little conversational exchange amongst themselves.

Some General Principles

On the basis of work carried out in a variety of contexts, and the recommendations of the Bullock

Report (1975), which gave considerable attention to language in the early years, it would seem desirable that nursery staff should:

1) give planned attention to children's language development. Without a deliberate language policy, it is likely that the level of verbal interaction in the nursery group will be lower than it need be;
2) provide as many opportunities as possible for children to be in a one-to-one relationship with adults in the nursery group. This will mean encouraging, in a controlled manner, the participation of adults additional to the usual staff in the group;
3) as far as they can, provide appropriate settings for adults to work with individual children and small groups. Sylva et al. (1980) comment that 'dialogue-inducing' settings are likely to be small, quiet rooms, intimate and home-like, with two or three children. In the Oxford study, some of the richest conversations took place in the home corner, or 'dens' which a small group of children had constructed on their own. Downes (1978) discusses how language can be encouraged in the normal 'work areas' found in the nursery group e.g. the sand area or home corner. Unfortunately, many nursery groups lack natural spaces where individual or small group activity can take place away from the usual bustle associated with a large number of children, and ingenuity is needed to create suitable settings;
4) seek a close partnership with parents, who play a major part in the child's language development.

Planned attention to language, a one-to-one relationship with adults, appropriate settings and parental involvement are particularly important in the case of children with emotional or social difficulties. Some children, especially those with a poor self-image, will benefit from being involved in varied language activities which introduce, at a level appropriate to the individual child, vocabulary and concepts relating to the self (see section on

'Play Activities').

Language Schemes and Programmes

The Bullock Report (1975) suggested that language should be learned in the course of using it in, and about, the daily experiences of the classroom and the home, but within this framework teachers might find support in some language programmes. Nursery staff in Britain are not greatly attracted to language schemes or programmes of a structured nature, such as have been produced in the U.S.A. Nevertheless, even if one does not accept a scheme in its entirety, or subscribe to the rationale behind it, many useful ideas can be gleaned from the available programmes, which may be discussed under four headings, although some of the schemes do not clearly come within a particular category:

1. traditional (informal) enrichment
2. planned language stimulation, not using one specific scheme
3. direct instruction
4. instructional dialogue

It is likely that most nursery staff, rather than choosing a particular emphasis, will prefer to combine all four of these approaches in varying ways.

1. Traditional (informal) Enrichment

This model sees help and encouragement from adults as providing the best opportunity for children to increase their linguistic skills (Parry and Archer, 1974). The emphasis is on flexibility of approach, free play and self-expression, incidental language learning in a appropriate environment rather than on specific language lessons with highly structured materials or situations, and on unobtrusive guidance rather than direction by the teacher. Most educationists would agree that, for some part at least of the school day, informal approaches and child-directed activities are desirable for young children, and many informal activities are included in the schemes discussed under 'direct instruction' and 'instructional dialogue'. However, nursery staff guided predominantly by the 'traditional enrichment' philosophy must be careful to ensure that language learning actually does occur. There are indeed many opportunities in the nursery group for such learning to take place.

Publications of Relevance

Schools Council Pre-School Education Project
Marianne Parry and Hilda Archer

1974a Pre-School Education London : Macmillan Education.

This is a report on the project's survey of 'good practice' in various nursery groups.

1974b Two to Five London : Macmillan Education.

A guide for nursery staff, which considers play experiences, particulary in the context of language development, and the use of basic materials in the nursery group. The guide is accompanied by four 16 mm. colour films.

2. Planned Language Stimulation (not using a pre-packaged scheme)

Some nursery groups, while not wishing to be tied to a specific language scheme, want to do more than rely on incidental language learning during the normal activities of the day. They prefer to devote some time, as a team, to the planning of language stimulation and thereby to ensure that each child is definitely involved in language activity. This approach has been adopted particularly in relation to socially disadvantaged children, and is illustrated by the work undertaken by S. Harvey and T.R. Lee. An account of this work, 'An Experimental Study of Educational Compensation' is given in Educational Priority, Volume 5 : EPA - A Scottish Study (London, HMSO, 1974). In this project, carried out in pre-schools in Dundee, there was no specific language programme, but language development was encouraged in the framework of an integrated scheme designed to enhance general cognitive development. 'Themes' were planned, usually lasting for a full week and maintaining continuity of emphasis on a single cognitive concept. Each theme was introduced by an activity or experience, and then the selected concept was dealt with from different points of view, i.e. through different senses, using varied play material, differently contrived situations and a wide range of songs, nursery rhymes and stories.

The 'cognitive discovery' approach, too, inspired by Piaget's work, involves the planning of appropriate activities by adults rather than the use of a pre-packaged scheme. Kamii and Radin (1970) and Kamii (1971 and 1973) describe the pre-school curriculum which they devised for four-year-old chilren. The general procedure was for the teacher to set up a situation or propose an activity, and to see how the children reacted before deciding what to pick upon in order to extend the child's thinking. Understanding through exploration and activity is stressed rather than the use of language for its own sake, the language being linked to the experiences offered.

3. Direct Instruction

A direct teaching model has been used by Bereiter and Engelmann in the U.S.A. (see 'Teaching Disadvantaged Children in the Preschool, 1966) and in later work by Engelmann and his associates (1970). This model, based on behaviour modification theory, aims at promoting language development through direct teaching of specific skills. It uses a demanding rather than a persuasive approach and requires imitative and structured, rather than individual and intuitive, responses from the children. The teacher takes on a highly directive role, making use of patterned repetition and extrinsic reinforcement as much as possible; children's success is judged in terms of how accurately they imitate the teacher's language model.

Another American programme using a direct instruction model is the Peabody Language Development Kit (PLDK) devised by L.M. Dunn and L.O. Smith in 1964 (Level P is designed for pre-school children). The PLDK is designed, through a series of 180 carefully sequenced daily lessons, to stimulate oral language development. It provides a variety of teaching aids, including pictorial material, puppets, life-sized plastic fruits and vegetables, magnetic shapes and strips, and recordings of different sounds. It aims to encourage creative responses as well as convergent thinking, and offers varied types of activities, including general vocabulary enrichment, the teaching of key sentence patterns and the use of language to serve many functions, ranging from logical and mathematical to social and emotional. A revision of the PLDK has been undertaken by the National Foundation for Educational Research, which has published a British Manual (Quigley and Hudson, 1974).

GOAL - Game Oriented Activities for Learning - is another American structured language development pack devised by M. Karnes, which although expensive is less so than the Peabody Kit. The publishers claim that GOAL is suitable for all children between the ages of 3 and 5 regardless of intelligence, background and handicap and can be used with children who have visual and hearing impairments. Six points are noted in the teacher guide to explain what GOAL does : it develops a desire to learn; it develops a positive self-concept and good emotional development; it develops good social skills; it enhances creative and problem-solving abilities; it promotes motor skills; and it encourages teachers and parents to focus on the language development of children. Reports from schools known to be using GOAL indicate that it offers considerable potential for teachers wishing to design programmes to meet the needs of individual children or small groups.

Some of the ideas from the direct instruction programmes have been incorporated in a more eclectic language programme described by D.M. and G.A. Gahagan in their book '<u>Talk Reform</u>'(1970). Although the Gahagans worked in London infant schools, many of their suggestions can be adapted for nursery groups. '<u>Talk Reform</u>' describes a language training programme (20 minutes per day) advocating a variety of activities, including games, picture stories, drama, small group discussions and direct instruction, with the main aim of improving (a) attention and auditory discrimination; (b) speech; (c) structure and vocabulary.

'<u>Teach Them to Speak</u>' (by G.M. Shiach, 1972) is another programme devised in Britain which relies heavily on formal training in language skills. The book presents a series of 200 lessons which aim to develop oral language in children aged four to seven years. No special kit is provided, and the materials needed can easily be collected or bought, e.g. picture cards, posters, colour cubes, hand puppets and various objects. The lessons, one for each day, last for about half an hour, and are designed to give a feeling of success through graded steps. There is constant revision, drill and repetition, with the emphasis on descriptions and explanations in well-structured grammatically complete and correct sentences. Stress is put on 'expansion' by the teacher, that is, modifying and extending the child's oral responses to achieve a desired sentence form. Some of the activities are somewhat stereotyped and unimaginative, and could be dull for both adults and children; but there is much useful material here for nursery staff to consider.

4. Instructional Dialogue

'Instructional dialogue' strategies have been developed in the U.S.A. by Marion Blank (1973) and in Britain by Joan Tough (1977b). The handbook of suggestions on language activities for disadvantaged children in their first year in the infant school (Downes, 1978), too, while adopting an eclectic stance, owes something to the 'instructional dialogue' approach.

Marion Blank's tutorial language programme is based on dialogue between teacher and child for about fifteen to twenty minutes each day. The main aim of this individual tutoring programme is to help the child to progress towards abstract thinking. The teacher uses no gestures, but helps the child to use language to complete the task set. The child is encouraged to extend his thinking beyond the concrete situation, by, for example, discussing alternative courses of action or attempting explanations of events. Errors made by the child in his verbal responses are used as a basis for developing thinking skills. Inexpensive and readily-available objects (e.g. paper, crayons, blocks, toys, simple books) are all that is needed for the programme. This approach, however, requires more adults to be available than is usually the case in most nursery groups.

Joan Tough's work as Director of the Schools Council '<u>Communication Skills in Early Childhood Project</u>', focusses on ways of discovering what children can do with language and how the teacher can stimulate children to use language for a variety of purposes meaningful to them and for extending their thinking. The following publications relating to this work are available (all by Joan Tough):

A. Books discussing rationale
   1973. Focus on Meaning. London: Allen and Unwin.
   1977a. The Development of Meaning. London : Allen and Unwin.

B. A Guide to the Appraisal of Children's Use of Language
   1976. Listening to Children Talking. London : Ward Lock Educational (for Schools

Council).

C. A Guide to Fostering Communication Skills 1977b. Talking and Learning. London : Ward Lock Educational (for Schools Council).

(A set of video-tapes is also available, published by Drake Educational Associates and Ward Lock Educational).

The handbook by Galen Downes (1978) focusses upon the vocabulary and language structures associated with logical thinking and reasoning. Its main aim is to help children to develop more elaborated speech, including more accurate descriptions and explanations and the use of questions to elicit information. It discusses the development of seven language skills (listening, naming, categorising, describing, denoting position, sequencing and reasoning) through activities and materials. The handbook contains a set of guidelines and suggested activities and games from which a selection can be made rather than a detailed, pre-sequenced 'package' of language activities. Teachers are encouraged to use the normal resources of the classroom to provide stimulation for language development, in addition to producing simple but imaginative materials themselves. Although designed for disadvantaged children in the early stages of formal schooling, many of the suggestions contained in the handbook are applicable to nursery groups.

Children with Severe Language Difficulties

Children with severe speech or language difficulties in the nursery group will need careful assessment, involving speech therapist, psychologist, medical officer or other professionals. In some cases, the emphasis will need to be on fundamental sensori-motor skills rather than on formal language training, and then on building up a basis of receptive language before systematic attempts are made to encourage speech (Reynell, 1973). Where the child has very poor language skills, schemes which assume a low starting point will be found useful. Two such schemes are:

1. 'Let Me Speak' by D.M. Jeffree and R. McConkey, published by Souvenir Press, London, 1976.
2. 'The First Words Language Programme', by B. Gillham, published by Allen and Unwin,

London, and University Park Press, Baltimore, 1979.

Conclusion

We have stressed that nursery staff can do much to promote language skills in the course of their daily work, and that they need to give a lot of thought to planning appropriate individual and group activities. Growing competence in understanding and using language will give the child much confidence and pleasure. We would also emphasise that the influence of the home on early language development is so important that nursery staff should seek to support the parents to the fullest extent, and encourage parental involvement as much as possible. Parents already play a considerable part in playgroups. Nursery schools should actively contribute to toy and book library schemes, and be concerned with a wide range of activities designed to encourage parents to interact naturally but purposefully with their children. Such positive interaction will be of great benefit to the child in his emotional and social development.

REFERENCES AND FURTHER READING

Bereiter, C.E. and Engelmann, S. (1966) Teaching Disadvantaged Children in the Pre-school. Englewood Cliffs, N.J. : Prentice-Hall.

Blank, M. (1973) Teaching Learning in the Pre-school: a Dialogue Approach. Columbus Ohio : Charles E. Merrill.

Bullock Report (Department of Education and Science, 1975) A Language for Life. London ; HMSO.

Cazden, C.B. and Harvey, D. (eds., 1979) Language in Early Childhood Education. Washington, DC : National Association for the Education of Young Children.

Downes, G. (1978) Language Development and the Disadvantaged Child. Edinburgh : Holmes-McDougall.

Dunn, L.M. and Smith, L.O. (1964) Peabody Language Development Kit. Nashville, Tennessee : Institute for Mental Retardation and Intellectual Development, George Peabody College for Teachers (distributed by NFER, The Mere, Upton Park, Slough, Berks SL12DQ).

Engelmann, S., Osborn, J. and Engelmann, T. (1970) Distar Language I and II. Chicago:Science Research Associates.
Gahagan, D.M. and Gahagan, G.A. (1970) Talk Reform. London: Routledge and Kegan Paul.
Gillham, B. (1979) The First Words Language Programme. London: Allen and Unwin.
Halsey, A.H. (ed., 1972) Educational Priority, Vol.1 EPA Problems and Policies. London:HMSO.
Harvey, S. and Lee, T.R. (1974) An experimental study of educational compensation. In Educational Priority, Vol. 5: EPA - A Scottish Study. London: HMSO.
Herriot, P. (1970) An Introduction to the Psychology of Language. London:Methuen.
Jeffree, D.M. and McConkey, R. (1976) Let Me Speak. London: Souvenir Press.
Kamii, C. (1971) Evaluation of learning in pre-school education; socio-emotional, perceptual-motor and cognitive development. In Bloom, B.S. Hastings, J.T. and Madaus, G.F.(eds.) Handbook on Formative and Summative Evaluation of Student Learning. New York: McGraw-Hill.
Kamii, C. (1973) A sketch of the Piaget-derived pre-school curriculum developed by the Ypsilanti Early Education Program. In Spodek, B. (ed.) Early Childhood Education. Englewood Cliffs, N.J.:Prentice-Hall.
Kamii, C. and Radin, N. (1970) A framework for a pre-school curriculum based on some Piagetian concepts. In Athey, I.J. and Rubadeau, D.O. (eds.) Educational Implications of Piaget's Theory. New York:Wiley.
Karnes, M. Goal Language Development Kit available from LBA, Park Works, Norwich Road, Wisbech, Cambridgeshire.
Lewis, M.M. (1968) Language and Personality in Deaf Children. Slough:NFER.
Myklebust, H.R. (1964) The Psychology of Deafness. New York:Grune and Stratton.
Parry, M. and Archer, H. (1974a) Pre-school Education. London:Macmillan Education
Parry, M. and Archer, H. (1974b) Two to Five. London:MacMillan Education.
Quigley, H. and Hudson, M. (1974) British Manual to the Peabody Language Development Kit (Level P) Windsor:Test Division, NFER Publishing Co.
Reynell, J.K. (1973) Planning treatment programmes for pre-school children. In Mittler, P. (ed.) Assessment for Learning in the Mentally Handicapped. Edinburgh and London:Churchill Livingstone.

Shiach, G.M. (1972) Teach Them to Speak. London : Ward Lock Educational.
Sylva, K., Roy, C. and Painter, M. (1980) Child-watching at Playgroup and Nursery School. London : Grant McIntyre.
Thomas, V. (1973) Children's use of language in the nursery. Educational Research, 15, 3, 209-16.
Tizard, B., Philps, J. and Plewis, I. (1976) Staff behaviour in pre-school centres. J. Child Psychol. Psychiat., 17. 21-33.
Tough, J. (1973) Focus on Meaning, London : Allen and Unwin.
Tough, J. (1976) Listening to Children Talking. London : Ward Lock Educational.
Tough, J. (1977a) The Development of Meaning. London : Allen and Unwin.
Tough, J. (1977b) Talking and Learning. London : Ward Lock Educational.
Woodhead, M. (1976a) Intervening in Disadvantage : a challenge for nursery education. Windsor : NFER Publishing Co.
Woodhead, M. (ed., 1976b) An Experiment in Nursery Education. Windsor : NFER Publishing Co.

CHAPTER 5

SPECIAL HELP IN THE CLASSROOM

Introduction

In previous sections of this book, a number of children have been discussed. Richard is shy and withdrawn, lacking in confidence and uninterested in other children. Jonathan clings to the teacher for reassurance but also has temper tantrums and outbursts of rather babyish behaviour. William is overactive, never settling to anything and constantly interfering with other children. Eric is disobedient, rude and aggressive. These four boys pose real but different problems to their teachers. What should they do about them?

Later on in this section you will find descriptions of a number of possible approaches. To start with, however, there will be a discussion of some general principles. Let us suppose first of all that you are faced with Brian in your group. What would you do to help him?

> Brian was recommended for speech therapy by his family health visitor at the age of two years six months. He appeared behind in all aspects of development, especially his speech, and he was given a priority place at nursery school, attending full-time from the age of three years six months. He has a younger sister, Susan, whom he treats rather roughly although he seems fond of her. He is an overweight, rather lethargic boy usually, but given to fairly violent temper tantrums when he becomes frustrated. As his speech is extremely poor and he is often in difficulties over making himself understood, his tantrums are becoming more frequent and occur at home as well as in school. He is well cared for physically

> but the home seems lacking in stimulation of any kind. His mother is young, but she too is overweight and is at times 'thumped' by Brian when he is in one of his tantrums.

There is much more that could be said about Brian but perhaps the above description enables some pointers to action with him to be indicated.

1. He needs stimulating, i.e. he needs the kind of activities that will attract his attention and encourage him to spend some time on them.
2. He needs help with his speech. Therapy is already being offered but a session once a week is not enough for Brian to begin to make good his very pronounced lag in speech development.
3. He needs to learn how to interact with other children so that the possibilities of frustration are somewhat reduced while, hopefully, his language development begins to catch up.
4. The signs of a coming tantrum or the situations which give rise to a tantrum need to be recognised so that avoiding action can be taken. With tantrums prevention is easier than cure.
5. His mother needs some guidance on how to cope with him at home.

So far, so good! But the pointers drawn up above are not very precise. It is not clear exactly what triggers off the tantrums, nor is it clear what Brian can do well. Neither his problems nor his strengths have been exactly noted. The best way to start to try to help Brian would be to complete the schedules (copies of which appear in Appendix A, pp. 257-289),intended to bring together just the sort of precise information which is required. Other people are involved, namely the mother and the speech therapist. The relevant schedules, when completed, would help to quantify what is happening at home and in the clinic as well as indicating who else might be able to help e.g. health visitor/school nurse (with advice to the parents) or educational psychologist (with advice to the teacher and parents).

Perhaps a combination of approaches is required for, indeed, there is not just one problem but a number. Descriptions of these approaches are to be found later in this section).

1. The teacher could use task analysis (pp. 163-174) to break down into simple steps actions such as putting on and taking off his shoes and his coat. His increased competence in the nursery setting might well help his tantrums.
2. A behaviour modification approach (pp. 128-163) could be tried to help encourage his speech. Wholehearted praise and recognition for his occasional one-word utterances might promote more and even longer communication.
3. Simple, imaginative play activities (pp. 92-128) might help his social development so that he learns to share and is confident enough to wait his turn.
4. Discussing his problems with Brian (pp. 177-202) may not be very helpful in this case as difficulties in communication could aggravate rather than alleviate the situation.

Sometimes one approach may seem to be the most likely to succeed, sometimes another, or a combination of approaches. What you have to do now is to read about the various possible approaches and decide which one appeals to you. Do not be put off by the feeling that a suggested approach is very different from your usual programme. It is usually possible to fit in a short session with the children in question on their own (or in a small group) or to give them the necessary guidance and encouragement (as when modifying behaviour) when supervising other activities. If you have a nursery assistant, the situation is much easier. You can either show her what you want her to do with particular children or ask her to cope with the rest of the group while you work with them.

The vital point is to plan your approach to the difficulty. The various schedules when completed should give you a good basis for any decisions you take, and you should note in the Record Book (pp. 290-302) what you hope to do, what you actually do, and what you achieve.

It is sometimes the case that behaviour can change surprisingly quickly when the real problem is identified and tackled. More often, however, change may be slow to come and you should be prepared to spend some time on the approach you have selected. It is difficult to say how long you should spend as this will vary according to the needs of the child you are working with and the techniques you have chosen. A good piece of advice is not to be too ambitious. It is better to work out a series of small objectives which can be comparatively easily reached than to set a goal which is so far from where the child actually is in his behaviour that it may not appear to be even relevant. Rather than setting as your aim, "to improve William's socialisation", it would be better to say, "to encourage William to play for 3 minutes alongside another child". The modest objectives gradually mount up until you realise the tremendous improvement in behaviour when you look back over the record booklet.

If the approach you select does not seem to be working at all, you must first of all consider if you are honestly giving it a chance. If you have decided before you begin that is all a waste of time, then you are very unlikely to succeed. A feeling that the approach is going to work helps you to persevere and achieve your goal. Again, you may not be implementing the approach properly. The methods suggested later in this section all require some changes from normal group procedure. It is unlikely that you are already doing all that they suggest; make sure that you have made the necessary adaptations to your normal approach. But if you have genuinely tried a technique and despite your efforts it has failed, then try another. What works with one child or with one teacher may not be successful with another and you will probably have learned a great deal about the child even if you feel you have not reached your objectives.

It is often argued that teachers and others do not have the time - or the opportunity - to work with one or two children when there are many others clamouring for their attention. Whether this argument is right or not must surely depend on how much time is involved. Children with behavioural problems may take up a lot of time if they are difficult to manage. Very withdrawn children may not be demanding in this respect but they cannot just be ignored. Often what is required is a change of attitude on your part.

Attitudes to Difficulties

Practically every child displays deviant behaviour

at one time or another. Most of these temporary difficulties are coped with adequately by giving unobtrusive support and encouragement. In some cases, however, problems persist or become more marked and children show more than a temporary upset. It is important

1. not to let the problem become magnified. If you look for difficult behaviour, you tend to see it and to miss the occasions on which it may not be in evidence. This is why precise description is so important (see above, pp. 82 and 84);
2. not to let the child's behaviour control your behaviour. Children learn very early how to get an adult's attention, or how to avoid it. It may be better to ignore attention-seeking behaviour, however spectacular, and to praise acceptable behaviour, even if it is minimal to begin with;
3. not to let the difficult behaviour rattle you. It is very seldom effective to have a confrontation with a child who is not behaving as the others are. Apart from the fact that you may not win, a clash of wills can escalate the problem or upset the other children. Rather, avoid the confrontation by the way in which you organise the activities in the nursery group (see below, pp.87-88);
4. not to let your routine or preferred way of working create difficulties. There are some children who do not take kindly to organisation. They may be dreamy, absorbed in a world of their own, impatient or impulsive. While not arguing for them to be allowed complete freedom, it could be suggested that perhaps their problems about conforming could be realised and the demands, at the beginning anyway, made realistic for them;
5. not to let any labels you attach to children get in the way of your objective view of them. It is possible to label children as 'naughty' and only to see them when they are being naughty.

Some of these points are illustrated by the

following example:

> Karen (aged 4½) is an energetic, talkative girl, described by her mother as "rather a handful". She was, until recently, an only child and has been overindulged by her father who sees her infrequently because of the nature of his job. In the nursery Karen appears to be constantly on the move, flitting from activity to activity and rarely completing anything. She demands her own way in most things and this leads to frequent clashes with children and adults alike as she will often resort to tantrums and physical aggression if checked in any way. Much of her behaviour, particularly in group situations, is deliberately attention-seeking and causes considerable disruption. Karen has good language skills and enjoys playing with water and constructional toys.

The nursery class which Karen attends is a large one with over sixty children attending at each session. The sessions are very tightly structured and children are expected to take up activities offered to them at a particular time and leave off when instructed to make way for other children. This fairly inflexible routine ensures that each child at some point in the week experiences all the activities available but, of course, makes little allowance for individual interests. Morning and afternoon sessions are similarly planned with some variations, depending on the availability of T.V. programmes for example, and include several periods when children are expected to sit fairly passively in groups.

For many children this organisation may be perfectly acceptable and it enables the staff to keep track of a large number of children and make sure that no aspect of a carefully thought out programme is being neglected. But for Karen the organisation is not entirely suitable. She is, as we have seen, a rather strong-willed little girl and the demands made upon her by the staff to take up a particular activity at a certain time lead to inevitable confrontations, which not infrequently result in loss of temper on both sides. Being an active child, Karen quickly becomes restless and bored in the numerous 'quiet' group times, and she has learned that shouting out and rolling around the floor quickly attracts the attention she craves.

However, when Karen is interested in an activity she becomes completely absorbed in it and can concentrate for long periods. This too has caused problems, as when she is involved with something Karen does not always attend to requests made to her by staff and her non-compliance is often seen by them as deliberate disobedience. The whole situation is frustrating to the staff and unsuited both to Karen's temperamental and developmental needs. The chances of a tantrum being triggered off are considerably increased and her lack of conformity is acquiring for Karen a reputation of being a naughty, as well as a difficult, child.

There are probably many different solutions to this particular problem, perhaps involving more relaxed individual work building on the good language and co-ordination skills which Karen does have. These possibilities will not be gone into here, although it is interesting to speculate on how a large organisation with a number of staff can be adapted to help individual children. The point is that in this case the school experience was to a large extent being wasted, as Karen was seen as being awkward to cope with, her lack of co-operation was being partly misinterpreted and her 'label', along with the group organisation, was effectively hampering any progress she might otherwise be making. Karen's teachers had adopted certain attitudes towards her, and, unfortuantely, they were not particularly helpful to her.

Some Further Thoughts on Organisation

The role of the nursery staff is primarily to bring about many different kinds of learning in the children with whom they work. They bring professional expertise to bear on the way the room is organised and the decisions taken in it. With young children, the goals set include social and emotional aspects as well as cognitive ones (Clift et al.,1980).

i. Classroom Management

The most obvious facet of classroom management is the organisation of the available space. You should ask yourself whether the way you have arranged the furniture, the storage space, the display areas and so on encourages the kind of controlled, co-operative behaviour wished or whether it invites a lot of movement in which disruption and aggression thrive and withdrawn children are overlooked.

The next point to consider is how effectively any help available to you in the classroom can be used, especially N.N.E.B. personnel. Even with only one other adult present, opportunities for making individual contacts materialise. You have to plan carefully to decide which of you will spend time with children who are having difficulties and what should be done. In this way, the children get the attention they may be striving for and they should also experience success and praise.

Thirdly, the attitudes of the other children to the children in difficulties need to be considered. How can situations be arranged so that those children are seen in the best light by the others? If children cannot share materials, is it realistic to expect them to wait until last to get their turn? How can surplus energy be absorbed while others are completing a task? Can withdrawn children be persuaded to play alongside other children as a preliminary to playing with them? If the children with special needs can appear to behave in a normal manner, this may prevent the group from closing its ranks against them.

Finally, instructions given should be clear and consistent. Children need to feel they are being treated fairly and should know what behaviour is not acceptable. It is better to say, "No", followed by an instruction to do something specific, than just to tell children to stop their activity. Too many negatives should be avoided. Try to present children with a new activity before they begin to mess around rather than wait for their attention to flag and the trouble to start. Vary the type of activities so that interest is re-stimulated.

ii. <u>Decisions in the Nursery Group</u>

Decisions in the nursery group are mainly about the nature of the individual and group programmes to be offered to the children. As with all other children, the programmes for those with behaviour problems need to be built around their strengths (see Assessment Schedule 3, pp.269-276), and to take account of their preferences while tackling their weaknesses. Teachers and others have to be ingenious in contriving materials and situations which are genuinely attractive to children in difficulties and which ensure that they will not fail. It is probably best to set up clear objectives beforehand which do not expect too much of them. Decide what you feel might be accomplished in a week, or a fortnight at the most, and then note whether or not these objectives are achieved. Not only do these decisions help to structure your work and enable others to offer support, they also simultaneously present you with a record of progress. If a desired objective is not obtained, consider why this has happened. Was the objective too difficult for the children to reach (e.g. you expected them to sit still for five minutes when their normal behaviour is that they barely sit at all)? Was the objective irrelevant to them (e.g. you wanted them to complete a jigsaw when they never of their own accord choose this activity)? Did they, in fact, achieve the objective but you missed it (e.g. the first move of a withdrawn child may be a tentative stretch of hand towards a toy or another child)? Would the children obtain the objective if you tackled it in another way? It is very easy to assume that, because children cannot or will not do a thing one way, they are incapable of doing it at all.

Once the children begin to co-operate with you, the objectives need not be so short-term. Records should still be carefully kept so that any slowing down in progress can be noted (see pp.29-31).

While overactive and disruptive children may need a number of brief experiences, withdrawn children may feel more secure if left longer on an activity, provided they are still involved in it. To cut down distraction, it may be as well not to get out too much equipment at any one time and to absorb the children's energy by getting them to help when necessary in the organisation. Again, the demands made on overactive, disruptive children should not be too high and praise should be given for co-operation. Withdrawn children are unlikely to help in this way but care should be taken that they always have the necessary equipment, so that they can model the behaviour of the others if they wish.

Too much emphasis may have been placed in the past on free choice of activity. The teacher's role must encompass the reasonable structuring of the activities to be offered so that all serve some specific purpose and the whole class gets as much out of them as they can. Studies of nursery school children (e.g. Thomas, 1973; Tizard et al., 1976) have revealed that contacts with adults are often limited and language experience negligible in a regime where self-chosen activities predominate. It is not the choosing element which is at fault but the kind of choice offered, so that some children may spend a lot of time on large apparatus, perhaps outside the classroom altogether, while never spending any time in imaginative play or in the book corner. Offering some different activities on different days might help here as would teacher participation, so that the full benefit can be extracted from the activity. Over-structuring should, however, be avoided.

iii. Planning Programmes
When actual planning of specific programmes based on suggested approaches in this book is considered, remember:

(a) these only apply to a small number of children in the class (as completion of the Behaviour Checklist (pp. 257-261) will reveal);

(b) they need to exist on paper, not just in your head;

(c) the children's progress through them has to be monitored at regular intervals and the programme adapted if necessary;

(d) you must feel that any programmes you adopt are likely to work,as nothing is gained by half-heartedly implementing something you do not believe in;

(e) have your aims and objectives clearly in mind.

Opportunities to help one particular child may be difficult to find. In open-plan premises in particular, it may not be easy to control an over-active child or establish a close relationship with a withdrawn one. The main opportunities may arise from working or playing with the child in question when he or she turns to suitable activities. Individual sessions lasting 4 or 5 minutes only may be enough to begin to change behaviour.

To sum up what has been said so far. What staff have to do would seem to be to:

(a) identify children in difficulty;

(b) assess the nature and extent of the difficulties;

(c) analyse the components of the skills to be acquired so that learning steps can be identified;

(d) plan appropriate programmes at the level of the children's functioning in such a way that they develop more skilled or more acceptable behaviour than shown previously;

(e) manage the group to the benefit of all those in it;

(f) observe the outcome of the programme and keep careful notes on how far it has been successful and what needs to be changed.

The best advice to give to teachers is to look for what children with behavioural problems can do or contribute and build up their strengths through praise until they form the bases from which their difficulties can be tackled.

Which Method of Helping should be Adopted?
We are anxious to avoid suggesting that there is one 'best way' of tackling children's problems. Everyone has different ways of working and children are highly individual. No one method will suit every adult and every child. By reading the following sub-sections of this chapter carefully, and chapter 6, you should be able to decide which method seems most likely to work in the case of the children you are considering. Indeed, a mixture of methods may be required and there is no reason why you should not adopt more than one approach. In this way, you can seize on a variety of opportunities to help.

REFERENCES

Clift, P., Cleave, S. and Griffin, M. (1980) The Aims, Role and Deployment of Staff in the Nursery. Windsor : N.F.E.R.

Tizard, B., Philps, J. and Plewis, I. (1976) Play in pre-school centres. I : Play measures and their relation to age, sex and IQ. Journal of Child Psychology and Psychiatry, 17, 251-264.

Tizard, B., Philps, J. and Plewis,I. (1976b) Play in pre-school centres. II : Effects on play on the child's social class and the educational orientation of the centre. Journal of Child Psychology and Psychiatry, 17, 265-274.

Thomas, V. (1973) Child's use of language in the nursery. Educ. Res., 15, 3, 209-216.

FURTHER READING

Hare, B.A., and Hare, J.,. (1977) Teaching Young Handicapped Children. New York ; Grune and Stratton.

Jeffree, D., McConkey, R. and Hewson, S. (1977) Teaching the Handicapped Child. London : Souvenir Press.

Webb, L. (1974) Purpose and Practice in Nursery Education. Oxford : Basil Blackwell.

(1) PLAY ACTIVITIES

When it comes to planning action with a particular child you may like to consider using an approach based wholly or partly on play activies. One of the aims of this section is to examine the kinds of play which have an important role in fostering the social and emotional development of children. Suggestions of activities for developing imaginative and co-operative play are included because they provide such a rich source of social learning opportunities for children with adjustment problems.

This section is in three parts:

I. General principles of using a play activity approach. Here we emphasise the importance of adult participation and take a broad look at some general principles to bear in mind when organising play activities for children with behaviour difficulties.

II. Imaginative Play. A discussion of the

value and functions of imaginative play for children with behaviour problems, together with practical advice for classroom activities.

III. Social Play. Activities for encouraging co-operation between children.

Most nursery staff are used to structuring play activities to suit the developmental level of their group and find the play approach attractive because it is so familiar. However, it is worth considering using some play activities in conjunction with some of the approaches outlined in other sections.

I. General Principles of Using a Play Activity Approach

It has always been emphasised in early education that play should be initiated by the children themselves; they choose what to play and how to play. They should be free from adult restraints and demands and be able to experiment in play without risk of failure. The sulky child forced to 'play' a game of picture lotto by an adult is not really playing. It has also long been assumed that 'play is the work of the child'. Thus, through play the child is able to practise old skills and develop new ones. By providing children with stimulating toys and surroundings it was believed that they would instinctively know how to play and, by playing, foster their social and intellectual development. Accordingly, many teachers have been loath to 'interfere' in the play of young children (recent research has shown as little as 2% of the nursery teacher's time to be spent actually playing with children), believing that the opportunity to play is sufficient in itself to encourage learning and emotional growth. However, the results of studies in which children's behaviour during play was observed have raised doubts about the ability of all children to derive benefit from purely self-initiated play. For example, it has been shown that socially disadvantaged pre-school children do not demonstrate a range of imaginative play nor do they participate in the variety of activities that advantaged children do. Another study demonstrated that working class children in pre-school centres chose to spend 75% of their time outdoors, thus failing to make use of the abundant constructional, creative and fantasy material provided for them inside. It seems that left to their own devices,with no adult participation, guidance or interest, some children are either unable or unwilling to use their opportunities for play to their best advantage. If children are going to develop intellectually, imaginatively or socially through play they need the stimulus of a friendly adult, not just as a provider of suitable materials, but as an active participant, otherwise their play may remain at a very low level and lack any kind of progression.

Play and Difficult Behaviour

Children experiencing social or emotional difficulties are often the ones least able to help themselves through play. Hyperactive children,for example, are not going to benefit from their play experiences if they do not stay in one place long enough to explore the possibilities of the toys and materials set out for their use.

> William is just such a child and is described by his teacher as being "like a wasp in a jam factory". He is boisterous and nearly always on the move, flitting from activity and rarely making use of the materials in an appropriate way. He can be destructive and is very wearing to both adults and children alike, as he disrupts group play continuously. Watching William is an exhausing activity in itself as an average two minutes taken from his teacher's notes will demonstrate. "William pushes his way into the house corner where he bangs the saucepans and kettle and throws them down. He runs off to the dressing up corner, grabs a cape and runs to an assistant to help him to put it on. He gallops around the nursery shouting 'Batman' and, as he passes an open cupboard,takes a swipe at the tins of powder paint. William runs into the cloakroom and jumps up and down on the wall bench. After being brought back into the playroom he returns to the house corner and pulls a doll's cot away from a child and jumps about in it!"

William comes from a materially very poor background and it could be that his behaviour is an understandable over-reaction to what must seem to him an overwhelming array of toys and activities.

His 'flitting' and disruptiveness are actually being exacerbated by his having free choice of such a wide range of toys.

Similarly withdrawn or highly dependent children may not know how to play with other children and if they remain totally overwhelmed by large numbers of boisterous, active youngsters, will have a reduced chance of developing socially.

> Richard is an only child who is over-protected by his mother. Despite the fact that he is a well-developed and sturdy four-year-old he is sometimes brought to the nursery group in a pushchair, or is carried part of the way. At home he plays mainly on his own indoors and even though there are children of his age who live nearby his mother does not encourage him to mix. In the nursery group, Richard is rarely seen to speak or to play with another child. He has one or two favoured activities, such as sand and water play, but will only choose to play with them if there are no other children present. His teacher has never seen him join in any imaginative play activities, in the house corner for example, and has noticed that when other children try to join him in an activity he will often walk away.

Obviously Richard has had little experience of other children and does not have the necessary social skills to either start or join in a game with any success. Without some guidance Richard's social development is going to remain at a very low level and his isolation may become self-perpetuating.

Observations of children at play, carried out by Margaret Manning in Edinburgh (1978),have revealed that aggressive children indulge in friendly co-operative games rather infrequently. They are not often found playing bus drivers, shop keepers, doctors or any of the variations of Wendy House games of mummy and daddy, visiting, cleaning, cooking and so on. It should not be assumed, however, that aggressive children would not like to play such games and would not find them rewarding,as can be demonstrated by the following example of Manning's:

> Alec was charging in and out of the Wendy House, where he upset pots and pans, threw dolls around and disrupted the game that

> was taking place. Surprisingly he eagerly accepted the suggestion of the teacher that he should play a game of mummies and daddies with the girl who was 'at home' and went inside saying, 'I'll be daddy'. Unfortunately, the teacher then went off to another part of the nursery leaving the two children alone in the Wendy House. There they sat for several minutes not saying a word to one another and totally unable to get the game going on their own. Yet, Alec still wanted to play because when the girl later 'went for a walk' with two of her friends he followed them and tried to join in, but without success.

Aggressive, disruptive children like Alec often lack the necessary ability for initiating and maintaining friendly domestic games, so that it may be necessary for nursery staff to actually teach such children how to play games like these. Staff should not just suggest games but should take part in them and actively keep them going when they are in danger of foundering through lack of inventiveness or expertise on the children's part. How different things might have been for Alec if his teacher had stayed and involved herself in the game she had suggested. Not only could she have set the game in motion, but by staying for a while she could have ensured that it did not peter out, either by suggesting a story line or taking on a role herself.

Play and Adult Participation

Some nursery staff have been reluctant to join in chidren's play, arguing that as soon as an adult participates the whole pattern of play changes; the children feel dominated by the adult's presence and either continually look to her for guidance or withdraw entirely. This is an understandable viewpoint, as the line between participation and interference is finely drawn. However, it is possible for adults to share in play without either directing or dominating. Careful observation and a knowledge of the individual children concerned will enable you to judge when to become involved and when to withdraw. The extent of your participation will be different with different children. With a shy, retiring child, like Richard for instance, you could play alongside him, making your own model or sandcastle. In this way you are presenting the child with several opportunities : he can carry on playing whilst absorbing what you are doing; he can imitate you; he can adapt your play and incorporate it into his own, either then or later; or he can share in your play or ask you to join in his. Most importantly, by playing alongside the child you show him that you value and enjoy sharing his play and this could be an important step in establishing a relationship with him.

In contrast, your involvement with highly active children may be of a different kind altogether. You may find you need to employ some of the techniques discussed in the section on Behaviour Modification in order to get the children to sit down and pay attention to toys, games or activities for increasingly longer periods. Initially, they will find these activities rewarding only if you stay and play with them and praise them for their efforts.

Whatever the children's difficulties, it is important not to be discouraged if they appear to ignore your presence or to reject your ideas and suggestions. If you have not regularly joined in children's play, it will take a while for them to accept you in this new role and establish a confident relationship with you as a partner in their activities. Once accepted as a participant, rather than as an onlooker or provider of materials, you will be in an ideal position to initiate play, help its development by your suggestions and maintain it through your continuing interest. Moreover, by involving yourself in play you are modifying the picture some children may have of you as a controlling and sometimes disapproving person. This may be particularly true in the case of aggressive or overactive children, who, because of their behaviour, often attract a great deal of negative attention from adults in the form of reprimands or punishments. It is, therefore, important that children with difficulties are not left to 'drift' either because the nursery group is committed to a 'free play' philosophy or in the fond hope that they will eventually settle in. Nor, on the other hand, should they be coerced into play activities that they are not ready for or find too stressful. (Individual play activities will be discussed later.)

Using Play Activities with Children with Behaviour Difficulties.

The structuring of play activities to aid developmental progression is nothing new and has long been recognised as good nursery practice, but using play, games and toys as a focused way to help children with behaviour or emotional problems requires a slightly different way of looking at things.

As part of the assessment stage you should already have gathered a great deal of information about a particular child or children whose behaviour is causing concern. Some of this will have involved observing children at play and your notes should, therefore, give you some indication of the kind of toys they find interesting and also the complexity of their play - is it at a very basic level or are they inventive and imaginative in their use of toys? This initial observation is important, so that if you do decide to use play techniques you do not choose activities which will either be too difficult or will fail to hold the children's interest. At first you should aim for activities that are well within the children's capabilities so that they are guaranteed the satisfaction of success. Gruadually, you can make the activities more demanding, so that as well as helping to remediate problem behaviour, the play will aid the children's development in other areas too.

Before going on to describe specific play activities in detail it will be useful first to look at some of the general principles you should bear in mind when attempting to help a child with difficulties. Although we will discuss these principles for the four broad categories of behaviour we introduced in earlier chapters, it should be stressed again that the children you are working with may not fit neatly into these pigeon-holes. Children often display a mixture of several kinds of behaviour, but you are in the best position to decide which sorts of behaviour are being the biggest hindrance to the child and you will need to plan your action accordingly.

Aggressive, Anti-social, Destructive Children

<u>Eric</u> (aged 4) is an aggressive, anti-social, disobedient and demanding child. He is often rude and abusive when thwarted or frustrated, and has frequent temper tantrums.

> He hits other children and finds it impossible to share toys, often over-reacting violently if his demands are not met. Although he likes to be the centre of attention, he shuns the physical contact offered by adults. He has good language and self-help skills and is an active child with good co-ordination.

Having a child like Eric in your group poses immediate problems, for you cannot allow his largely unprovoked aggression against other children to go unchecked. Inevitably when young children play together some conflicts and disagreements are to be expected, but if force becomes an established method of getting their own way, children like Eric risk social isolation, as other children will fear them and avoid their company. Eric needs to learn very quickly that kicking, hitting and biting are not acceptable behaviour and this is best achieved by removing him immediately from any such situation. This should be done in a matter of fact way, with the minimum of fuss and without accompanying comments such as "naughty boy" (see section on Behaviour Modification on "sit and watch"). It is not feasible or desirable to ban children like Eric from playing with other children as they need to learn from contact with others that there are effective, alternative methods of getting along which do not involve force. Until he has gained some measure of self-control Eric will need to have a much more structured day, with less free time than other children.

1. At first Eric should always be included as a member of a small supervised playgroup, where with guidance from a friendly adult he can begin to learn other ways of relating to his peers and can be immediately praised for any amicable behaviour. By keeping him constantly busy and in range of an adult, the number of opportunities he has for exhibiting his hostility are considerably reduced.
2. He should not be included in activities that ask too much of him too soon and which will lead to frustration or encourage destructive behaviour, e.g. group play with blocks or games involving long waits between turns.

3. He needs plenty of opportunity to let off steam in an acceptable way, e.g. large floor cushions are good for vigorous but safe bouncing.
4. Situations which have led to difficulties in the past should be avoided or better still altered in such a way as to defuse their potential for disagreements. For instance, if squabbles have occurred on several occasions because there are only two spades in the sand tray, the obvious solution is to provide enough spades for all the children who play there at any one time. This is easily done if the equipment involved is cheap and readily obtainable, but poses problems if the object in question is an expensive item such as a tricycle. However, the promise of five minutes uninterrupted play on the tricycle is a reward worth considering for good behaviour. Alternatively, the person on outside duty could arrange a rota of all those wishing to ride the coveted bike, perhaps using a cooking 'pinger' to time rides and signal when time is up.
5. In large groups, such as story time, he should be kept as near to the teacher as possible so that he can have an unobstructed view of what is going on and is less likely to hit another child for getting in his way.
6. Other adults must be kept fully in the picture about the strategies of management which are adopted with an aggressive child. It is important that all concerned are in agreement about how the child should be handled and stick to any decisions taken, as maintaining a consistent approach is a prerequisite for success.
7. Children such as Eric can be very upsetting, but it is important that adults around him do not resort to smacking him as he needs to learn that physical force is not the best way of handling things.

8. In the early stages aggressive children in a group should be given first 'go' at any activity they are involved in, whether it is stirring cake mixture or a game of lotto. Of course, they have to learn to delay gratification, to take their turn and wait patiently, but this should be a gradual process (see Section on Behaviour Modification).

Destructive Children

Usually a distinction is made between aggression and destructiveness: an aggressive child generally attacks other children without provocation whereas a destructive child tends to break up equipment and playthings. At an earlier developmental stage children enjoy pushing over towers of bricks or flattening sandcastles but normally they move on quickly from this stage and building up takes precedence over knocking down. The play of truly destructive children consists almost entirely in the pleasure of dismantling or destroying toys. Why does this happen? It may be that from their point of view they have exhausted the play possibilities of a particular game or toy. If they are encouraged to explore other aspects of a toy or given more challenging activities, the destructiveness may cease. At the other extreme, frustration sometimes causes children to destroy toys that are too difficult for them in much the same way that older children (and adults!) may upset a games board when they are losing. Yet another possibility is that children who have been reprimanded by the teacher or turned out of a game may nurse resentment and vent their feelings, not by directly attacking those responsible, but by destroying constructions or hurling toys about. You should guard against confusing destructiveness with mere clumsiness as children are often unaware of the need for care when handling fragile objects and may not have attained the fine motor co-ordination necessary to examine things without breaking them. Curiosity and a wish to explore the inner workings of things may also lead children to dismantle objects which as yet they are not capable of putting back together again. This is where your close observations of the circumstances in which children show their destructiveness should give you some indication of where the problem lies and how you can best help.

Destructiveness brought about by frustration or boredom is most readily helped by ensuring that the child is guided towards games and toys that are of the right developmental level. For example, it is easy to see why a child who cannot complete a simple formboard has difficulty with a twenty-piece jigsaw and resorts to hammering the pieces together out of sheer frustration. An observant adult would encourage such children to try puzzles with which they would have a chance of success.

For children who enjoy dismantling objects, there are many take apart toys on the market, ranging from simple graded peg and ring people (Brio) to quite complicated trains and lorries connected by easily removable nuts and bolts. Diverting their interest into toys that can be legitimately taken apart may reduce the frequency of disasters occurring with more precious items.

Experience of handling animals, such as guinea pigs or rabbits (gerbils and hamsters are really too small and quick for nursery age children) can be valuable in demonstrating to clumsy children the need for care and a gentle touch.

Dealing with children who use destructiveness as a means of 'retaliation', either against their peers or you, can be difficult. A further reprimand or attempts to control the behaviour may lead to another bout of destructiveness elsewhere in the nursery. Trying to make children clear up the mess they have made or to apologise may be met with defiance. The more you demand, the more adamant a child may become and a situation is quickly reached where neither party can back down without loss of face. Solutions, such as diverting the child's aggression into more acceptable channels (e.g. hammering at the woodwork table) may work in the short term, but will probably have little lasting effect. It is more than likely that, when faced with a similar situation in the future, the child will again resort to destructive behaviour. Rather than discouraging or diverting the retaliatory destruction, your attempts to help would be better directed towards breaking the behavioural deadlocks these children find themselves in over and over again. Activities described in the section "Problem-Solving Approaches" might effect a lasting behaviour change than would benefit both the children and yourself. This section describes methods aimed at improving the child's social relationships with others, both nursery staff and children, thereby reducing the need for the child to indulge in destructive outbursts. Alternatively, you may like to consider some of the play activities described later in this section, which emphasise the quieter co-operative aspects of pretend play and which may be applied equally well to aggressive and withdrawn children as well as those causing problems because of their destructiveness.

Restless, Overactive Children

Earlier in this section we described William, a highly overactive child, who was never still for a moment and who needed constant adult attention if he was not to cause chaos in his nursery group.

> Nicola (aged 4) has many characteristics in common with William although her restlessness is not nearly so extreme. She is nearly always on the go, rarely completing an activity before moving on to something else. Nicola comes from a caring home and although she is clean and tidy on arrival this rarely lasts long as she seems to attract mess of all kinds and is soon liberally spattered in paint, milk, clay etc. By the end of the session she is often without coat, cardigan, hair ribbons, shoes and socks as they have been taken off and dropped in whichever area she was passing through at the time. She tends to favour outdoor play, possibly because of the greater freedom of movement it allows her and does not show more than a fleeting interest in table-top activities.

Children such as Nicola and William have been rather aptly described as being "all beginnings and no endings". In William's case the multitude of toys and activities available in the nursery group actually worsened his behaviour and the 'flitting' from one thing to another seemed to be related to the number of new activities with which he had suddenly been presented. Nicola, on the other hand, if left to her own devices would spend a large proportion of her time outdoors, racing around, failing to take advantage of the other amenities. Neither child is going to attain the habits of concentration and attention so vital to later learning if they never come to realise that quieter activities, such as jigsaws, drawing, constructional toys etc., can be rewarding too. What can be done to help overactive children like this?

1. To begin with they need several short play sessions during which they have the exclusive attention of an adult, who will immediately praise every sign of co-operation and attention, however fleeting these may be at first. It is a mistake to attempt too much too soon and the children should be allowed to move off after a short period to do something else. Gradually, over a period of weeks, the demands upon their concentration can be increased, but they should be encouraged to achieve and value results even if initially this only means completing a simple inset tray.
2. Ideally, all distractions should be deliberately reduced in these sessions, either by using a screened-off corner or a table facing a wall with nothing in view but the toy or activity in hand.
3. What may be needed to hold the attention of a distractible child is a toy that gives big results for little effort, such as jack-in-the-box or pop-up cone tree. Since these children are also attracted by novelty another way of gaining their co-operation in the first place may be by providing a toy or game not normally available in the nursery group. Provided that presentation is carefully thought out and repeated attempts are made with toys and activities of the right developmental level, the child should begin to take part in longer and longer play sequences.

Shy/Withdrawn Children

It is all too easy to overlook shy withdrawn children such as Richard in the bustle of a nursery session, as they do not make the same demands upon your attention as an aggressive or restless child does. If, after a suitable settling-in period, a child you have been observing remains isolated from others, then you should intervene as the child needs help in overcoming these fears before the withdrawal becomes self-perpetuating. Your attempts to integrate a shy child more fully into nursery life will have to be carefully timed and structured very gradually, beginning with activities in pairs perhaps before any involvement in larger groups.

1. From your observations try to gauge whether the child has shown any interest in a particular toy or activity that will serve as a useful starting point. You may find the child is hovering near a favoured activity,and a wistful expression or a glancing eye movement may indicate that you are on the right track.
2. In the beginning you may have difficulty in getting any response but do not try to force the child's involvement with you as this may make the situation worse. If a child shrinks from physical contact, stares blankly into space when spoken to, or refuses to take an outstretched hand, persist quietly and gently with your efforts until you get some response, however small, that you can praise. Your first attempts may not be highly successful but do not withdraw in frustration as this will only reinforce the child's isolation and make it more difficult to establish contact when you next try.
3. Face-to-face confrontations can be very threatening for shy children, and so it may be better to place yourself beside them and avoid staring directly at them when you speak. Puppets, either the usual glove variety or a hand-and-arm puppet like Emu, can be useful props. Children may respond to a puppet, perhaps only waving to it or shaking its hand at first, even though they will not communicate directly with you. If you use a puppet be sure you give children a chance to respond by leaving some gaps in the conversation. They may not be talking only because they cannot get a word in edgeways.
4. Try to encourage the child in turn-taking activities as it is sometimes easier to produce a physical response rather than a spoken one. You could, for example, take it in turns to:

   (a) blow bubbles for bursting;

   (b) roll marbles down a run;

(c) build towers of bricks and knock them down;

(d) keep a water wheel turning by pouring water.

You can devise many more reciprocal games of this kind using the toys you have available.

5. Look critically at the layout of your room and the kind of materials and activities you provide to see if they can be modified to increase the likelihood of co-operation and social play occurring between children. For example, you could put out floor jigsaws for groups of children to complete, or provide very large sheets of paper for group painting or collage sessions. Try letting several children make one large junk model on the floor rather than individual ones at a table. With a little thought and ingenuity you can easily contrive more situations to foster social play amongst children in your group.

Immature/Dependent Children

Anxiety and a certain amount of 'clinging' behaviour are to be expected when young children are left by their mothers for the first time. Sometimes, however, the problem continues and you may find you are being followed around by a child who has the persistence of a terrier.

> Jonathan (aged 3½) is a small, sickly-looking child. His allround development was at such low level that the health visitor arranged for an educational home visitor to provide tuition and stimulation prior to his enrolment in the nursery. On arrival he cries and frequently clings to an adult for assurance. He cannot attend to his own needs and his inability to communicate adequately makes it difficult for other children to include him in their activities. On some days he wanders aimlessly around the room, oblivious to all that is happening around him, and is unresponsive to commands and questions.

To lessen dependent children's reliance upon you and promote their self-confidence and initiative requires similar tactics to those employed with shy children.

1. Try to include dependent children in small groups of children younger than themselves, preferably involved in a messy activity which requires two hands (such as clay, water, or sand) making it easier for you to slip away.
2. Often such children are physically timid and possibly clumsy, having had restricted opportunities to indulge in the normal childhood pursuits of climbing, swinging or rough and tumble play. Increasing physical confidence may have a beneficial effect that spills over into other areas of a child's functioning. You could begin by encouraging the child to jump off the lowest part of the climbing frame, to run about with you outside: to push the swing etc. Gradually increase your demands, encouraging more daring feats, such as jumping down from a higher part of the climbing frame, and at the same time reducing the amount of help you give so that eventually they will manage independently.
3. Sometimes dependent children are lacking in self-help skills, perhaps because everything in the way of dressing and washing has been done for them by over-solicitous parents. Task analysis (pp.163-174) is a good way of teaching children to manage these important skills for themselves, thereby lessening their dependence on you. Another alternative you could consider is making a big rag doll, with removable clothes, which incorporates all the common fastenings (e.g. press studs, zips, laces, buttons, hooks and eyes etc.) for the child to practise on.

In the following pages we are going to examine in some detail the kinds of play which have an important role in fostering the social and emotional development of children. The emphasis is placed largely upon ways of encouraging imaginative and social play because these provide such a rich source of social learning opportunities for children experiencing difficulties with their behaviour. For the sake of clarity, imaginative and co-operative play will be discussed separately, although the distinction is rather artificial as there is obviously a great deal of overlap between these categories and also with other areas of play.

II. Imaginative Play

All nursery staff are aware of the value and functions of imaginative play in early childhood but it is worthwhile to look at the way such play can help children with behaviour difficulties.

1. Imaginative Play Helps to Promote Thought and Language.

Communicating with shy children, such as Richard, can be a problem, as they will often not respond to direct approaches made by adults or children. Using puppets, however, can be a useful ploy in getting withdrawn children to talk as most children are fascinated by puppets and will chatter quite happily to them.

Because imaginative play is based on plots and themes, it requires the unfolding of longer sequences of activity than other sorts of play and helps children to develop the ability to organise and plan ahead. This aspect of imaginative play has particular relevance for overactive children, like Nicola and William, who engage in continuing restless behaviour, requiring little or no reflective thought. Recent research has shown that helping and encouraging overactive children to take part in domestic and fantasy play increases their concentration and reduces their restlessness. In marked contrast to the kind of rough and tumble play they previously favoured, they become absorbed for longer periods in make-believe play and are able to resist distractions and interruptions from their immediate surroundings. This proved to be the case with Nicola, whose teacher involved her in regular role-playing games over a period of several weeks. Every afternoon Nicola joined a group of about six children in the 'quiet area' and for ten minutes they were led by an adult in a variety of imaginative games. These included acting out small scenes from everyday life, such as a trip to the shops in town or a day at the sea-side, as well as more adventurous themes involving Red Indians or jungle animals. Nicola greatly enjoyed these sessions and joined in with gusto. Although she still favoured outside activities, she was beginning to play for longer periods in the Home Corner and was most attentive during story time, where previously she had been very disruptive.

2. Imaginative Play Helps Children to Understand Others.

By adopting roles in imaginative play, children learn to put themselves in another's place and they get some idea of what it feels like to 'be' mummy, daddy or baby. Through such experiences they gain understanding of the role in question and its attendant responsibilities as well as of the relationships of people to each other. They are also acquiring skill in looking at situations from different points of view, for sometimes they are the 'baddies' and sometimes the 'goodies'. It is possible that children who have learned to see the other child's point of view through make-believe are less likely to be physically aggressive or vicious in their behaviour. Another of the hidden assets emerging from these games, and which is linked to role play, is the increase in sharing and taking turns which you will find. This is not an easy skill for a small child to learn and aggressive children often fail to master it.

Role play also offers the withdrawn child the opportunity of trying out a new, more assertive role (perhaps that of 'Batman' or 'teacher' for example) within the safety of the Wendy House or den. Domineering, aggressive children also learn to accommodate to the demands of the game and to the ebb and flow of the mood of a small group, for without some co-operation the game cannot continue.

3. Imaginative Play Offers the Chance of Practising New Skills

By imitating adults and adopting their roles, children can practise skills they will need later on. These can be of a practical nature such as dressing, washing and cleaning etc.and, perhaps more importantly, also social skills such as holding a conversation, sharing, concern for others, leadership and co-operation. Often, children with behaviour problems are totally lacking in some of these basic skills, the aggressive child like Eric using force to get his own way or the shy child, such as Richard, being unable to start and continue a conversation. Through imaginative play children can learn from adults and children alternative and more appropriate ways of responding.

4. Imaginative Play Helps Children Come to Terms with their Anxieties
During play children are free to act out, at their own pace,situations which may have worried or disturbed them, thereby lessening their potential for upsetting them on subsequent occasions. Make-believe can act as a safety valve for children as they can play out in an acceptable way some of the violent impulses they may feel. Children can be angry towards their dolls or imaginary characters, and screaming or hitting can all be part of the game without any harm being done, as no real people are involved.

Unobtrusive observation of this kind may furnish you with insight into the problems of home or school that are worrying children and which may have some bearing on their current behaviour. Take for instance the case of a child who is feeling very jealous of a new baby in the family. You may notice games in the nursery in which imaginary crying babies or dolls are always scolded or spanked or suffer dreadful punishments. Not only does this suggest that the child wants more attention but it opens the way for introducing more pretend play that will help the child to cope with the role of big brother or sister. Play that offers the child possible ways of sharing in looking after the baby will help in regaining lost self-esteem and in handling the understandable annoyance at the new-comer more constructively.

The Role of the Adult in Encouraging Make-believe Play

Observation. Watching children playing make-believe games is an art in itself, as you have to take care to be unobtrusive and blend into the background. For nursery staff it can be an especially difficult task, as with many children and a high noise level, it is hard to keep track of a particular child, especially when there may be many other demands upon your time and attention. It is,however, a very valuable exercise to set aside five or ten minutes to watch children weaving through the group in free play.

There are several points you should look out for and make note of:

1. does the child you are watching eagerly

join in imaginative play or instead hang about at the edge of the group looking on but not participating?
2. does the child initiate make-believe games or latch on to an established group?
3. does the child always insist on the dominant role, or can a minor role be accepted if insisted upon by playmates?
4. does the child offer to swop roles with other children, taking turns to be the leading light?
5. does the child find a corner and develop solitary play situations?
6. does the child spend most of the time in wild, chasing games of soldiers, Star Wars, Batman etc., with little story line or development?

At this stage it is probably best not to try to introduce a solitary child into a group or to interfere when a rumbustious child is seemingly spoiling the game for others. When you have observed for a while you will quickly begin to pick up play themes, recurring speech patterns, signs of fear or hesitancy and the level of plot complexity. Then you will be in a better position to intervene usefully by offering help and alternative game suggestions.

Set out in Table 5.1 is a simplified guide to the stages of imaginative play, which may be of help when observing children. It should be stressed that imaginative play develops gradually and does not suddenly jump from one stage to the next. You may find when observing children that they incorporate elements from several stages, but with practice you will be able to judge at which level the majority of play takes place.

Table 5.1 Stages of Imaginative Play

<u>First level</u>	Pushes car along (no other actions associated with driving a car). Pretends to feed self, to be asleep, to get washed etc.

Second Level	Imitates a single action, e.g. dusting; ironing; steering; digging. Simple pretend play, e.g. puts doll to bed (maybe upside down), uses box as car.
Third Level	Sequences pretend play - prolonged make-believe involving several 'events' in order, e.g. feeds doll, undresses it, washes doll, puts it to bed. Involved in make-believe play with imaginary characters and imaginary objects, e.g. can pretend to drink from imaginary cup or drive an imaginary car.
Fourth Level	Dresses up and adopts a role, e.g. bridge, doctor, policeman. Uses 'play' voice and appropriate actions. Play is on a particular theme, involves several children and could extend over a period of days.

Participation. The child's world of make-believe is often viewed as a 'secret domain' which should be free from adult participation or interference. It is often said that adult involvement alters the situation, inhibiting rather than promoting children's imagination. Despite the fact that there is a great deal to be said for children being free to develop play as their own imagination dictates, this opportunity on its own may be insufficient for children with behaviour problems. As mentioned earlier, some children are unable to sustain imaginative sequences, particularly those of the quiet, domestic variety, either because they quickly run out of ideas or because they lack the social skills necessary for maintaining a co-operative activity. This may be because these childre have not been encouraged in make-believe before joining the nursery group; perhaps their parents may not have realised the value of such play or may not have had the time to encourage it. Some children have not had the opportunity to watch older brothers and sisters playing and, therefore, have lacked a model to copy. Your participation in the play situation may enable you to introduce elements of imaginative play which may be missing and act as a model that can subsequently be copied.

Planning Activities to Stimulate Imaginative Play. From your observations you should have discovered whether or not the children you have been watching are making the most of their play opportunities. You may find, for instance, that the withdrawn child indulges only in solitary make-believe or that the imaginative play of a hyperactive child, like William, consists almost entirely of running around in a cape shouting, "Batman!" If on the basis of your observations you decide to intervene, you will need to plan carefully in advance what you hope to achieve and how this can best be done within the framework of your particular group. Some suggestions will be offered as to how you can incorporate these activities into your normal routine, but there can be no hard and fast rules about this, as nursery groups will differ in both organisation and in the number of adults available. Many of the activities suggested will be familiar to you and you may feel that you are already doing most of them, but it is intended that you should use them in a much more structured and systematic way than is usually the case, focussing on the deficiencies or difficulties children may be facing in their play.

Group Size and Composition. Most of the activities are designed for small groups of five or six children working with an adult for 20-30 minutes per session. In a group of this size there are sufficient children to ensure plenty of interaction but not so many that some children never get a chance to participate. This number should not be too overwhelming for quieter children and allows them the chance to remain on the periphery of the action without causing undue concern, as even if they do not become involved they may be absorbing a great deal and this will be reflected in later play.

> Richard is an example of a little boy who perfectly illustrates this point. He was, as you may remember, a shy child who chose mainly solitary activities and had rarely been observed to speak to or play with another child. For several weeks his

> teacher included him in a small group of four year olds who met for twenty minutes each day and took part in a variety of role playing games and activities. Richard did not join in at all but sat unspeaking and watched the games intently. During all this time his teacher continued to observe Richard in free play sessions and found that a remarkable change was taking place. He was becoming much more outward going,to the extent that one member of staff had to reprimand him for being giddy and noisy. He began to challenge other boys for the use of the nursery's only bicycle and was seen in the playground taking charge of a small group of children, leading them around in a line chanting and singing a song. For the first time he joined in playing imaginative games with other children in the domestic corner and was overhead making up a story whilst playing with the doll's house.

This example shows that even shy children have the capacity for make-believe but may need some form of encouragement or model to follow before they can easily become involved. Richard not only found himself playmates but was trying out new words and increasing his vocabulary, as well as becoming more assertive and self-confident.

Try to ensure that all the children in the group are at about the same level of play and do not include very young children who may not be ready for group play and may be disruptive as a consequence. Similarly, gathering together in one group all the children you consider to be having difficulties could be a recipe for disaster. You will have to use your judgement and try out various combinations of children until you achieve fairly balanced groupings.

Suitable settings. Ideally, the activities should take place in a quiet area screened off from the main body of the room. Some nursery groups have separate story or quiet rooms which could be used; otherwise you could improvise by re-arranging large items of furniture to create a private space free from distractions. This is especially important for overactive children, whose concentration may be easily lost if they can see interesting activities elsewhere in the room.

Organisation. Some nursery groups may be lucky enough to have a high ratio of adults to children so that it is relatively easy for one adult to work undisturbed with a small group for part of the session. If you are working with only one other person, small group work can pose problems. However, if all the children come together for story time or singing then this could be your opportunity to take your group off elsewhere for twenty minutes or so, leaving the other adult in charge of the remainder. You could also consider, if you do not do so already, inviting mothers as helpers to either the morning or afternoon sessions. If they come in on a regular basis then you can use the times when there are extra adults around to work with your groups.

Again, some nursery groups have a rota system whereby every adult is responsible for particular activities in different areas of the nursery each week (e.g. outside play, messy activities such as sand, water, clay or a collage and model building area). Perhaps in this case, one adult could oversee two adjacent areas, freeing someone else to take over the play sessions with a small group. Adding the play sessions to the weekly rota would also give each adult a chance to plan activities for the week ahead rather than it being the responsibility of one person. This system has the added advantage that all the personnel would be involved at some stage and would be fully aware of the problems and progress of individual children.

In nursery groups where each adult is responsible for a particular group of children with whom she is expected to complete some daily activity, then it should not be difficult to introduce group play sessions at these regular 'get togethers', providing, of course, that the numbers in the groups are not too large.

Suggested Activities for Imaginative Play Sessions

Overleaf is a list of activities for you to try out in your play sessions. Although by no means comprehensive, the list of games will act as a starting point and, no doubt, as you progress they will be transformed and elaborated upon by the children taking part.

1. Developing Awareness of Feelings

One of the difficult skills that children must learn as they grow up involves understanding the messages people send to each other without words. Facial expressions, body positions and gestures all convey messages about the way people feel. Children discover these clues to others' emotions slowly and learning what facial expressions signal is perhaps the easiest part of the process to begin with. You can help children develop sensitivity to another's feelings by increasing their awareness of the facial and bodily expressions of those around them through games and activities. Poorly adjusted children may not be aware of the effect of their behaviour on others, and games which increase their awareness of other children's feelings will aid their emotional and social development.

Faces Game. For this game you will need a large mirror, pictures cut out of magazines showing different facial expressions and stories illustrating some of the different moods children experience (see booklist at end of section). The idea is to demonstrate different moods to children through your own facial expression and have them guess what you are feeling. You could show happiness, sadness, anger, surprise or disgust, talking about each of them as you go along. See if the children can pick out examples of each type of face from the pictures you have collected. Let them imitate your expressions and watch themselves in the mirror as they do so. Ask questions and give examples of the different faces people use on different occasions, e.g. "What kind of face do you have when its raining and you cannot go out to play? Show me a 'sad face'" or "Ooh, some of your dinner fell off the plate and made a mess on your dress! Show me a 'disgusted face'. Now clean it all up and show me a 'happy face'". Once you have led the way the children may make up their own stories and suggest the faces to go with them. Read stories that demonstrate different emotions and ask the children to show you how the characters felt (e.g. how did Baby Bear feel when he came home and found his chair broken? Show me a sad face).

By watching you pretend you are sad or happy or angry, and by imitating your facial expression and looking at their own in the mirror, children will begin to learn to identify the expressions of others around.

2. Role-Playing Games

The idea of these games is to encourage children to try out a variety of roles and thus extend the repertoire available to them in make-believe play. Being able to adopt appropriate roles in pretend play opens the door to additional ways of making contact with other children and of learning further roles along the way. A child who quickly grasps what is involved in a game of 'spacemen' or 'school' is able to move smoothly into a small group and be accepted into the game, unlike the little boy, Alec, who wanted to be 'daddy' but did not know how to go about it.

(a) Who am I?

In this game you mime the activity of someone at work for the children to guess. Keep the mimes simple at first and ensure they are concerned with a familiar person or event, e.g. a policeman controlling traffic, a bus conductor, a road mender, a milkman, a postman. The child who guesses correctly mimes the next person for the group to guess. Initially you may have to offer suggestions and even the mime, encouraging the child to copy your actions.

(b) What am I doing?

This is a similar game but this time you mime an action the children will be familiar with from everyday activities for them to guess. The child who guesses correctly mimes the next action, e.g. eating, washing up, driving a car, knitting, sewing etc.

(c) Bag of Hats

Children seem attracted to hats of all kinds and often will happily assume a new identity with the addition of the correct headgear for the occasion. Collect as many hats as you can, e.g. for a nurse, king or queen, fireman, policemen, cowboy, sailor, soldier, a bride, a bridesmaid, a spacemen, a motor cyclist, a witch or wizard, a magician; and for home roles, a lady's hat and a man's hat or cap. Put all the hats in a large bag (a black plastic refuse bag would be ideal) and let the children pull out one at a time. When they put on the hat help them to act out the character as suggested in the examples below:

Nurse's hat - have the children pretend to be ill. Ask the nurse to look at their tongues, feel their pulse, take temperatures etc. The nurse can pretend to administer medicine to make them better.
Fireman's hat - all pretend to smell the smoke - dial 999 for the fire brigade and make loud siren noises as the fire engine arrives. Help the fireman to put up his ladder, unroll his hosepipe, rescue the family and put out the fire with plenty of swooshing noises for the water.

(d) Acting-out Stories
Most children in a nursery group will have joined in with actions to favourite rhymes and songs such as 'Incy Wincy Spider' and 'Row row row your boat' and so it should be a relatively easy step to acting out simple stories with several characters. A familiar tale is much easier for children who are playing a role for the first time, as they are less self-conscious if the story is part of their world (good examples are the Three Billy Goats Gruff, Goldilocks and the Three Bears, the Three Little Pigs). Be sure to read or tell the stories aloud several times first and afterwards encourage the children to remember the correct sequence of the plot by discussing the reasons behind some of the events in the story. For instance, "Why did the Billy Goats cross the bridge?" or "Why did little Bear start to cry?" or "What happened next?" etc.

At first the whole group can go through the actions of the story together, e.g. all standing up and looking big and strong when Father Bear is mentioned or making themselves small and using a tiny voice for Baby Bear. Later the children can be assigned individual roles and act out the appropriate part as you tell the story.

Only a minimum of props are required. In the 'Three Billy Goats Gruff', for example, a small table will serve as a bridge for the troll to hide under, whilst the goats walk across the top. Do not be tempted to use costumes as they distract children from the story, and in the limited time available may cause more trouble than they are worth.

Once the children have gained confidence by acting out familiar stories they will find it easier to draw on their own powers of inventiveness and you can then move on to acting out familiar or recent events that have happened in their lives, such as a birthday party, a visit to the hairdresser or a trip to the seaside.

(e) Puppets

Some children feel less inhibited about acting a story or singing a song if they can do it through a puppet rather than by themselves. If this is the case, it may be better to introduce puppets in an earlier play session before attempting to act out fairy stories.

Puppets can be easily made from old socks, mittens or old rubber balls on sticks. You may be lucky enough to have a puppet theatre or a three-sided screen that doubles as a shop or a theatre. If not, a large box, with the bottom folded inwards, standing on a table, will do just as well. Drape a piece of material over the back of the box, so that the puppeteers are not seen by the audience.

The children can make the puppets sing, enact nursery rhymes or even act out simple stories, as suggested above.

(f) Play themes using small scale toys

For these sessions you will need a collection of small scale toys such as cars, lorries, trains, boats, miniature dolls such as Play People, together with plasticene or playdoh, lego, wooden blocks and shapes.

The idea is to act out small plots or themes (based, if possible, on the children's interests) in which the miniature people are made to talk and engage in make-believe roles and the play materials are used imaginatively as props.

Have a clear idea of the theme you intend to use, beginning with simple everyday occurrences, such as a shopping trip to town, and in later sessions move on to more exciting plots such as pirates, witches or rocket trips to the moon.

For a game of pirates, for example, you could use a large sheet of blue paper for the sea, plasticene for islands and sharks, lego or wooden blocks for boats and play people for the pirates. The ships can sail along with the pirates keeping a look out for a treasure island. Suggest adventures they could have on the way : a man overboard, sharks coming, a storm, rescue at sea and so on. Finally, they reach the island and dig up the treasure. Encourage each child to help in the construction of the boats, islands and sharks and to adopt a role and talk as though he were a character in the story you are unfolding. They can also be shown how to simulate the sound of waves and wind and teach them 'pirate' phrases such as "Yo ho ho and a bottle of rum" and "Shiver me timbers".

Small scale play themes such as pirates can easily be transformed into large scale versions by the provision of suitable props for the children to use, such as eye patches, headscarves, gold earrings, card-board swords and moustaches.

By carefully planning activities you should be able to encourage skills and help the children learn to play with their peers and to work through some of the feelings or rivalry and jealousy that are common in this age group. But this can only happen if you do not overwhelm them by making the games another duty or task to be mastered. Be careful not to dominate the game or organise the play too highly so that it turns into a chore or a drill. You need to be able to recognise the moments when you may be pushing too hard and when a quick change of direction can make all the difference in helping a child to use to the full what you are offering in your play sessions together. Play may be the main 'business' of childhood, but if it is not fun it is not really play.

III. Social Play

We will now turn our attention to activities aimed

at promoting social play, i.e. activities based on interaction between two or more children. It is only at the beginning of a child's fourth year that co-operative play begins to emerge and even then it rarely involves more than two children who may not stay together for very long. Only among the older four and five year-olds does group play become increasingly common, involving up to six children playing together for much longer periods.

There is some evidence (Sylva et al., 1980) which suggests that the most natural and fruitful grouping to encourage amongst pre-school children is the pair. Observations in playgroups and nurseries revealed that not only did play between two children enhance social interaction, but that the highest proportion of challenging and complex play occurred while the children were in pairs. They concluded that nursery staff should encourage children to play in pairs as this might foster interpersonal skills and improve the intellectual level of their play.

It is worthwhile considering some of the many reasons why social play is particularly important for children in this age group who are experiencing difficulties.

1. Shy children may isolate themselves from other children by deliberately choosing solitary activities such as painting at an easel or completing an inset tray. Thrusting them prematurely into a group of children may totally overwhelm them and only increase their isolation. A less stressful way of easing them into nursery life may be to engineer play activities for them that follow the normal stages of development of social play. Thus the first step would be to encourage them to build a block castle or draw on a large sheet of paper with one other child. Each need only be concerned with his/her bit of it but working together with another child greatly increases the chances of them co-operating to produce the finished article, particularly if you suggest a few different types of buildings they could make or an idea of a picture to draw. Once a child is used to the idea of playing alongside another child you can try introducing activities that really

do require co-operation such as simple picture dominoes or lotto or other basic board games. By providing rewarding alternatives to solitary play you may find the child manages the transition into group play much more easily than would otherwise be the case.

Remember Jonathan, the withdrawn, immature and dependent little boy whose problems were compounded by his poor language skills? On entry to the nursery his play was at a very low level. He would suck and chew toys baby fashion and would throw a tantrum if other children tried to join in with his play. After a period of observation his teacher planned a programme of activities for Jonathan designed to take him through some of the earliest stages of play in an attempt to improve his level of social development. To build up a trusting relationship with him she began by playing some of the games mothers play with small children whilst simultaneously trying to encourage his speech. Gradually, over a period of two terms, the games became more demanding and other children were introduced into the sessions. To begin with, one other child stood and watched and later he sat down and was included in the activity. By the end of the school year Jonathan was able to participate quite happily in a game of picture lotto with a group of children, chatting both to them and to his teacher.

2. Children who are boisterous and aggressive may be rejected by all but a few like-minded children because of the wild rough and tumble games they favour. Aggressive children are often very selfish, wanting their own way, rarely considering another child's point of view and backing up their demands by force. To some extent all young children are selfish, but generally as they grow older they learn to adapt and find more socially acceptable ways of resolving situations than by hostility. Social play can be a valuable tool in helping aggressive children to share and take turns, which in the long run makes them easier to get on with. You could, for

instance, teach such children simple board games so that they are bound by a clear cut set of rules and turn-taking is essential for the game to continue. Once they have mastered the rules, on the poacher turned gamekeeper principle you could then suggest that, since they are so good at the game, they should teach another child how to play. This will boost their self-esteem and allow them to show off their prowess in an acceptable way rather than proving themselves by boasting and physical domination. Even though they seem unlikely candidates, aggressive children often prove to be surprisingly good instructors of tasks or feats at which they are adept.

3. Many resless overactive children spend most of their day in physical pursuits, running, climbing and swinging and often have difficulty in adjusting to school later on because they find it difficult to sit still and concentrate for more than a few minutes at a time. Some of the table-top activities suggested further on would be useful in introducing children to the quieter sedentary occupations that will be expected of them later. Initially you may have to play the games or do the activities with them, so that they are praised sufficiently for their efforts and will then come to find the activity rewarding in itself.

   William, for instance, was given ten minutes of exclusive attention everyday by an adult in the peace and quiet of the Head's office with a toy, book or game of his choosing. His concentration during these periods was much greater than his teacher had originally thought he was capable of sustaining, and it began to spill over into the rest of his day. Having once experienced the satisfaction of completing a jigsaw with the help and praise of an adult, he began to try others on his own and eventually would persevere even with quite difficult ones.

Fostering Social Play

In a sense all play can be 'social' play. Many imaginative play activities, for example, are particularly suited to getting children to play together. To begin with, however, it is a good idea to direct children towards activities which really do need two children and are not capable of being played by a child on his own. You are, in effect, 'forcing' the children to play together as the activity can only continue if both take part. Ideally, the first games should not involve one child waiting for a turn while the other plays, and neither should you have to stay and direct operations. One other point to bear in mind is that the children should be able to cope with the action or actions that the activity demands. Children who are frustrated by a difficult physical element in a game will stop playing.

Set out below are a few suggestions for both energetic and table-top games, chosen because of their intrinsically social nature. This is not meant to be a comprehensive list and it is likely that you will have many ideas of your own which will extend these basic suggestions or add to them. It is also a good idea to take a close look at all your games and equipment and evaluate them in terms of their potential for increasing co-operative play. For instance, many of the normally solitary activities such as drawing, painting, modelling in clay or plasticene etc., can easily be adapted for two by providing larger sheets of paper or bigger boards. A little thought about the activities provided and the layout of your room can greatly increase the likelihood of co-operative play developing and thriving in your group.

Energetic Activities

Push carts and tyres on castors. Toys like this, where one child pushes whilst the other rides, are greatly enjoyed by children and the activity can be extended by introducing an imaginative element, e.g. pretending it is a bus or a train.

Rocking boats. A much safer, if more expensive, version of the old fashioned see-saw. Rockers, whether of metal or wood, lend themselves to all kinds of fantasy play and children have to co-operate to produce the rocking motion.

Ball games. Simple throwing, catching and kicking games between two children are as much social play as they are good outlets for surplus energy. Very young children may need to practise throwing and kicking with you first, to ensure they have sufficient skill to maintain a game with another child without becoming frustrated. Large foam balls (made by Combex) are ideally suited to a young child's first attempts at throwing and catching, as they do not hurt if they accidentally hit a child in the face.

Table-top Activities

Apart from games with rules, which will be described separately, most table-top activities do not usually require two children. However, you should encourage children to play together in other activities, even ones which they could play by themselves.

Drawing. Give a pair of children a large sheet of paper they can both draw on without getting in each other's way. Suggest a particular scene for them to draw themselves, each child being responsible for a different part, or draw an outline yourself for them to colour in. Perhaps you could make this joint activity rather special by allowing them to use felt tip markers (if these are not normally available) or a special set of new, unbroken crayons.

Large jigsaws. Large table or floor jigsaws, which can be worked on by two or more children, could be made available as well as the more usual small inset variety.

Games with Rules

Even young children can master the rules of simple board games, which once learned greatly increase the range of social activities available to them. Admittedly, at first you will have to spend some time explaining the rules and acting as referee, but as the children's ability to play correctly increases, you should be able to leave them to it.

Games for two are best to begin with, as the more children taking part, the longer each will have to wait for a turn with accompanying impatience. They should have a minimum of rules and for this reason a home-made game may be preferable to a commercially produced one, as even a simple game such as 'Snakes and Ladders' has too many rules for a beginner to grasp all at once.

<u>A basic game for beginners.</u> You need two strips of card, each divided into about 10 squares, and a die marked with three red and three green spots. The children take turns in throwing the die, but only move forward one space when the green spot is uppermost. The first child to reach the end of a strip is the winner.

The game has only ten squares, so that it does not go on long enough for the children to lose interest. Having the squares in a straight line makes it easier for children to see and understand the rule of moving from start to finish. Replacing the die numbers with spots allows children to get used to throwing the die without necessarily being able to count.

The game can be made more interesting by using toy cars instead of counters with a picture of a garage at the end of the strip for them to 'drive' into; having plastic frogs hopping to a pond; plastic spiders climbing drainpipes; mice going up a grandfather clock etc.

Once the basic idea of the game and rules are understood, you can make more complicated versions by having a longer course; varying the shape of the course by adding bends and loops; having only one course that children race along together; using a die with dots, perhaps only 1 and 2 dots to start with; introducing hazards such as ladders that take the counters back several spaces, etc.

<u>Other Games</u>

You probably already have simple dominoes (either the picture, shape or touch varieties), lotto games and Pelmanism, but it is worth looking at other more complicated games such as ludo, to see whether or not you can make a simpler version yourself. If you are stuck for ideas it may be useful to scan the pages of Educational Supplies catalogues for inspiration.

Obviously it would be impossible to cover all the various kinds of play activities which could be used constructively to help children overcome the emotional and behavioural difficulties they may be experiencing in the nursery group. However, it is hoped that you will find the suggested games and activities useful when planning a programme for an individual child.

Included at the end of this section is an annotated list of several books which contain many more ideas for play activities than can be included here. Also appended is a list of children's books which may be useful starting points for imaginative play.

BIBLIOGRAPHY

Freyburg, J. (1973) Increasing imaginative play in urban disadvantaged children through systematic training in J.L. Singer (Ed.) The Child's World of Make Believe: experimental studies of imaginative play. New York : Academic Press.
Garvey, D. (1977) Play. London : Fontana/Open Books.
Gould, R. (1972) Child Studies through Fantasy. London : Quadrangle Books.
Jeffree, D.M., McConkey, R. and Hewson, S. (1977) Let Me Play. London : Souvenir Press.
Manning, K. and Sharp, A. (1977) Structuring Play in the Early Years at School. London : Ward Lock Educational.
Manning, M. (1978) Exploratory study on the management and treatment of difficult children in a nursery school (personal communication).
Marshall, H. and Hahn, S. (1967) Experimental modification of dramatic play. Journal of Personality and Social Psychology, 5, 119-122.
Saltz, E., Dixon, D. and Johnson, J. (1977) Training disadvantaged pre-schoolers in various fantasy activities : effects on cognitive functioning and impulse control. Child Development, 48, 367-380.
Singer, D.G. and Singer, J.L. (1977) Partners in Play. New York : Harper and Row.
Smilansky, S. (1968) The effects of sociodramatic play in disadvantage pre-school children. New York : Wiley.
Sylva, K., Roy, C. and Painter, M. (1980) Childwatching at playgroup and nursery school. London : Grant McIntyre.

FURTHER READING

Jeffree, D.M., McConkey, R. and Hewson, S. (1977) Let Me Play. London : Souvenir Press.
Written for parents, teachers, nursery assistants and playgroup leaders of handicapped children. Contains a programme of games devised to encourage motor and sensory skills, intellect, imagination and social confidence.

It was developed through the Parental Involvement Project of the Hester Adrian Research Centre at the University of Manchester.

Manning, K. and Sharp, A. (1977) Structuring Play in the Early Years at School. London : Ward Lock Educational.
Based on the work of six hundred teachers who took part in the Schools Council Project on the Structuring of Play in the Infant and First School. It describes ways in which teachers can structure play by the provision of materials and their own involvement. Examples of play situations that teachers can adapt for use in their own classroom are included.

Riddick, B. (1982) Toys and Play for the Handicapped Child. London : Croom Helm. As well as describing the developmental needs of babies through to 5-year-olds, also provides a 'consumer's guide' to choosing and buying toys.

Singer, D.G., and Singer, J.L. (1977) Partners in Play : a step-by-step guide to imaginative play in children.
This book sets out the basic principles of fantasy play, and presents in a step-by-step format, explicit games to stimulate the various senses and encourage make-believe for the 2-5 age group. Included are indoor and outdoor games and activities suitable for the solitary child or groups.

(2) BEHAVIOUR MODIFICATION

INTRODUCTION

Mark is an overactive, uncontrolled and rather awkward little boy. He rushes around the nursery at high speed, bumping into furniture, knocking over a half-assembled tower and then disrupts the activities of another group of children playing quietly in the Wendy House. Despite strenuous efforts and repeated requests by the nursery staff to slow down and join in with the others for a reasonable length of time, he continues to be a very disruptive influence in the nursery. The staff feel that he is basically unhappy about not joining in with the other children and that he rushes around a lot in order to gain attention from them and from the staff. They believe that he *can* be helped but are at a loss to know where to start and what to do to help him.

Those who believe in behaviour modification techniques would suggest a course of action to help Mark along the following lines.

Firstly, Mark's behaviour needs to be carefully observed over a period of time, with sample observations being taken each morning for a few minutes in each hour. The aim is to try to find out when he seems more active than usual and what conditions seem to trigger off this overactivity. His quieter moments will also be noted and the circumstances in which he slows down, perhaps when he comes across a favourite toy or has contact with a particular friend. On the basis of these observations, collected over a series of days or weeks, the conditions which seem to make Mark's behaviour better or worse can be discovered. The observations will also show Mark's normal behaviour level, and will act as a 'baseline' on which a programme of retraining or intervention can be built, making the most of the situations where his behaviour is nearest to acceptability. Some suggestions follow as to what you could do if you had a child like Mark in your class.

First of all, you must decide what it is you want Mark to do. This is the goal towards which you are aiming and the programme you devise is intended to encourage Mark towards the behaviour you would like to see - for example, sitting in his seat for a reasonable period of time. How would you set about it?

Restrain Mark in a firm but gentle way and make him sit down at a table. Keep him there for a few minutes and then give him a reward, perhaps a smile and a hug, and then allow him to run about for a few minutes (a further reward). A little later in the morning restrain him again and reward him in a similar fashion. You may go on like this for several days.

When Mark shows a tendency to approach a chair, reward him with a wave and a smile, or give physical prompts (i.e. point at a chair and tell him to sit down). In the early days of the programme he should be rewarded each time he slows down and approaches a table or chair in a controlled way. What you are doing is building up his good behaviour-establishing a number of good responses that will result in his becoming more controlled and more able to join in with the other children. Naturally, you give him a lot of praise and attention if he sits down.

If Mark does anything constructive, like helping in a game involving children, reward him. He may be merely approaching other children in a controlled fashion and picking up a toy that has fallen on the floor. Reward him strongly - give lavish praise, even though this may appear inappropriate for such a trivial act. In terms of Mark's behaviour, it is not trivial, it is a very big step forward and possibly the beginnings of a major improvement that will be maintained.

Mark's behaviour must be monitored carefully (i.e. observations of his behaviour must be continued on a daily basis and his record kept up to date) so that you will have an objective statement of any change (for better or worse) in his behaviour. If at the end of the programme his behaviour has not improved as much as you had hoped, you will have to try again, perhaps modifying the programme somewhat. With a good deal of persistence and skill on your part, Mark's behaviour should improve and, though progress may be painfully slow at first, a change will almost certainly be achieved.

To summarise the approach that you have adopted with Mark:

Question: What did you do for Mark?
Answer: You SATIM down!

You helped him become more controlled and able to sit down and concentrate and enjoy games with the other children by applying the following procedures to his problem behaviours:-

S ystematically observing
A ssessing and analysing
T argetting (i.e. setting a goal for him)
I ntervening and systematically training
M onitoring, reassessing and changing the intervention.

The approach is largely based on the assumption that most of our behaviour (whether this is 'good', 'bad' or inappropriate) is learned. Thus the degree to which a child joins in the activities in the nursery group will be the result of the success or failure of the social learning experienced in the home, nursery and elsewhere. The essence of the behaviour modification approach is put succinctly by Vance Hall (1977), ".... behaviour modification, as the name implies, is concerned with changing behaviour in desirable directions, that is, increasing the strength of appropriate behaviours and decreasing the strength of those that are inappropriate".

Behaviour modification is, therefore, a very 'common-sense' approach. It deals with the realities of the child's behaviour as you observe it and aims to devise a sensible course of action to help the child, within the confines of what can be done in the classroom or group. It places great emphasis on the importance of the real-life situation. In essence it says, "Here is the child, this is how he or she usually behaves and this is what we will attempt to do to help this child". It recognises the paramount importance of parental influence - much work has been done in training parents as behaviour modifiers - and aims to help the child deal with real-life problems in a better way. Nursery staff, if they decide to adopt this approach, will be concentrating upon the child's present behaviour in the nursery environment and will be seeking to arrange conditions in such a way that the child's problem behaviour can be controlled and modified for the better.

Time and Staff Involvement

Very often, the use of behaviour modification will merely involve giving a little more structure to the activities that are carried out normally in the nursery. In fact, the techniques will be more readily understood if you try to relate them to your daily nursery activity. For example, you may wish to encourage a shy child to involve herself more in playing constructively in the Wendy House with a group of other children. The changes that you make might be merely to concentrate more attention on this one child by prompting and rewarding her actions in a more systematic way than you do with the other children in the group. Again, if you have an aide, or if more than one teacher is working in the room, you can arrange for individual attention to be given to the child in question either by yourself or by someone else who fully understands what you are aiming to do.

Outline of the Rest of this Section

It is not possible here to give a comprehensive review of behaviour modification. What we have tried to do is to select those procedures that seem to be most appropriate for helping young children in a nursery setting.

The rest of the section is divided up as follows:-

- Part I — discusses the basic principles which underlie behaviour modification
- Part II — deals with methods of observation, assessment and measurement
- Part III — examines methods of encouraging or increasing appropriate behaviour
- Part IV — looks at methods of discouraging or decreasing inappropriate behaviour
- Part V — describes some applications of behaviour modification techniques to typical problem behaviour
- Part VI — outlines the specialised technique of TASK ANALYSIS

Do not be put off by the apparent length of the section as a whole. What we suggest you do in your initial reading is to quickly review Parts I, II, III and IV. Then read Part V fairly thoroughly as this will give you a good idea of how the method is put into practice. At a later stage in your reading you will want to read all the parts more thoroughly but remember that you are not expected to plough laboriously through it from first to last. Part VI on task analysis can be treated largely as a separate entity, though many of the basic principles described in Part I will be relevant to it.

PART I

BASIC PRINCIPLES

1. Reinforcement

The idea of reinforcement may be stated simply as follows:- if behaviour is immediately rewarded, then it is more likely to be repeated. For instance, if you smile at your next door neighbour in the morning on the way to work and she smiles back, you are much more likely to smile at her again the next morning than if she had frowned and looked away. Put in another way, the fact that she smiled back at you reinforced your act of smiling at her.

Reinforcers (rewards) have been classified in a number of ways, but for the practical purposes of applying behaviour modification techniques they may be thought of as tangible (or material) rewards such as food, drinks or tokens and social rewards such as praise, a hug or other signs of approval. Often reinforcers are presented together; thus good behaviour might be rewarded by giving a child a sweet and a hug and saying clearly what it is that is being rewarded. In broad terms, reinforcers will determine future behaviour. Both children and adults will tend to repeat behaviours that they feel have brought them a reward, and they will tend not to repeat behaviours that are not rewarded.

Some basic principles of reinforcement are given below, but a word of caution might be given at this juncture. Though these principles have been tried and tested and found, on the whole, to be true in controlled experimental situations, the chances of obtaining success in applying them in 'real-life' will depend a great deal on your skill in observing the child's behaviour, analysing this carefully and designing an appropriate plan to intervene and help the child. Thus much depends on your own intuitive skill and experience with young children. The following principles will only succeed if you can begin to work out their appropriate application in the particular setting that you are in and with a particular child's behaviour problem in mind (see also Sarason et al., 1972).

(i) Reward Appropriate Behaviour

Ensure that you only reward the behaviour that you want to increase. If you give children rewards for the sake of keeping them quiet (e.g. sucking a sweet does prevent children from crying out and tends to keep them preoccupied with the pleasant taste), you may be inadvertently establishing bad behaviour. Thus, if the child threw a temper tantrum prior to being given the sweet, there will probably be another temper tantrum because this brings the very pleasant reward of a sweet. An appropriate behaviour to reinforce might be sitting quietly and looking at a toy; this can be rewarded with a smile of approval and perhaps some verbal points.

(ii) Reward Appropriate Behaviour Immediately
This is very important. The reward should be given immediately after the good behaviour has occurred so that the child does not produce another piece of behaviour before receiving the reward. That is to say, the good behaviour alone must be rewarded. If a reward is delayed until the end of a piece of activity and you decide to reward the child because of good behaviour 'on the whole', you will in fact be rewarding both the good and the bad behaviour that occurred during that activity.

(iii) In the Early Stages of Changing Behaviour, Reward the Good Behaviour Each Time it Occurs
When the process of learning good behaviour is in its early stages, a reward should be given every time the good behaviour occurs. If rewards are given inconsistently, the child will become confused about what is being rewarded and what is not. Take advantage of encouraging an appropriate piece of behaviour each time it occurs at the beginning of the programme.

(iv) In the Later Stages of Changing Behaviour, when the Good Behaviour Begins to Occur Frequently, give a Reward on Fewer Occasions
Put in another way, reward the good behaviour now and again once it begins to occur at a satisfactorily high level. It would appear from learning theory that once a 'good' behaviour has reached a certain level it is sufficient for the child to know that a reward will be coming sooner or later, and giving a reward each time will devalue it. Commonsense tells us that a child who has received twenty smarties during a session will find the twenty-first smartie less attractive than the first few - though this does, of course, depend on the particular child's capacity for smarties.

(v) Tangible and Special Rewards when Applied Together will Often be More Reinforcing than if One of these Alone is Given
The aim of carrying out a behaviour modification programme is to obtain appropriate behaviour for its own sake. That is, the well-adjusted behaviour is seen as being rewarding in its own right and the reward is not allowed to become an end in itself. It is the social approval of the child's classmates and the adults with whom there is interaction that should be the ultimate rewarding factor.

With this in mind, it is useful to pair tangible rewards with social reinforcers when this is possible. In practice in the nursery setting it may be difficult or inappropriate to supply some tangible reward. Thus, it may appear unfair to other children if one child alone is given a sweet or drink whilst the rest go without. In that case you might use token rewards such as stars and points, in combination with social reinforcement. There is a wide variety of possible rewards, ranging from things the child can eat or play with to opportunities to help the teacher or take part in a favourite activity. The important thing is to find out what the child would like, as only then is the reward truly rewarding.

How do we decide on an appropriate reinforcer? Remember these four methods:-

(a) ask the child what he or she really likes;

(b) ask the parents or friends of the child what he or she likes;

(c) do a preference check (try out many rewards before arriving at a choice);

(d) apply the Premack Principle; where no appropriate rewards can be decided upon, use part of the child's behaviour that occurs frequently to reinforce another less frequently occurring behaviour(thus overactive children may be taught to sit attentively for a short period of time if they are allowed on occasion to rush around - the "rushing around" acting as a reward in this instance).

<u>Summary : Positive Reinforcement</u>

Positive reinforcement of a behaviour means that the reinforcer (reward) given after the behaviour has occurred is pleasant for the child, so that the behaviour will tend to occur again. By applying positive reinforcement to good behaviour, you increase the probability of that behaviour occuring again. Thus, by smiling and saying "Good boy, you are paying attention so well", you will encourage the child to repeat the good behaviour of sitting and attending. Remember the basic principles of reinforcement: reinforce when the desired behaviour occurs, and <u>each time</u> it occurs at first; give the reinforcement immediately after the desired behaviour then gradually tail off giving the reinforcement once the behaviour occurs frequently and appears to be well established.

2. Extinction and Punishment

(i) Extinction

Extinction means removing the conditions that maintain or increase the likelihood that certain behaviour will occur. In other words, it means withholding a reward which has been given on previous occasions so that the behaviour which the reward has been helping to maintain will tend to die out (i.e. be extinguished). To extend the example given previously, if your next door neighbour ceases to smile back at you each morning, you will tend not to smile at her on subsequent mornings. That is, your response of smiling will be extinguished.

Ignoring bad behaviour may not be a good example of extinction. Thus, for the sake of peace and quiet, we may ignore a temper tantrum or aggressive display by a child in the hope that this bad behaviour will simply go away if we pay no attention to it. However, we may find that the behaviour is so intolerable on the following day that it simply cannot be ignored. So the removal of attention is inconsistent and the behaviour will not be extinguished because it is still, on occasion, bringing the child the reward of gaining attention sooner or later. Thus, if the removal of attention is to be applied to a problem behaviour, do it consistently. If you want to extinguish a certain behaviour, you must make sure that it is never rewarded when it occurs. A good idea may be to reward other behaviour which stops the child carrying out the undesirable behaviour. (These points are discussed further in Part IV of this section pp.149-153.)

(ii) Punishment

This is, perhaps, the method most often used in an attempt to change or modify children's behaviour. It is used in one form or another by almost all parents and teachers at some stage. Punishment can obviously be used to control immediately the problem behaviour, but the effect of punishment would appear to be to suppress the behaviour problem for the time being (e.g. until the punisher leaves the room), not to change it fundamentally over time. To extinguish the behaviour might be more satisfactory.

PART II

METHODS OF ASSESSMENT AND MEASUREMENT

In behaviour modification, measurement is important. It involves counting the number of times a certain type of behaviour occurs and recording how long it lasts on each occasion. We will describe some convenient methods of collecting and recording observations of a child's behaviour in as simple and straightforward a way as possible, but because behaviour is so complicated, it may take you a little time to get used to measuring it. What you have to do is to define, count, record and chart the behaviour. These steps will now be discussed in detail.

1. Defining and Counting Problem Behaviour

In order to define behaviour objectively it must be broken down into units that are specific and observable. A child could be described as 'aggressive' or 'naughty', or his/her behaviour could be said to be 'disturbing others', but none of these descriptions tells us accurately what the child actually does or what the consequences of his/her behaviour are. They are merely labels which describe in a very general way what may be a wide variety of different kinds of behaviour. Listed below are a number of examples of poorly defined behaviour and opposite is given a clearer and more specific description of what the observer really meant. The definitions given on the right hand side can be more readily recognised and counted.

	Poorly Defined	Clearly Defined
(a)	Poor attitude	Refuses to join in group activities such as playing in the Wendy House or ball games unless given the dominant role. Refuses to allow other children to take their turn as leader of a group activity.

	Poorly Defined	Clearly Defined
(b)	Immature	Clings to adults a lot, frequently whines and asks to be cuddled. Tries to climb up on adult's lap and seeks comfort, unlike most other children of a similar age.
(c)	Is cheeky and insulting	Talks back to staff when not appropriate, e.g. says 'why should I' when instructed to sit down, or refers to characteristics of others.
(d)	Cannot concentrate	Flits from activity to activity all the time, and cannot settle down to play quietly and constructively for more than a minute or two at a time.

By following the clear definition, it becomes possible to <u>count</u> the number of occurrences of this type of behaviour. For example, you may decide to count separately the number of occasions of clinging (C), whining (W) and demanding (D) that occur during the whole or part of the session. A record chart can then be drawn up with different categories for each type of behaviour, as shown on the following page.

You can design your own record charts or follow the examples given in several of the references at the end of this section (e.g. Walker and Shea, 1976). Again, you must decide beforehand exactly what kinds of behaviour will be denoted by the code letters. In this particular instance they could have been as follows:-

<u>C</u> - <u>clinging</u> to adults' clothing or body as they pass by; trying to grasp hand or arm of adults to draw their attention etc.

<u>W</u> - <u>whining</u>: speaking to adults or other children in a self-pitying way; making complaining noises, grizzling

Behaviour Record Chart

Frequency of Clinging, Whining and Demanding

Observer's Name .... Date ....

	MONDAY			TUESDAY			WEDNESDAY			THURSDAY			FRIDAY		
	C	W	D	C	W	D	C	W	D	C	W	D	C	W	D
Observation Interval (e.g. whole of morning session or 10 a.m. to 11 a.m. etc.)															
Total number of occurrences															

Child's Name (or code) ....

D - demanding comfort and attention; a direct appeal to adults to be allowed to sit on their lap or close to them; asking to be cuddled or comforted.

The particular codes and the number of different categories that you adopt is a matter for you to decide. It may be convenient to have just one category - where the behaviour is a very specific one - or you may select two or more types of behaviour to concentrate your attention upon. Essentially, you will want to collect as much information as is necessary for you to plan a sensible course of action to change the behaviour in question.

2. Recording Different Aspects of Behaviour

(a) Frequency

Here, the observer keeps a tally of the number of times a specific behaviour occurs over a certain period of time (per hour, morning, day or week). The nursery staff could have a pencil and pad always to hand. They can then keep a record of how often a child gets up, talks out or hits another child. An alternative would be to have a simple digit counter such as a pocket calculator or other device which could be used to keep a record of the particular behaviour you have decided beforehand to observe. The behaviour record chart described above is one example of how to count the frequency with which a selected behaviour occurs.

(b) Duration

This simply involves recording how long a particular behaviour lasts and may be achieved by the use of a stopwatch or by the use of a wristwatch with a seconds hand. Very often a simple frequency count will not provide sufficient information about a behaviour. For instance, a child may cry or whine for quite lengthy periods at a time, and we need to know how long these periods are. A drawback to duration recording is that it requires the nursery teacher to concentrate her attention on the one child for the necessary length of time, and she may simply be too busy to do this. When there is more than one adult in the room, of course, this difficulty can be avoided.

(c) Type of Recording

(i) Continuous
As the name implies, a continuous record of the child's behaviour could be kept (i.e. you watch all the time) but this is virtually impossible to achieve in practice. Extensive recording of behaviour might be possible if there were teams of observers available,but we are faced with a situation where there will normally be only a nursery teacher and aide or playgroup leader and helper to share out the observation between them, whilst trying to carry out all sorts of other jobs. One way out of this difficulty is to take sample recordings of the problem behaviour.

(ii) Time-sample recording
Sample Recording
In this situation the observer watches the child for a certain interval of time every so often e.g. the nursery teacher will keep an eye on a particular child for five minutes at the end of each half-hour throughout the whole session, and will note down whether a particular behaviour occurs, and how often. In this way a record can be built up of how often a particular type of behaviour occurs during that session.

Fixed-interval Recording
Here, the observer notes down at the end of a fixed interval of time say, every 2 minutes for half an hour at a time, what the child is doing. The nursery teacher might want to obtain a record of how much time a child spends 'on-task', for example, when painting or drawing.

Minute	2	4	6	8	10	12	14	16	18	20
Behaviour	+	+	-	-	+	-	-	-	-	+

A record sheet like that above allows the observer to record the behaviour of the child at two-minute intervals for a period of twenty minutes. At exactly two-minute intervals the observer looks at the child and awards a '+' if the child is actually doing the task or a '-' if not. What goes on during the two-minute period is ignored.

(d) <u>When to Record</u>

(i) Any problem behaviour should be observed as much as possible, but when time is limited you may have to observe at set times only or for short intervals at random during the whole session. If a problem behaviour occurs infrequently but is very severe you might be limited to observing it just when it occurs and describing the situation that gives rise to it, i.e. where it happens, others present, what actions seem to trigger it off, how long it lasts, how you usually try to cope with it and so on. If a problem behaviour occurs very frequently, then observing it for short periods during the session, as described above, may give a good estimate of its seriousness. Try to work out a timetable for watching that will give a number of observations as representative as possible of the problem behaviour.

(ii) Before an intervention is planned, you will need to obtain a '<u>baseline</u>' of the behaviour that you hope to change. The baseline is the record of how often the problem behaviour occurs before you begin to try to change it. The baseline will help you to compare the behaviour before, during and after the intervention. It is difficult to give any definite guidance as to how long a realistic baseline period should be. It will vary with the type of behaviour that is being observed as well as practical considerations such as the time available for observation. If a behaviour occurs fairly frequently, e.g. at least half a dozen times in any one observation period, then a good estimate of the usual level of occurrence should be obtained after a week or ten days.

On the other hand, if the behaviour only occurs fairly infrequently but is nevertheless causing concern, a much longer period of observation might be needed. For example, a child may be wet only once or twice a week. You should also try to assess the intensity or seriousness of difficult behaviour as well as how often it occurs (frequency) and how long it lasts (duration). If a child behaves so badly as to cause injury to another, then you might decide that no baseline is necessary and begin the intervention right away.

(iii) Observation should be continued <u>during and following</u> an intervention programme. This will enable you to monitor how the intervention is progressing, that is, assess whether it is having an effect on the problem behaviour. This raises the question of how long an intervention programme should be persevered with before it is abandoned or changed. Clearly, if a particular programme has not altered the behaviour in any way after several weeks, then it should be abandoned and the whole problem reviewed afresh. If, however, the intervention is having some success, but only to a limited extent, you may wish to change the approach based on new information that has come to light or on an intuition on your part that a change of procedure might lead to greater success. As you try out programmes, you will begin to see when and how they could be improved.

3. Graphing

(a) It will be very valuable for you to graph the information that you have recorded for the child. This will give you a visual representation of the situation, and will show clearly the changes, if any, that you have brought about by your programme. The general form of the graph could be as shown in Figure 5.1(a)

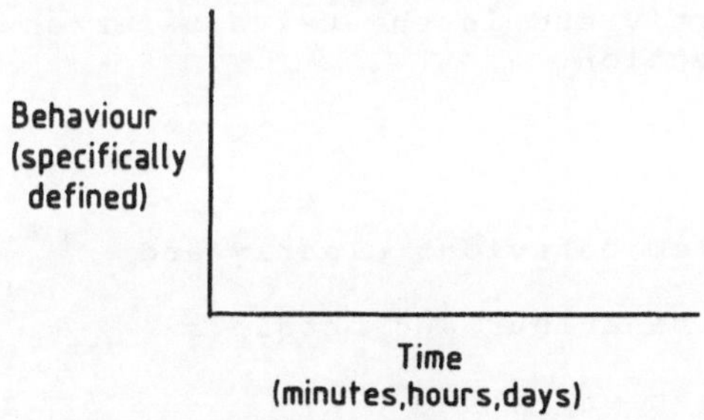

FIGURE 5.1 (a)

(b) Figure 5.1(b) gives a hypothetical graph for a child's time'out of seat' for the baseline period and during the intervention.

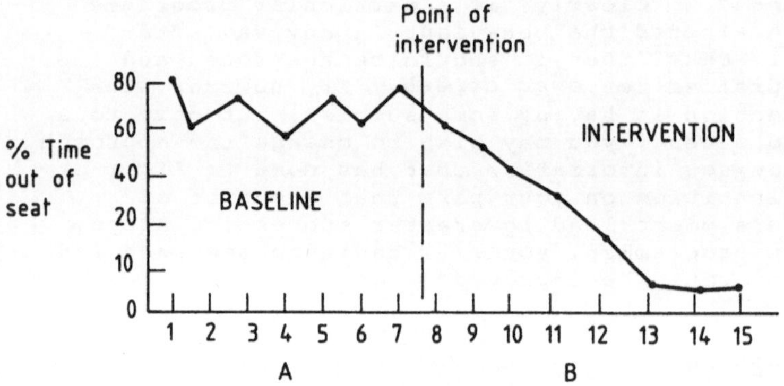

FIGURE 5.1 (b)

This graph shows that during the baseline period (A) of seven days the child spent approximately 60 to 80% of time out of seat but that level dropped dramatically to stabilize at about 10% during the following eight days (B) when intervention was taking place.

Further examples of how to graph your information will be found in Part V and in the texts referred to at the end of this section.

<u>Summary of Procedure</u>

1. Define the problem behaviour clearly and objectively
2. Observe current behaviour and obtain a baseline
3. Graph the information
4. Plan the programme of intervention (i.e. decide what you are going to reward)
5. Introduce the programme and monitor the behaviour by continuing to graph what happens

PART III. METHODS OF ENCOURAGING OR INCREASING CERTAIN BEHAVIOUR

1. Positive Reinforcement

This procedure has already been discussed (pp.132-136) and simply involves rewarding appropriate behaviour after it has occurred. Commonly used rewards or positive reinforcers are material rewards such as food or drink, and social rewards such as praise, a hug or a smile. The principles of reinforcement outlined in Part I should be borne in mind when applying positive reinforcement. Staff should decide on the particular kind of reward to use, e.g. ten minutes of free play activiy following some good behaviour, and how to schedule this reward (i.e. decide beforehand how often the child will be allowed this free play activity). A positive reinforcement programme might be used to build up appropriate behaviour such as obeying the teacher's instructions or joining in the nursery activities with the other children.

2. Differential Reinforcement

It has been found that it is relatively easy for an adult to increase or decrease behaviour that children are already showing. Thus staff might decide to increase the behaviour of a child when he or she is playing quietly and cooperatively and decrease the child's aggressive tendencies or overactivity. They could do this by paying a lot of attention to the child when he or she is actually producing the desirable social-play behaviour - by smiling and saying 'very good' etc. - and ignoring the child when overactive or demanding of attention. In this way the occurrence of appropriate behaviour is increased and that of the inappropriate behaviour decreased by 'differential reinforcement'. There are many studies which show the value of this method. It is used every day by teachers and other nursery staff, but for behaviour modification it needs to be rather more systematic than is usually the case.

3. Shaping, Prompting and Fading

Shaping

Shaping means systematically rewarding approximations of the desired behaviour until gradually the proper desired behaviour is achieved and then firmly established. It is used to develop behaviour which the child is seemingly unable to learn or has difficulty in learning. Rewards are given as the child's behaviour more and more nearly approximates to what you want him to do.

The steps in shaping behaviour are usually:

(i) select the behaviour you want the child to achieve;

(ii) obtain baseline information (i.e. what the child is now doing which is closest to what you want done);

(iii) select reinforcers (rewards);

(iv) reward successive approximations of the desired behaviour each time they occur until the child achieves the desired behaviour;

(v) reinforce the newly established behaviour each time it occurs;

(vi) maintain the level of the new behaviour by rewarding it now and again.

Shaping has been used, for example, to develop a child's speech where there is difficulty in this area. Typically, an adult would sit with a child and point to an object such as a spoon or knife and ask the child to say what it was. Responses might approximate the correct word such as "'poon" or "'oon", and each better approximation is rewarded by giving the child a sweet or drink and a smile or hug.

Shaping might also be used to change social or play behaviour. Thus a child who has difficulty in joining in ball games with other children might be helped by shaping any good play patterns shown. For instance, a child may have rather poor co-ordination, and tend to dash around in a random fashion during a ball game played by children in a circle. The unco-ordinated child could be helped by the staff encouraging him to stand with the others, giving clear directions when and where to run and rewarding with praise each time the correct behaviour is shown. By doing this successively with each aspect of the game, the child's behaviour can be shaped into an appropriate pattern for the play activity.

Prompting and Fading

When children are slow to produce something near to

the desired behaviour, thay may be prompted by the teacher to do so. Thus, in the verbal shaping procedure described above, the teacher might supply a prompt by pointing at the spoon, saying 'spoo ..' and allowing the child to join in to finish the word off.

In the example of shaping play behaviour, the teacher might help children by pointing to the spot they are supposed to run to and saying, 'Go on, run over there'. Further physical prompts might involve guiding the children's throwing action or guiding them through other actions involved in the game.

Fading refers to the gradual phasing out of the verbal or physical prompts given by the teacher to the child. Thus, the teacher might begin to point to the spoon and not give a verbal prompt. In the example of the ball game, the teacher might stand back and give fewer verbal instructions to the child, thus allowing him to carry on on his own.

4. Modelling or Imitation

One of the most frequently used methods of encouraging new behaviour is that of modelling. The child's attention is directed to appropriate behaviour in adults, other children or the group, and he is encouraged to copy this behaviour or model his behaviour on theirs. In this way, the child will:

(i) acquire new behaviour;

(ii) unlearn some of the inappropriate behaviour previously shown;

(iii) be encouraged to go on and develop further appropriate behaviour.

Before you try to encourage modelling, you should consider whether:

(a) the child is sufficiently mature to be able to understand what he is imitating and why this is desirable;

(b) the child will be rewarded for imitating desirable behaviour or whether this will be done 'for its own sake'. (In this case it might be wise to reward the child in the initial stages, but to gradually fade out the reward);

(c) the model really is a 'good' one. Thus, a child may imitate a lot of another child's behaviour, but only parts of the latter's behaviour may be desirable i.e. guard against a child imitating undesirable as well as desirable behaviour.

Again, staff should remember that in all their actions and attitudes they are acting as models for the children. Thus, it is not a good thing for adults to express anger or irritation however badly behaved a child may be, since this emotional behaviour may well be copied by the children. If children think it appropriate to express anger by shouting (or physically attacking others), they may be basing their actions on the teacher's behaviour.

Summary : The Importance of Feedback

If you decide to employ any of the approaches described above, it is important that children should know why rewards are being given and how their behaviour is improving or deteriorating. That is to say, you must comment on their behaviour thus providing feedback for the child or the nursery group so that they will get some indication of how they are progressing and for what they are being rewarded or not rewarded.

This leads us to another important idea about learning. Generalisation is the process by which a response or a piece of behaviour that is rewarded or reinforced in the presence of one stimulus will occur when another different but related stimulus is presented. Generalisation is a useful process since it cuts out the need to learn the same behaviour again each time a new stimulus or situation that requires the same response occurs. An example of generalisation is when a child learns originally to drink from a bowl or plastic cup and this later and very quickly leads to drinking from a cup or glass tumbler. It can be encouraged by drawing the child's attention to the similarity between the new activity and what he can already do.

Inappropriate generalisation may be avoided by teaching a response or behaviour consistently in the setting for which that behaviour is appropriate. Teaching a child to use the toilet may be brought about by helping in the initial stages with clothes and other necessary actions in the toilet itself rather than in another room and subsequently allowing the child to go to the toilet.

Ways of encouraging or increasing behaviour have been described in general terms. How they are actually implemented will depend on the child, the nursery environment and your skills and preferences in applying the techniques suggested. Remember that you must plan carefully in advance how much time you can spend in trying out any method with a child and always select rewards that are suitable for that particular child. An outline of the steps involved in the behaviour change process will be provided in summary form at the end (p. 163), but we will now go on to consider methods of discouraging or decreasing behaviour that you do not want.

PART IV. METHODS OF DISCOURAGING OR DECREASING UNDESIRED BEHAVIOUR

In this part we will expand on methods that could be used by nursery staff to decrease behaviour that is unacceptable or disrupting. Examples of such behaviour are extreme overactivity (a child rushing around in an unco-ordinated and seemingly meaningless fashion), incessant whining and clinging behaviour, frequent crying, aggression (hitting or bullying other children) and so on.

1. Encouraging Incompatible Behaviour

One way to combat disruptive behaviour is to reward incompatible behaviour. That is to say, a behaviour that makes it impossible or difficult to indulge in the negative, unacceptable behaviour is strengthened. Thus, a teacher may reward a child for sitting quietly by smiling and showing approval, but withdraw this rewarding attention when the child gets up and rushes around. Encouraging incompatible behaviour is a positive method of decreasing unacceptable behaviour and does not involve any punishment of the child.

2. Extinction

Another procedure that could be used to cut down undesirable behaviour is to withhold any reward given to the inappropriate act. Thus, a teacher may have paid attention to children each time they whined or started to cry so that the attention became reinforcing. By ignoring children when they begin to whine and attending to them when they are not whining, the teacher may be able to extinguish the whining. Again, temper tantrums are often brought about by the child wishing to gain attention, and withdrawal of that attention during the tantrum will often lead to the extinction of that behaviour.

There are some difficulties involved in the use of extinction with children in a nursery classroom or group. One of these is that a teacher cannot ignore a child when he or she is genuinely distressed and in need of reassurance. It must fall on the nursery staff to judge whether a child's behaviour shows that he or she is genuinely in need of comfort.

A second difficulty is that the rest of a group may provide rewards for children's extreme behaviour by giving them attention (laughing and talking to them) so that some reinforcement is still being given for the undesirable act. Adults might combat this by asking the others to help by not giving the children in question such attention.

Finally, nursery staff should be aware that the severity of temper tantrums or of bad behaviour will often increase when attention is first withdrawn. When beginning the process of withdrawing attention, therefore, staff should not weaken and give in to an increased display of bad temper or emotion, but persist until the behaviour settles down or clearly needs some other method of coping with it.

3. Restraining

Clearly, there are times when children will have to be restrained physically by the nursery staff. If one child attacks another with a toy or in some other way, the child will have to be immediately restrained before any serious physical injury can result to the other child. When restraining children to prevent harmful behaviour you should bear the following in mind:

(i) only use restraint when strictly necessary and only just enough to stop an attack;

(ii) explain as far as possible to children why they are being restrained.

Often it will be effective merely to use verbal restraint (e.g. wagging a finger at a child and saying, 'You must not do that') so it is essential that children should be able to understand what it is that they are doing wrong. Very young children are often unable to do this, but there are ways of helping the child to achieve more insight (see section on 'Problem-Solving Approaches' pp.177-202).

Restraint can also be used to begin to change behaviour as well as just to prevent its occurrence. When used along with an insistence that children should 'sit and watch' (see below), restraining should encourage calm and controlled behaviour. That is, the adult ceases to restrain children only when they have calmed down and are sitting watching others at play.

4. 'Sit and Watch'

Young children who are slow to develop acceptable patterns of play can often cause considerable disruption in the nursery. Nursery staff are sometimes advised to redirect or distract children who are misbehaving. This might involve the teacher telling a child, "No, don't throw the toys about like that. Come over here and play with this toy instead". This approach can be very demanding of the staff's time, however, and may often be inadequate in dealing with severe disruptions.

The technique of 'sit and watch' was developed by Porterfield et al. (1976) to combat just such disruptive behaviour. 'Sit and watch' involves the adults following the steps outlined below:

1. the nursery staff explain briefly to the child (we shall call her Jenny) the behaviour that is inappropriate and why it is inappropriate e.g. "No, don't snatch the toys from the other children, ask them if you can borrow the toy or ask me if you can have it";

2. Jenny is then moved to the edge of the play area, without close company or play materials. The nursery staff then instruct her to sit and watch the other children at play, e.g. "Sit and watch how the other children ask for the toys that they want";

3. when the staff are satisfied that Jenny has observed the other children at play for a brief period (usually less than one minute), they ask her if she is ready to rejoin the play activity, e.g. "Do you know how to ask for a toy now?" If the response is positive the child is allowed to rejoin the game. If the child says 'no' or makes no response she is told to sit in the same place

and watch the play activity for a little longer. This is repeated until a positive response is given by the child that she understands how she should play with the other children;

4. when Jenny returns to the play activity the nursery staff give her praise and positive attention for playing appropriately, e.g. when she asks for a toy, the staff might say, "Very good, you asked for the toy that time".

Nursery staff should give some comfort to children who are upset or crying whilst they are sitting and watching the other children at play. If they continue to be very upset during this period, however, the staff might take them to a 'rest area' (e.g. a chair at the far end of the nursery which is screened off from the play area) and say, "Have a little rest here before you go back to watch the other children playing". When children have calmed down sufficiently (usually after a few minutes), they may return to their spot to sit and watch the play activity, and the procedure described above is followed once more.

5. Reducing Anxiety

A child who shows fear or anxiety at the approach of an adult might be helped by the staff planning a series of gradual approaches to the child to overcome this feeling. The staff might sit down well away from the child and smile and wave reassuringly, later they might beckon the child or move slightly nearer at a slow and relaxed pace, later still they might walk up quietly to the child and stroke an arm reassuringly. By gradually increasing the directness of approach, the nursery staff would hope to reach the point where they could walk directly up to the child and even give a reassuring hug without being afraid of frightening the child. This method of overcoming fear is known as 'systematic desensitisation'.

Summary : Which Procedure to Use?

All of the procedures outlined above have, at one time or another, been used as a means of discouraging problem behaviour in young children, with varying degrees of success. More than one of the procedures might be used together with a particular child or several different procedures tried one after the other if little success is achieved with the first method tried. A great deal will depend, once again, on the skill of the nursery staff in using the various approaches consistently and realise istically, i.e. they must be applied properly and be manageable in terms of time and commitment. It would be helpful if you were to read some of the numerous case studies showing the application of those methods which appear in the books mentioned at the end of this section. We will now go on to look at how some typical problem behaviour that might be encountered in the nursery could be coped with using some of the behaviour modification methods.

PART V. TYPICAL PROBLEMS

In the previous parts of this section we have described the underlying principles, ways of assessment and some of the methods of behaviour modification. These should form the basis of your plan of action.

It is possible that you may need outside help in coping with problem children but often you will be in the best position to help them as you have much more contact with them than anyone from outside the nursery group. Nursery staff soon acquire an intimate knowledge of children's problems and what their likes and dislikes are. Enlist the help of your colleagues whenever possible to aid in gathering basic information about children's behaviour and perhaps to help with carrying out any intervention planned. Once the problem behaviour has been defined and described and the baseline information obtained, you will have to decide which approach to try out with the child. It would be sensible to start off by trying to modify relatively simple problems, using very basic techniques such as positive reinforcement or extinction, until you are sufficiently practised and feel able to cope with comparatively difficult procedures.

What approach should you use? This will depend on several factors, including the type and severity of the problem, and the time and resources available to you.

As outlined in Chapter 2, most of the problem behaviour encountered in the nursery group will fall under the following four main categories:

(i) shy/withdrawn/timid

(ii) immature/dependent

(iii) restless/overactive

(iv) aggressive/anti-social/destructive

However, it is not sufficient merely to label a child as belonging to one of the above categories. You must state precisely what behaviour makes you conclude that a child is having problems and define the difficulty in as much detail as possible. Thus shy, withdrawn children may be described as being very reluctant to approach or talk to adults or other children, to spend a good deal of time (say how much) on their own, and to shun joining in general activities with others. There may be specific times or situations when this behaviour is worse than usual, e.g. the child may dislike mixing with a large group of children playing outside in the yard, but be reasonably willing to play with one another child in a quiet part of the nursery. The same procedure holds good for the other three categories - describe specifically and clearly what behaviours are being exhibited and how severe they are.

A child may show behaviour that falls into two or more of the above categories. Thus, a child may be very restless and overactive and also have a tendency to be aggressive and destructive. You should describe the observed behaviour in detail and not worry too much about which category it falls into in the main. You have then to decide which particular aspect of the behaviour you are going to tackle first.

We will now go on to give some examples of the action that might be taken to help.

(i) WITHDRAWAL AND ISOLATION

The Problem

Anna is a very timid and shy little girl. Outside she is more often than not to be found standing alone in the yard when most other children are playing noisily and happily together. In the nursery she seems to seek out the quieter spots and rarely talks to or approaches another child. She is not fearful of the staff and will approach them from time to time but not as much as the other children do.

(a) Behavioural Method Used
The nursery staff decided to try out a behaviour modification approach to help Anna become less isolated and to help her interact more freely with the other children.

(b) Definition of Behaviour
If Anna was not interacting with at least one child on the occasions when she was being observed, the staff recorded an instance of isolated behaviour. If Anna was with a member of staff, there had to be at least one other child present for it to count as social behaviour. Social interaction was defined as talking to or playing with another child, not merely being close to one.

(c) Measurement of Behaviour
The staff used a time-sampling procedure to measure Anna's isolated behaviour throughout the nursery day. Observations of her behaviour were made on average every twenty minutes during the nursery day. About fifteen observations per day were made, therefore. Observations were carried out for ten days to give a baseline of Anna's isolated behaviour. The information obtained was graphed (p.156).

(d) Procedures and results
The staff decided to use a simple positive reinforcement procedure (p.145). Thus every time Anna approached another child, talked or began to play with children, she was praised by the teacher who would smile and say, 'Well done, Anna. I'm glad to see you are joining in with the others'. (The reward would be varied, e.g. giving a hug or allowing Anna a favoured activity.) Reward was only given when Anna indulged in some form of social interaction or other. In a situation where there was very little initiation of the desired behaviour by the child, the staff might decide to use prompts. Thus, Anna could be taken by the hand and guided to where a group of children were playing and helped to join in by the teacher demonstrating how to play the game. As soon as Anna began to approach play situations spontaneously, the prompts were to be gradually faded out.

After fifteen days of this procedure, the graph the staff had drawn up (Figure 5.2) throughout the intervention programme showed that the frequency of Anna's isolated play had decreased dramatically following the introduction of the programme.

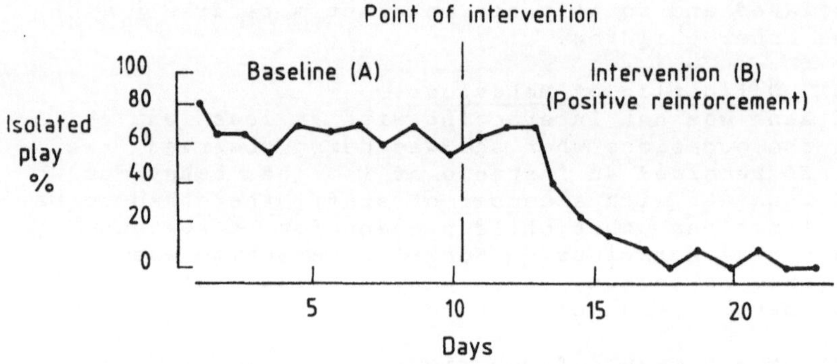

FIGURE 5.2 THE FREQUENCY OF ANNA'S ISOLATED PLAY

Figure 5.2 shows that the percentage of time Anna spent playing in isolation, after an immediate increase, decreased on average from about 70% to 10% following the introduction of the positive reinforcement procedure.

(e) Stopping the Programme
The nursery staff decided to discontinue the programme at this point, since the amount of time that Anna spent playing on her own was less than that of several other children in the nursery and was well within the range of what would be considered to be normal. After three weeks they carried out a further ten days observation (a post-intervention check) and found that Anna still only spent about 20% of the time playing on her own, so no further special action was considered necessary.

(ii) IMMATURE, DEPENDENT BEHAVIOUR

The Problem

Malcolm is three and a half years old but seems more backward than the other children of the same age. He frequently whines and cries and seeks comfort from the nursery staff who find that they have difficulty in carrying on with their work because of his clinging behaviour. The staff propose trying to modify Malcolm's whining and clinging behaviour.

(a) Behavioural Method Used
The nursery staff decided to use an extinction procedure (p.149) to try to stop Malcolm's whining and clinging behaviour. They noted that as soon as one of the staff gave him some attention, his whining would stop and he would cling to the adult for comfort. Extinction would consist of withdrawing this attention and comfort.

(b) Definition of Behaviour and Measurement
The staff collected baseline information about Malcolm's whining and clinging behaviour using a time-sampling procedure over a period of eight days. Observations were made at various intervals but on average about every 15 minutes. Eighteen observations per day were made. Whining was defined as any verbalisation that was complaining and delivered in a tremulous, emotional manner. Clinging was defined as approaching an adult and seeking attention by pulling at clothes or limbs or attempting to climb on the adult's lap. The information was graphed.

(c) Procedure and Results
The staff decided on the following procedure. Each time Malcolm whined he would be ignored by the staff, who would normally have asked him what the trouble was and probably approached him. If Malcolm came to them, they would gently but firmly refuse him physical contact and perhaps move away from him. They decided to try out this procedure for a period of fourteen days.

Figure 5.3(a)and(b) shows the effect that this procedure had on Malcolm's behaviour.

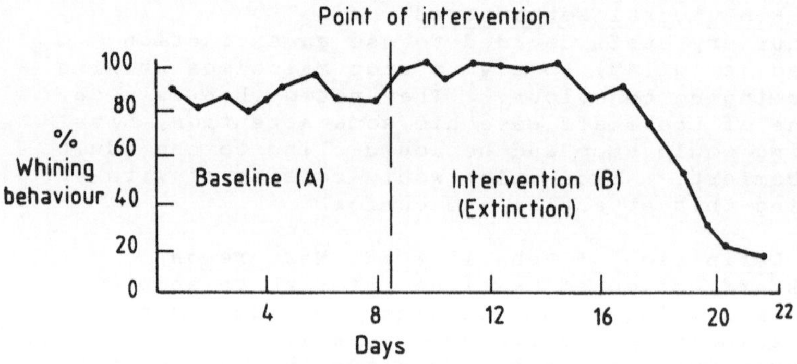

(a) Malcolm's whining behaviour

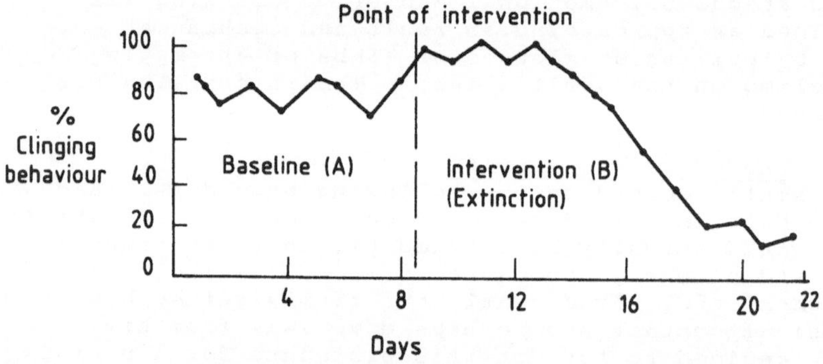

(b) Malcolm's clinging behaviour

FIGURE 5.3

The graphs show that the programme had little effect on Malcolm's whining and clinging during the first few days. In fact, it seemed to increase the frequency of the behaviour but after about eight days the extinction procedure began to take effect, and the frequency of both unacceptable behaviours declined to quite a low level.

(iii) RESTLESS, OVERACTIVE BEHAVIOUR

The Problem

Lucy is a very restless, fidgety and generally overactive little girl. She rushes about the nursery in a random fashion disturbing other children who are playing quietly. She cannot keep still for a minute, and staff are constantly checking her and attempting to keep her quiet by involving her in some play activity, but sooner or later she leaves that activity and dashes to another part of the nursery.

(a) Definiton and Measurement of Behaviour

The nursery staff decided to try a behaviour modification procedure involving elements of restraining (p.150) and differential reinforcement (p.145).

The staff used the percentage of time that Lucy spent in constructive play activity, whether on her own or with other children, as a measure of Lucy's appropriate behaviour. Observations of Lucy's behaviour were made at fixed intervals, every half-hour during the nursery day. Twelve observations per day were recorded over a period of 10 days. This baseline information was graphed.

(b) Procedures and Results

Restraining. At certain times during the nursery day (every hour), Lucy was restrained by a member of the nursery staff at a table where a game was laid out. Restraining involved one of the staff sitting or squatting by Lucy and making sure that she did not dash away from the table. Each time she attempted to do so, the adult would put an arm around her, gently prevent her from going and attempt to bring her attention back to the game. After about five minutes Lucy was allowed to run about as she pleased for a few minutes.

Differential reinforcement. At other times, the staff would reward Lucy with praise, a hug, and occasionally a sweet when she was sitting quietly or playing in a relatively controlled way. That is, any behaviour shown by her that was incompatible with rushing around the nursery was rewarded.

Staff continued to observe and record Lucy's behaviour and noted every half hour whether she was taking part in constructive play or was behaving in a controlled manner. The graph was continually added to. After twelve days of applying these procedures, they were withdrawn and a further six days (second baseline) of Lucy's behaviour were observed. After this second baseline period, the procedures were reintroduced and observations of Lucy's behaviour again collected as before.

Figure 5.4 illustrates graphically the information collected on Lucy's behaviour. It shows that the percentage of time spent in constructive play or controlled activity increased as a result of the action taken by the nursery staff. When the intervention was stopped, however, Lucy's constructive activity soon declined again. Upon reintroduction of the procedures, however, Lucy once more began to spend more time involved in constructive activity and less time in uncontrolled random activity.

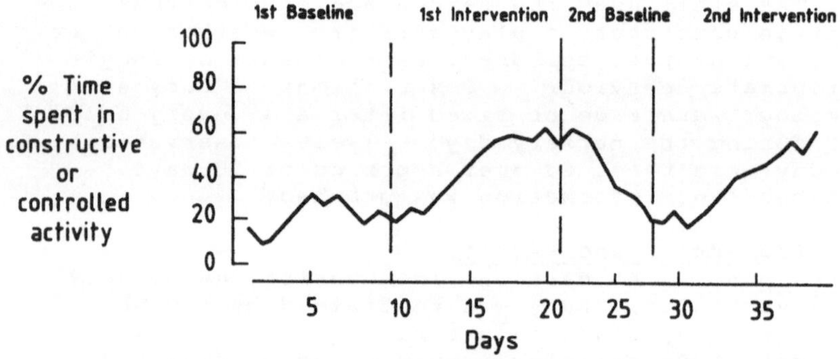

FIGURE 5.4 LUCY'S CONSTRUCTIVE ACTIVITY BEFORE AND AFTER INTERVENTION

(c) <u>Stopping the Programme</u>

Over the following weeks, the staff made more baseline observations and re-introduced the intervention on two further occasions before they were satisfied that Lucy's behaviour had settled down at a point where she spent some two-thirds of her time being reasonably controlled. This was felt to be the best that could be achieved at this stage and certainly represented a marked improvement over her previous behaviour.

(iv) AGGRESSIVE, ANTI-SOCIAL, DESTRUCTIVE BEHAVIOUR

The Problem

Frank is difficult to cope with in the nursery. He uses little speech and resorts to pushing and shoving when he wants to join in an activity. He snatches toys and equipment from others, only to throw his prize down and rush off. He has no respect for the other children's activities, and , because of his behaviour and the fact that he is a big boy, some of the more timid children are afraid of him. Children who try to stand up to him come off badly and finish up in tears usually.

(a) Behavioural Method Used

The staff decided to try a blend of differential reinforcement and shaping. They had noticed that water play attracted Frank, although his participation frequently ended with the soaking of other children and the flooding of the surrounding area. The staff decided to reinforce Frank's acceptable water play and use it to improve his communication and his interaction with others.

(b) Procedure and Results

Careful records were kept over a number of days of Frank's behaviour at the water tray. He was observed by a member of staff each time he went there and, as trouble was not long in breaking out, the whole episode was recorded each time. Records showed that his behaviour deteriorated according to the number of children present and the equipment available. Frank seldom used his hands to splash with but would throw or pour water from various containers. Graphing was carried out to show the length of time Frank spent at the water tray before he either rushed off or began to throw water about. As staff always had to keep an eye on him, gathering information was no problem.

The intervention programme consisted of a member of staff inviting Frank to come to the water tray when the other children were involved elsewhere. Most of the equipment had been unobtrusively removed. The adult played in the water with her hands, talking to Frank about the feel of the water, its appearance and other related topics (rain, seaside, bath etc.). Frank proved to have things to say in these circumstances, although he had difficulties in expressing himself clearly. He was helped without being nagged and new vocabulary was gradually introduced. Play moved on to using a colander and objects that sink in water or absorb water. The length of time Frank spent at the water tray lengthened considerably - and, as a bonus, the water stayed longer in the tray. The sessions were still, of course, brief (between 1 and 10 minutes). One other child was then encouraged to join the member of staff and Frank and, although Frank did not welcome the intrusion to begin with, he began to realise that another pair of hands and other ideas added to the game. The adult showed by her behaviour how the other child could be brought in and how equipment could be shared. When more children were added to the group, there was a tendency for Frank to become aggressive again, but he was encouraged to show them what he could do with the apparatus and was found to be urging others not to spill the water.

(c) Stopping the Programme
The work in the water tray was only a very small beginning and there was a great deal still to be done to help Frank. It had, however, shown that

1. he could continue to play for longer than the staff had thought possible;
2. he could use spoken language when he wanted to, thus giving staff the opportunity to shape his speech and extend it;
3. he could interact positively with other children.

The intervention programme was considered to be successful as far as it went. However, a positive reinforcement programme was now required to establish the behaviour (i.e. rewarding the acceptable behaviour) and then to maintain it in the absence of the members of staff. The programme, therefore, had to be adapted and continued.

In this part we have given some brief descriptions of the procedures involved in some hypothetical cases of behaviour problems. To get a better grasp of how the behaviour modification approach can be used, you should look at some of the case studies described in the reference books given at the end of this section. These will contain more detail of what behaviour modifiers actually do and will serve as guidelines for you when you plan your own programmes. A summary of the steps involved in behaviour modification is given overleaf.

Summary of the Steps Involved in the Behaviour Change Process

1. Define the problem and select a target:-

   (a) state clearly and objectively what the problem behaviour is;

   (b) select a target or level that you wish that behaviour to reach; you should be able to see the behaviour and count it

2. Use objective measurement techniques

   The process of measurement involves:-

   (a) defining

   (b) counting

   (c) recording

   (d) graphing

3. What to do about the behaviour

   You can either:

   (a) leave it alone (i.e. you wish the behaviour to be maintained at its present level)

   (b) increase it (i.e. teach new behaviour or develop infrequent behaviour)

   (c) decrease it (i.e. eliminate or reduce the level of the behaviour)

4. Continuously monitor the behaviour

   Keep records of the behaviour before, during and following and intervention.

PART VI. TASK ANALYSIS

1. Introduction

In essence, task analysis is concerned with breaking down a complex piece of behaviour into recognisable smaller pieces of behaviour. The 'task' may be the act of putting on an overcoat to play outside or washing one's hands after a messy activity. In the latter instance the task might be broken down into the discrete steps of approaching the sink, putting in the plug, turning on the tap, grasping the soap, soaping and scouring hands, rinsing and drying hands, removing plug and rinsing out the sink after use. With a behaviour problem such as extreme overactivity a relevant task might be getting the child to sit attentively at a desk or table in order to play with a puzzle or join in a group activity. Here the task (of sitting down attentively) might be broken down into approaching the table, pulling back the chair, positioning the body immediately above the chair, grasping the table for support and finally easing down into a sitting position with eyes focused on the puzzle.

This process of breaking down the task into seemingly trivial steps may seem at first sight to be complicating the learning process unnecessarily but we hope to show later on that there are sometimes good reasons for doing so. The important thing to remember is that you are trying to establish a 'good' piece of behaviour (the task), and that for a particular child the learning of the task may have to be broken down into simple steps that can be systematically linked together into a coherent whole. The process of linking these simpler bits of behaviour together has been fairly widely researched by teachers and therapists concerned with mentally retarded or handicapped children and has been called 'chaining'. We will discuss some of the ideas and examine some of the problems involved in the chaining of responses below, but to re-emphasise the basic point - in task analysis we aim to <u>analyse a fairly complex piece of behaviour into smaller component parts in order to institute a systematic training programme to enable the child to learn the complex behaviour</u>.

2. <u>Chaining</u>

Chaining as a method of teaching a skill involves writing down in a series all the steps involved in attaining the end or target behaviour. Thus the steps can be seen as a series of objectives to be reached by the child. Basically there are two kinds of chaining : forward chaining and backward chaining.

<u>Forward Chaining</u> involves breaking down the task into a series of steps, the first of which must

be attained before proceeding to the third, and so on until the target is reached.

Example 1
Removing a sock using FORWARD chaining

A. Sock moved down to ankle
B. A + sock pulled over heel
C. A + B + sock pushed down to toes
D. A + B + C + removes sock from toes

To use this method,the child would first be encouraged to carry out step A and rewarded for doing it. When A is established, B is tackled in addition, also using reward. And so on.

Backward Chaining involves starting at the end and working backwords so to speak. Thus, the task could be analysed as follows:

Example 2
Removing sock using BACKWARD chaining

Begin with the sock already pulled down to the toes, then the sequence becomes:
A. Removes sock from toes
B. Removes sock from toes and heel
C. Removes sock from toes, heel and ankle
D. Removes sock completely

Chaining is most usefully employed where steps can be put in an unvarying and fairly close time sequence. Thus, long delays between one or two steps in a task would make chaining a less appropriate method to use.

Hemsley and Carr (1980) say that there are no clear-cut research findings to show whether forward or backward chaining is the more reliable or efficient method, but that, on the whole, backward chaining is the more dependable method. The reason given for this is that starting with the almost completed task is a more rewarding situation for the child.

In the early years at school a number of important skills can be learned by chaining, including tying laces, using scissors, throwing and catching a ball. In their turn, these become part of more complex activities, such as printing and writing, and playing ball games. As Gagné (1976) puts it, " .....chains of motor responses become the components of motor skills, often as 'part-skills'. The latter are combined into organised motor performances which learning and continued practice invest with characteristics of smoothness and precise timing".

The Essentials of Task Analysis

Gardner and Tweddle (1978) suggest that there may be three levels of complexity in task analysis.

1. First Order task analysis involves a simple transfer of learning from one objective to the next.
2. Second Order task analysis uses a particular teaching method (e.g. chaining, shaping and fading).
3. Third Order task analysis includes prompting procedures.

Examples of these three levels are given below.

(i) FIRST ORDER TASK ANALYSIS

The important factor here is that the task is broken down into several steps, and each step is an objective which has to be attained before the child proceeds to the next one. That is to say, a sequence of objectives is drawn up, as in the following illustration concerned with learning to kick a ball.

Programme 1

A. Kicks stationary ball with preferred foot
B. Kicks slow rolling ball with preferred foot
C. Kicks fast rolling ball with preferred foot

The rationale here is that the learning of A will make it easier to learn B, i.e. there is a transfer of learning from A to B to C.

(ii) SECOND ORDER TASK ANALYSIS

Here, the way in which the task is analyzed is governed closely by the nature of the method used to teach the task. Shaping (p. 145) as a technique has been found to be particularly useful for this level of task analysis. An example given by Gardner and Tweddle of learning to thread a needle involves grading the teaching materials in order to shape the child's activity.

Programme 2 : Threading a Needle

A. Threads needle with ½" diameter hole with thin string
B. Threads needle with ¼" diameter hole with thin string
C. Threads needle with ¼" diameter hole with thick sewing cotton
D. Threads darning needle with thick sewing cotton
E. Threads darning needle with thin sewing cotton
F. Threads sewing needle with thin sewing cotton

Using such a programme would involve some preparation of materials but it may well ensure that the child learns the required skill (threading a sewing needle) more rapidly and with less frustration than might otherwise be the case.

(iii) THIRD ORDER TASK ANALYSIS

This type of task analysis uses physical prompts to help the child acquire the skill. Though prompting can be used at the second order level as well, it is used to a greater extent at this level. Thus, when a child fails to learn a task at the first or second levels, it might be necessary to introduce a programme where a lot of physical prompting is given, as in programme 3 below.

Programme 3 : Removing a Sock (using physical prompt)

A. Removes sock from toe when told to with physical prompt (i.e. teacher takes child's hand and guides it through the action of removing sock)
B. Removes sock from toe when told to with gestural prompt (i.e. teacher imitates the necessary action)
C. Remove sock from toe when told to with gestural prompt (i.e. teacher points at the sock while saying, 'Take off your sock')
D. Removes sock from toe when told to without prompting.

The sequence is then repeated to remove sock from toe and heel and so on.

A point to watch when using prompts is to ensure that not too many prompts are given i.e. use only as many physical or gestural prompts as are necessary and gradually reduce these (fade them out).

3. Some Applications of Task Analysis to Typical Problems

Case 1. Overcoming shyness and isolation and teaching ball skills

Jimmy is a shy and isolated child who is often to be seen sitting or standing on his own when most of the other children are joining in games and noisily enjoying themselves. Even when Jimmy joins in the fun, he is so awkward and clumsy that he more often than not spoils the game for the other children. The nursery staff decided that they would approach his problems in two stages:

1. by teaching Jimmy to approach others and join in games more readily, thus overcoming his shyness,and
2. by teaching Jimmy some basic skills necessary to enable him to join in ball games.

The following programmes were devised.

Stage 1 : Overcoming shyness and isolation

The staff used a shaping procedure to increase gradually Jimmy's approach to and contact with other children. Each time Jimmy glanced at or took a tentative step towards the other children, the staff would reward him by saying, 'Good boy, go and join in', or smiling and waving him on. When Jimmy went for long periods without giving even these first steps, the staff would approach him and gently guide him (i.e. prompt) towards the other children and perhaps say, 'Come on Jimmy, let's see you join in the fun with the others'. As soon as Jimmy showed a fairly consistent tendency to approach others, the staff gradually faded out the physical promptings but continued to give him verbal praise and encouragement when he displayed this behaviour.

Stage 2 : Teaching Ball Skills using 1st, 2nd and 3rd order task analysis

Overlapping with Stage 1, as soon as Jimmy showed

more and more tendency to approach the other children, the staff devised the following programme to teach Jimmy the elements of throwing a ball.

Throwing

First Order Task Analysis

A. Throws large ball underarm using both hands to adult.
B. Throws bean bag underarm using preferred hand to adult.
C. Throws small ball underarm using preferred hand to adult

Second Order Task Analysis (using shaping)

A.
(1. Throws large ball underarm with both hands (any direction)
(2. Throws large ball underarm with both hands into large basket nearby
(3. Throws large ball underarm with both hands to adult close by

B.
(1. Throws bean bag underarm with preferred hand (in any direction)
(2. Throws bean bag underarm with preferred hand into basket nearby
(3. Throws bean bag underarm with preferred hand to adult close by

C.
(1. Throws small ball underarm with preferred hand (in any direction)
(2. Throws small ball underarm with preferred hand into large basket
(3. Throws small ball underarm with preferred hand to adult close by

Third Order Task Analysis

A1
((a) Throws large ball underarm (any direction) with both hands with physical prompt (i.e. stands behind child and physically guides his arms through the action of throwing the ball)
((b) Throws large ball underarm (any direction) with both hands with gestural prompt (i.e adult imitates the action of throwing the ball)
((c) Throws large ball underarm (any direction) with both hands when asked to without prompting

((a) Throws large ball underarm into large basket
(nearby with both hands with physical prompt
((i.e. adult stands behind child and points
(him at the basket and physically guides his
(arms through the action of throwing the
(ball)
(
A2 ((b) Throws large ball underarm into large basket
(nearby with both hands with gestural prompt
((i.e. adult imitates the action of throwing
(the ball into the basket)
(
((c) Throws large ball underarm into large basket
(nearby with both hands when asked to without
(prompting

A3 and so on ......

The third order task procedures (i.e. the same procedures as for the second order but incorporating physical prompts, gestures and verbal commands) are then repeated for each of the other steps in the process. Because Jimmy was so poor at throwing, the third order task procedures were felt to be most appropriate for him and the programme began with them.

Stage 3 : Maintaining Skills
Over several weeks of training Jimmy's behaviour was observed at intervals; any tendency to withdraw from contact with the other children or to give up trying to throw was countered by introducing an appropriate training session.

Case 2. Teaching Attention and Cooperation and Developing Coordinated Movement in an Overactive Child

Sally is a very restless and overactive little girl. She seldom sits still for more than a minute and cannot concentrate or pay attention to any one activity for very long, despite the efforts of the staff. She seems to have boundless energy and enthusiasm, but she expresses herself in a totally unco-ordinated way by rushing around the nursery, bumping into furniture and other children or crawling aimlessly over the floor or apparatus.

The nursery staff decided to try to teach Sally how to pay attention, be more cooperative and develop more smoothness and coordination in her movements.

A. <u>Teaching Attention and Cooperation</u>

Sally is asked:

1. (a) 'Come over here' and is physically guided to a chair

   (b) 'Come over here' and is gestured towards a chair

   (c) 'Come over here' without any physical or gestured guidance from the staff

When 1(c) has been successfuly achieved, the staff proceed to the next stage.

Sally is asked:

2. (a) 'Come over here and sit down' and is physically guided to the chair and gently made to sit down

   (b) 'Come over here and sit down' and is gestured towards the chair and motioned to sit down

   (c) 'Come over here and sit down' without any physical guidance or gestures

Each step is practised, obviously, until the child has achieved it, before going on to the next step.

As soon as 2(c) has been successfully carried out, the staff proceed to the third stage.

Sally is asked:

3. (a) 'Come over here, sit down and watch me for a while', and is guided to the chair, encouraged to sit down and persuaded to watch the staff member completing a task (e.g. doing a simple drawing). Any attempt to get up and dash away is countered by gently restraining her

   (b) 'Come over here, sit down and watch me for a while', and is made to do so by the use of gestures rather than physical guidance or restraint

   (c) 'Come over here, sit down and watch me

for a while', without any physical guidance or gestures being used

Again, each step may have to be repeated several times before the staff are satisfied that they can proceed to the next one.

At the same time as teaching the later stages of developing attention and cooperation, the staff try to encourage Sally to move in a more controlled and coordinated way and to avoid rushing, falling and bumping into people and objects.

B. Developing Controlled and Coordinated Movement

The staff devised the following series of activities for Sally. Again, physical guidance and gestures were used for the initial steps before Sally performed the activities on her own with only verbal instructions from the staff.

1. Walks along a simple obstacle course which requires her to go under, over and between suitable obstacles (e.g. desks, chairs or benches)

   Step (a) with physical guidance
   Step (b) with gestures
   Step (c) verbal instructions only

2. Walks up and down stairs

   Step (a) with physical guidance
   Step (b) with gestures
   Step (c) with verbal instructions only

3. Climbs up and down a small step ladder

   (Steps (a), (b) and (c))

4. Runs along an obstacle course

   (Steps (a), (b) and (c))

5. Hops along obstacle course, first on right foot and then on left foot

   (Steps (a), (b) and (c) as appropriate)

6. Jumps forward ten times, both feet together, then backward ten times, both feet together

(Steps (a), (b) and (c) as appropriate)

7. Jumps over a skipping rope held stationary one foot above the floor

(Steps (a), (b) and (c))

8. Jumps over skipping rope rotated slowly by helpers

(Steps (a), (b) and (c))

9. Skips on her own using rope

(Steps (a), (b) and (c) as appropriate)

<u>Summary : Points to Bear in Mind</u>

The use of procedures such as chaining and shaping in a teaching programme may be a new departure for you, and you should remember that certain basic elements must be present before these procedures can be effective. Some of these basic elements are listed below. The child must have:

1. the verbal and general ability to understand the task;
2. the physical attributes necessary to do the task;
3. the motivation to learn, and the alertness necessary to perform the task;
4. rewards for any improvement, however slight;
5. adequate rest periods between intensive training sessions;
6. a variety of materials to make learning more interesting;
7. both tangible and social rewards at appropriate times;
8. adequate opportunity to practise the skill;
9. the realisation that learning a new skill is rewarding in itself;
10. a good model that can be imitated;
11. sympathy and understanding when having difficulty with parts of the task;
12. enjoyment and happiness whilst learning.

Task analysis and its associated techniques have been widely applied in a variety of settings over the last few years and there are a number of good training manuals and books available for the interested reader. It is recommended that you read at least one or two of the references given at the end.

Conclusion

It is good advice to suggest that if you are thinking of using any behaviour modification methods in your nursery group, you might be wise to discuss your intended programme with an educational psychologist if this is possible. Talking things over can help to clarify matters in your own mind as well as opening out other possibilities.

There may be a problem of time in some cases. It would be inadvisable to spend too much time concentrating on one individual to the detriment of the other children. You may have to adapt your programme once you have worked out how much time you can justifiably spend on the child with the problem. In some instances this may be no more than a few minutes each day. However, even a few minutes' application of a well thought-out intervention programme may produce dramatic changes in that child's behaviour over several weeks.

Some of the methods described in this section may be difficult to apply in your particular setting or with a particular child. You will have to use your experience and judgement to pick out what is practical and what is not, but do not do this 'out of hand' without a thorough analysis of the situation. Many of these methods really do work, but only if they are used properly.

The other children in the nursery might well be used to help their classmates to become better adjusted. The children will be of particular help when a technique is embedded in a play-situation which will often have to involve other children in order to structure a game (e.g. chaining the teaching of ball skills).

It is important to keep parents as fully informed as possible about what you are doing. Consult the parents at all stages, gain their agreement and try to involve them in the assessment and intervention that you will be carrying out.

A further point that may bother you is whether it is ethical to apply what may seem to be highly manipulative techniques to a child's behaviour. The answer to this is that behaviour modification must always be humanely and thoughfully used. Any procedure that might indirectly exacerbate a child's problem should be considered unsuitable. In reality most of the techniques are not 'manipulative' in a derogatory sense but merely constitute a systematic way of teaching a new behaviour pattern that will make the child a good deal happier in the long term.

Finally, many of the procedures of behaviour modifcation (e.g. rewarding good behaviour)are very 'common-sense' notions, and often those attending a course on the application of these techniques pass the remark, "...well, we do all that already, anyway". Without wishing to appear too defensive, we say that, in fact, this is not usually the case! Yes, it is true that many of the ideas underlying behaviour modification are familiar in everyday life and are rooted strongly in 'common-sense' (and this is to be welcomed since it probably means that many of these ideas are closely related to the fundamental laws of behaviour), but it is the systematic, structured and consistent manner in which these ideas are applied that makes behaviour modification a distincitive new approach to the treatment of behaviour problems in young children.

REFERENCES

BEHAVIOUR MODIFICATION

Hall, Vance : In Axelrod, S. (1977) Behaviour Modification for the Classroom Teacher. New York : McGraw Hill.

Porterfield, J.K., Herbert-Jackson, E. and Risley, T.R. (1976) Contingent Observation : an effective and acceptable procedure for reducing disruptive behaviour of young children in a group setting. Journal of Applied Behaviour Analysis, 9, 55-64.

Sarason, I.G., Glazer, E.M., and Fargo, G.A. (1972) Reinforcing Productive Classroom Behaviour. New York : Behavioural Publications, Inc.

Walker, J.E. and Shea, T.M. (1976) Behaviour Modification : a practical approach for educators. St. Louis : C.V. Mosby.

Recommended Books (good outlines of applications of Behaviour Modification)

Axelrod, S. (1977) Behaviour Modification for the Classroom Teacher. New York : McGraw Hill.

Herbert, M. (1978) Conduct Disorders of Childhood and Adolescence. New York : Wiley.
Vargas, J.S. (1977) Behavioural Psychology for Teachers. New York : Harper and Row.
Walker, J.E. and Shea, T.M. (1976) Behaviour Modification : a practical approach for educators. St. Louis : C.V. Mosby.

FURTHER READING

Blackham, G.T. and Silberman, A. (1975) Modification of Child and Adolescent Behaviour. Belmont : Wadsworth.
Cambrill, E.D. (1977) Behaviour Modification : Handbook of Assessment Intervention and Evaluation. Washington : Jossey-Bass.
Hersen, M. and Barlow, D.H. (1976) Single-Case Experimental Designs. New York : Pergamon.
O'Leary, K.D. and Wilson, G.T. (1975) Behaviour Therapy : Application and Outcome. New Jersey : Prentice-Hall.
Willis, J. and Giles, D. (eds) (1976) Great Experiments in Behaviour Modification. Indianapolis : Hackett.

REFERENCES

TASK ANALYSIS

Gagné, R.M. (1977) The Conditions of Learning (3rd Edition) New York : Holt, Rinehart and Winston.
Gardner, J. and Tweddle, D.A. (1978) Some Guidelines for Sequencing Objectives. Training document, available from School Psychological Service, Walsall.
Hemsley, R. and Carr, J. (1980), and Tsoi, M. and Yule, W. (1980) - Chapters in Yule, W. and Carr, J. (eds.), Behaviour Modification for the Mentally Handicapped. London : Croom Helm; Baltimore : University Park Press.

FURTHER READING

Ainscow, M. and Tweddle, D.A. (1979) Preventing Classroom Failure : An Objectives Approach. Chichester : Wiley.
Burland, J.R., Brown, T.W. and Mendham, R.P. (1977)

Steps to Self Sufficiency : a training manual developed at Chelfham Mill School, Devon, and available on request.

(3) PROBLEM-SOLVING APPROACHES

Introduction

Philip (aged 4½) is a very active, lively boy who likes to be the centre of attention. He demands his own way frequently and if he is thwarted or frustrated he is abusive to staff and children alike and often hits out in temper. Philip sometimes takes it upon himself to 'punish' other children for what he sees as misbehaviour on their part, usually picking upon younger, weaker children. His teacher, Mrs. G., frequently finds herself intervening in problem situations which have been provoked by Philip's behaviour, either pacifying children in tears or sorting out squabbles and fights. Philip always manages to come up with some justification for his behaviour.

It often seems to be the case that children, like Philip, whose behaviour is a cause for concern repeatedly find themselves in the same kind of situations and always meet their difficulties in the same way with the same disastrous results. For example, if Philip wants to play with a trike that another child is riding, he has been known to try and push the child off and forcibly wrest the trike from him or her. The other child then either retaliates or becomes upset and Mrs. G. is called upon once again to act as arbiter or comforter. Behaviour such as pushing, grabbing and hitting are very common in three-year-olds, but generally, as children develop they learn to adapt their behaviour and try other ploys to get their own way, such as offering to share or to give a toy in return. Some children, however, get stuck in a 'rut' and like Philip their only means of 'solving' a problem may be to use force because they cannot readily adopt new strategies for resolving their difficulties.

Like Philip's teacher when faced with unacceptable behaviour you may find yourself saying, "Stop it, Philip, you must not hit (push, grab, kick etc.). David, wait until he has finishing riding the trike and then you can have a turn." We often make demands upon children to stop hitting, kicking or whatever "because I say so" perhaps adding the rider "you might hurt him" or "you will have to learn to share and take turns". But, in all probability, when in similar circumstances the child will do the same thing again. All Philip learned from Mrs. G's interventions was that she was not very pleased with him. Although she intended to help, her actions were not successful in achieving lasting positive changes in his behaviour. This was largely because her direct commands and comments on what he 'ought' to do in his position gave him little help in sorting out the situation for himself because all the thinking had been done for him.

As an alternative to imposing external solutions on Philip's problems Mrs. G. sometimes adopted the role of arbitrator, helping to sort out the argument and explaining why a particular behaviour was not acceptable. Although this was an improvement on the 'because I say so' approach this method had only limited success. Typically, if Philip had worked himself into a temper and was upset, a lengthy explanation of the rights and wrongs of the matter washed over him and he understood very little of what his teacher said and failed to grasp the underlying principles of her reasoning. This is not to say that she should not have offered such explanations, but it may have been better to delay them until tempers had cooled and the children involved were in a more receptive frame of mind. At least, in her role as arbitrator Mrs. G. gave Philip a chance to explain himself and his grievances and become involved in working towards an acceptable solution, but even so she felt that this approach, although an improvement on the 'because I say so' method, was doing little to change Philip's behaviour for the better.

What Does the Problem-solving Approach Offer?

The problem-solving approach has a great deal in common with the arbitration method outlined above. However, in this approach the adult's role is rather different. Instead of suggesting the most acceptable answer to a problem or explaining why particular actions meet with disapproval, the adult acts as a guide in encouraging the children to think up their own ideas of resolving the situation to everyone's satisfaction. The adult helps the children to think about alternative courses of action for themselves, to look ahead to possible outcomes and on this basis to choose the best solution. This does not involve teaching children specific solutions to specific problems but rather assisting them to think up their own options and their consequences, i.e. teaching children how to think, not what to think. The implicit philosophy on which the method is based is that if one wishes to change the behaviour of children one must influence the thinking which controls the behaviour. As demonstrated by Philip, merely prohibiting a behaviour does not prevent its re-occurrence, largely because the thought processes, which produced the behaviour in the first place, remain unaltered. The problem-solving approach, if used effectively, aims to develop flexible thinking and demonstrates to children that there is more than one way of solving a personal problem to their own and everyone else's satisfaction.

Perhaps this can best be illustrated by showing how Mrs. G. could have used problem-solving to sort out Philip's dispute over the tricycle.

> Philip, you may remember, had wanted to ride on the trike which David was pedalling around the playground. He ran over to David and tried to push him off but David retaliated by kicking Philip, and both children end in tears. Mrs. G. comes over to sort things out.
>
> Mrs. G. : Philip, what happened when you tried to push David off the bike?
>
> Philip : He kicked me.
>
> Mrs. G. : How did you feel when he did that?
>
> Philip : It hurt, he made me cry.
>
> Mrs. G. : I know you wanted to ride the trike and pushing was one way of getting it, but can you think of another way?
>
> Philip : I could hit him.
>
> Mrs. G. : Yes, you could hit him, but what might happen if you do?
>
> Philip : He'd hit me back.
>
> Mrs. G. : He might, so hitting isn't such a

good idea because he might make you cry again. Can you think of a different way?

Philip : I could ask him.

Mrs. G. : Yes you could. Why not ask David and see what he says?

(She calls him over)

Philip : Can I have a ride on the bike please?

David : No! (Philip begins to get cross again)

Mrs. G. : Oh dear, he said no. Well, Philip, I know you're upset now but I bet if you think really hard you'll find a different idea. You've tried asking, what else could you do?

Philip : (After several seconds) Can we take turns? I'll have a little go and then you have it back?

David : All right.

Mrs. G. : Good boy Philip, you thought of a different way all by yourself. Do you feel better now?

David and Philip : Yes.

In this situation Mrs. G. did not simply put a stop to the kicking and pushing, nor did she tell them to stay away from each other or even direct them by suggesting other activities. Instead she brought both children together and guided Philip in thinking through the problem for himself. She did not tell him what to say or what to think; she merely used the circumstances to direct him towards a successful outcome to the problem. This is important, since it is much more likely that Philip will act upon a conclusion if he has worked it out for himself than if he is given a ready-made solution by an adult. It should also be noted that Mrs. G. did not reject Philip's negative suggestion out of hand but encouraged him to judge its merits in the same way as more acceptable ideas.

Which Children will Benefit from this Approach?

Although so far we have only looked at an example of an aggressive child, the approach can be used equally well with any children who are having difficulties in adjusting to the nursery group. Withdrawn children, for example, may not know how to join in a group game because of their very limited social skills, and simply thrusting them into a group activity and hoping for the best may leave them floundering. The problem-solving approach used in conjunction with some of the play activities (see pp. 92-128) offers opportunities for you to help withdrawn children become more adaptive and socially outgoing.

The problem-solving approach aims to develop logical thinking, but it should be stressed that you should not expect too much rational behaviour on the part of very young children. Learning to think logically takes time (even adults do not always act on the basis of reason) and you should be prepared to accept and encourage partial responses and partial understanding of the concepts involved.

To work successfully, this approach requires a child to be competent in certain language skills and also capable of grasping the concepts involved in logical thinking (e.g. Why did I fall off my bike? I fell off my bike because I was going too fast). For this reason it may not be the most suitable method to use with very young children or children who are slow developers, particulary if their language is immature. With these qualifications in mind, we suggest that the problem-solving approach gives nursery staff a framework for teaching children the skills necessary to deal with social difficulties.

Using the Problem-solving Approach in the Nursery Group

The problem-solving approach has two main components, both of which should run concurrently if maximum benefit is to be gained.

1. Group Activities

In order to develop the language and cognitive skills necessary for successful problem-solving, children need experience of practising these skills within the security of a small group. The group sessions involve a variety of activities and games which will be outlined in detail later on in this section. They are specifically designed to enhance children's awareness of the effects of their behaviour on others and to help in understanding that problems can have a number of different solutions. The basic principles of this approach are derived from a nursery programme developed by George Spivack and Myrna Shure. There are three stages of activities.

A. developing basic language skills;
B. developing an awareness of others;
C. using the skills from the first two stages to solve hypothetical problems.

2. Adopting the Problem-solving Style
Although you are teaching the skills and techniques by means of group activities, if they are to be effective in positively changing a child's behaviour, you will have to ensure that what has been learned in the group generalises to the remainder of the child's day. Once you are familiar with the basic principles of the approach you should be able to incorporate them into your daily routine. Thus when problems arise between children, you should be on hand to prompt them in working out a solution. A consistent application of the techniques in guiding children through the real life difficulties they encounter during the day will lead to their more successful handling of similar situations in the future.

The remainder of this chapter is devoted to practical guidelines for implementing both parts of the problem-solving approach in your nursery group.

1. GROUP ACTIVITIES

Organisation

The games and activities of stages A, B and C(see above) are designed for group sessions with 6 - 8 children for ten to fifteen minutes a day. Suggestions concerning the settings, composition and organisation of small groups are to be found in the section "Play Activities" (pp. 113-115) although it is worth mentioning several points in particular here. All the activities require the children's participation, so it is best to try and achieve a balanced group of responding and non-responding children, as the former are a great help to the latter. Have the quiet children sit in the middle of the group near the front, so that you can encourage them to whisper in your ear if they are too inhibited to respond in front of the others. Similarly, if you have disruptive children in your group you may consider having them sitting next to you in order to maintain their attention more easily. It is probably unwise to gather all the children you consider to be having problems into one group. Later on you will find suggestions on handling the kinds of difficult behaviour you may encounter in the group sessions (pp. 195-197).

Sequencing of Activities

The activities of each stage, and the stages themselves, are based on a step-by-step progression so that success in the later games is dependent on a good understanding of the earlier ones. For this reason it is important that the activities are introduced in the sequence suggested, although you may need to spend several sessions on some of the topics, and on revision, if it is apparent that the children have not mastered a particular concept. For this reason, many of the activities include suggestions to extend the game, for example, by introducing a different set of pictures, and you can probably think up some more variations yourself.

Materials for Each of the Stages

Most of the materials needed for the activities are those normally available in nursery groups and are listed below.

Stages A and B (Language and Awareness Games)

Several sets of large pictures, preferably coloured, mounted on card and covered in clear plastic. You should try to collect a set of each of the following:

- pets
- food (fruit, sweets, vegetables)
- faces (children who are smiling, laughing, crying, afraid, angry etc.)
- action pictures (children who are running jumping, eating, skipping etc.)
- toys (for boys and girls)
- forms of transportation

The faces and action sets should include pictures of different children doing the same thing.

Also required are a hand mirror, a glove puppet, two small collections of objects (e.g. hats, paintbrushes, cars, dolls) and an apple or an orange.

Stage C (Problem-solving)
In this stage you can, if you wish, use pictures of children at play to illustrate the hypothetical problems you will be presenting to the group. These may be more difficult to obtain but there are several possible sources you could consider:-

(a) old educational supplies catalogues which include pictures of children playing with toys and equipment (e.g. Community Playthings, Abbatt toys, Galt Early Stages);

(b) the early books of the 'Dominoes' or 'Through the Rainbow' reading schemes, which contain coloured photographs of children playing;

(c) the school library service will often provide, on request, a box of discarded picture books suitable for cutting up.

Stage A : Developing Basic Language Skills
The activities described in this section introduce the basic vocabulary upon which the problem-solving approach is based. Some children may be sufficiently competent in their use and comprehension of language to by-pass this initial stage. If, however, you are at all uncertain about your children's abilities, it is best to take them through the programme from the very beginning, as success in the later activities is dependent on these early skills. The goal of all these activities is to teach children to use language as a tool to solve personal problems. Thus absolute grammatical accuracy is not required, provided that a child has grasped the particular concept involved, e.g. "I've not got no cars" is just as acceptable as "I haven't any cars" as long as the child understands the concept of negation.

(a) 'Is' and 'Is Not'
Children have to be familiar with the concept of negation if they are to decide not to do something in favour of something else, e.g. "I'll not hit him, I'll ask him to share."

Begin the activity by pointing to individuals in the group and saying, for example, "Tracey is a girl, Gareth is a boy, James is a boy etc." Go around all the children in the group and reinforce the idea by having them tap their knees if you point to a girl and raise their hands if you point to a boy. Next introduce the work 'not' by pointing out that Tracey is a girl, she is not a boy and repeat with the other children. Let the group have fun with the word 'not' by naming silly things they are not, e.g. "Gareth is not an elephant, Gareth is not a dustbin etc." To maintain interest give the children objects (e.g. hats and cars), and ask who is and who is not holding a car/hat. To encourage them to take notice of others ask individual children what another child is holding, e.g."Robert, is Jane holding a car?" or "Lisa, point to someone who is not holding a hat, etc." The game can be extended by using pictures from the faces and action sets. The children can point to someone who is smiling and someone who is not smiling, a child who is running and one who is not running etc.

(b) 'Or'
If children are to learn to think of alternative solutions to a problem they must be able to use the word 'or' correctly, e.g. "I can hit him or I can ask him to share or I can swop cars with him".

Introduce 'or' by asking questions such as:

"Am I pointing to Richard or am I pointing to Susan?"
"Is Peter standing up or is Peter siting down?"
"Am I holding a pencil or am I holding a book?"

Reinforce the words learned in the previous game in the answers you model:

"Good Mark, I'm holding a pencil, I'm not holding a book."
"Peter is not standing up he is sitting down."

Use pictures from the food and pet set and ask:

"Is this a cat or is this a dog?"
"Is this an apple or is this a banana?" etc.

Go around the group asking individual children a variety of questions using 'or'.

(c) 'Same' and 'Different'
These words are important in naming new and different alternatives and in being able to discriminate between them when solving problems. They also have a part to play in demonstrating individual preferences, for instance, different children like

different things; some children like playing with dolls and some do not; not everybody likes the same thing.

In this activity try to keep the focus on children and the things they do. A good way of introducing the words is by performing various movements (waving, patting your head, standing up, nodding your head etc.,) and first of all having the group do the same thing as you and then asking them to do a different action from yours. Each child can take turns to come out and perform an action, the group first copying the action and then doing a different action. In this way the children are not only thinking about the words 'same' and 'different' but are also given the opportunity to think about what other children are doing.

The game can be extended by using pictures from the action set and letting the children make pairs of pictures sometimes illustrating the same action and sometimes two different actions. Make sure you reinforce the words by continuously monitoring what the children are doing (e.g. "Yes Richard, you have chosen two boys doing the same thing. This boy is running and this boy is running") and also by questions (e.g. "Are these girls doing the same thing?").

(d) 'Happy', 'Sad' and 'Angry'

As part of this approach involves demonstrating to children how their behaviour can affect other children's feelings, by making them upset, angry or happy, they need to know the various adjectives used to describe emotions, as well as the ways these feelings are expressed.

Use pictures from the faces set to demonstrate expressions such as laughing, crying, smiling etc., and talk about the relationship between facial expressions and emotions, e.g. we smile when we are happy and cry when we are sad etc. Demonstrate a range of facial expressions yourself and see if the children can identify your emotions from your face. Encourage the children to make the same faces as you and let them see themselves in a mirror. Ask questions and give examples of the different faces people use on different occasions, e.g. "What kind of face do you have when someone gives you a birthday present? Show me a 'happy' face". "How would you feel if you lost your mummy in the middle of town when you were out shopping? Show me a 'sad' face", etc. Once you are certain that the children have mastered the basic vocabularly move on to the next stage.

Stage B : Developing an Awareness of Others

(a) How Can we Tell?
Attending to another child's feelings and preferences is an important element in developing children's abilities to solve personal problems successfully. Understanding words such as 'happy','sad' and 'angry' help children to learn that different people feel differently, that feelings change and that it is possible to find these things out by watching, listening and asking.

The first activity demonstrates to children that watching is one way to find out how someone feels. Show the children a picture of a smiling boy and ask, 'How can we tell if he is happy or sad?' Point out that we can tell he is happy because we can see him smiling. Repeat with pictures of sad and angry children, emphasising that we can tell how they feel because we can see with our eyes whether they are frowning, crying, laughing etc.

Listening is another way of finding out how people feel. Show this by covering your face with a book and laughing loudly. Ask the children whether you are happy or sad and how they can tell? Emphasise that they can tell not because they can see you with their eyes but because they can hear you with their ears. Cover your face again but this time cry and repeat as for laughing. Let the children take turns to cover their faces and laugh or cry. The rest of the group have to guess how they are feeling.

See if the children can think of another way to find out whether someone is happy or sad. If no one replies, tell them that the third way is to ask. Go around the group asking the children how they feel and encourage them to ask one another.

(b) Individual Preferences
The aim here is to show children that not everybody chooses the same thing, as young children frequently assume that others would choose what they choose and this can lead to faulty conclusions. These games offer guidance on how fo find out what other children like and the children take an active role in doing the asking. Throughout, the point is made that different people like different things and this is perfectly all right.

Choosing Game. Use pictures from the food or pets

set and present them to the children in pairs, e.g. cat and dog, ice cream and crisps, chips and biscuits etc. Let children in the group say which of the two they would prefer. Point out that not all the children choose the same thing, some prefer cats and others dogs. Repeat with several pairs of animals/food asking all the children in the group individually. Encourage the children to say what they think others would choose, e.g. "Brian, what do you think Alan would choose, a cat or a dog?" When Brian has guessed let him see if he was right by asking Alan himself what he would really like. Repeat this with other children, making it clear that asking is an important way of finding out what others like.

Do you Like? To reinforce the idea that not everybody likes the same thing let the children ask each other questions about what they like, e.g. "Kevin, do you like sweets? Do you like cars? Do you like dolls?" Allow the children to get carried away with the phrase "do you like?" and ask other children as many questions as they can think of.

(c) Why - Because Game

If children are to understand how their behaviour affects others then they need to know something about causality. Children who realise, for instance, that the reason why their playmates hit them is because they hit first, will be more aware of the consequences of hitting and a better judge of the usefulness of this tactic next time around.

This game aims to establish the connection between 'why' and 'because' and for it you will need a glove puppet. Have the puppet introduce itself and explain that it has come to play a game with the children. To begin, the puppet makes a statement, such as "I'm tired" or "I'm hungry", and the children are prompted to ask "Why?". The puppet replies "Because I went to bed late" or "I didn't have any breakfast", etc. If you play the game with the puppet first, the group will more easily grasp what is required of them. After several such statements and questions, the game changes and the children are encouraged to think of reasons for the statements themselves. E.g. the puppet says "My friend Jean won't come out to play today. Does anybody know why Jean won't play out? Perhaps she won't because ......" At this point the children have to think of as many different reasons as they can. For instance, she is not feeling well, it's raining, her mummy won't let her,etc. Repeat back to the children all the reasons they come up with for each statement. Carry on until the children run out of reasons and then have the puppet make a new statement and repeat the game again. The game can continue with the children making statements and the puppet asking 'Why?'.

Thinking of alternatives in this way is good practice for later when the children have to think of alternative consequences and solutions to problems.

(d) Fairness

Fairness is an important concept in learning to take into consideration the rights of other children and in being sensitive to their feelings. Included in these activities is the notion that sometimes being fair means having to wait.

Divide up an orange or an apple, explaining that there is one piece for everyone in the group, but they are not to eat them straight away. Point out that it is fair for everyone to have one piece, but if someone takes two then it is not fair as someone will have to go without and this will make them unhappy or angry. Demonstrate by handing round the apple/orange so that the adult has two pieces and someone else none at all, and show how this can be put right so that everyone has a fair share. Go on to give other examples of what is fair and what is not fair, such as two children wanting to look at the same book or play with the same toy. Encourage the children to say what would be the fair thing to do under the circumstances.

To illustrate that being fair sometimes entails waiting, you can make up a little story about a trip to the seaside. Make a pretend car out of chairs or boxes that will seat only half the children in the group. Explain that there is only room for some of the children so that you will have to make two journeys, some going on the first trip and some on the second. Choose half the group and pretend to set off with them to the seaside, going through the motions of driving and paddling in the sea before pretending to return. Ask the group who should go on the second trip,explaining that it would not be fair for some children to go twice. Name some of the children who went on the first trip and some who did not and ask whether it would be fair for them to go on the second journey. Make a second trip with the children who were not chosen the first time. Fairness is not an easy concept for children of this age to grasp and even though some children will understand the idea they will still find it difficult to put into practice.

Stage C ; Problem-solving
The aim of these group sessions is to enable children to think of alternative solutions to hypothetical problems and to encourage them to appreciate the consequences of their actions. The activities in this section are divided into three parts:

(a) alternative solutions;

(b) alternative consequences;

(c) pairing solutions and possible consequences.

It should be stressed that, in working through a problem, the children should be guided to think of their own solutions and consequences. Never tell the group what you consider to be the best solution but allow them to work this out for themselves with your help.

How to Organise these Group Sessions
Children of this age cannot be expected to understand hypothetical problems without some assistance from props or visual aids. You may find that the group will solve problems more readily if you choose two of them to 'act out' examples of problem situations. This need not be anything very elaborate; you could, for example, choose one child to sit and look at a book and ask a second child to snatch it from her. Having watched an actual demonstration of a problem the group may then be able to talk about how the first child might feel, what might happen next and so on. By using role play in this way to illustrate typical problems, children may find it easier to relate the hypothetical problems to situations in real life.

Alternatively, you may want to use pictures and photographs to illustrate difficult situations. These pictures do not need to depict an obvious problem as you can utilise any pictures of children playing and define the problem verbally when you show it to the group. For example, a picture of two children eating biscuits could form the basis of a story in which one child snatches a biscuit from the other. You can then talk about the story in the light of what is fair and what might happen as a consequence. Inventing a problem situation from a picture is not difficult and although suggestions will be given you can, if you wish, make up a variety of problems which are typical of your nursery group.

(a) Alternative Solutions
The aim here is to use the basic word concepts learned earlier to guide the children towards thinking in terms of alternatives. In each session the children are either shown a picture depicting a common problem or act out a problem and then are asked to think of as many different ways as possible of solving the problem.

A typical example might be a situation involving two boys playing with a box of bricks. Tell the children that David and Gareth have both been playing with the bricks, but now that it is time to put them away Gareth does not want to help. The problem is how can David get Gareth to help him clear away? The story is discussed in terms of what is fair and what is not fair and the group is told that the idea of the game is to think of lots of different ways for David to get Gareth to help him. Each solution offered is repeated to the group and they are urged to think of what else David can do to get Gareth's co-operation. When ideas of what to do are no longer offered, the children are asked what David can say to Gareth and the solutions are enumerated once again.

At this stage children will often suggest a variation of the same solution rather than a different one. The most common variations are: giving something (give him a sweet, give him your car); telling someone (tell his daddy or his mummy, tell the teacher); hurting (hit him, kick him, bite him). Let the children do this for a while and then classify their statements so that they learn to distinguish between mere variations and solutions that are categorically different. For instance, "Giving Gareth a car or a sweet or a crisp are all 'giving something'. Can anyone think of an idea that is different from giving something?"

Again, if 'giving something' is suggested as a solution, you should point out to the group that not all children like the same things. Before offering to give a sweet or a toy they would first have to find out if the other child wants or likes what is being offered by asking. Sometimes children appear to give seemingly irrelevant solutions to the problem ('cry' or 'be good' for example), in which case you will have to question the children as to why they think this is a good idea by asking them to tell you more about it.

It is important to accept all the children's ideas at this point without making any value judgements, so that 'hit him' is just as relevant as saying 'please' and should be included in the list of solutions offered. Later on, both forceful and non-forceful solutions will be looked at in the light of their consequences.

Listed below are some suggestions of problem situations which you can use in these sessions. They can be illustrated either by pictures or by children 'acting out' the situations you describe for them. As mentioned earlier you may make up your own little stories if you wish.

(i) A boy wants his friend to help with clearing away the toys.

(ii) A child wants another to sit down and stop blocking the view of the picture book being read to them by an adult.

(iii) A child wants to ride on a bike (swing, scooter, cart, rocking horse etc.) that another child is already playing with.

(iv) A child wants another child to play with in the Wendy House.

(b) Alternative Consequences

In the next few sessions the children are presented with similar problems and again asked for solutions, but here your aim is to teach them to think in terms of the consequences of particular solutions. Through questioning (e.g. "What might happen next if you hit her?"),the children are encouraged to think for themselves, weigh the pros and cons of an action and then decide whether or not their idea was a good one. This is perhaps best illustrated by the following example:

> Either show the group a picture of two children standing by a rabbit hutch and tell them that the boy wants the girl to let him feed the rabbits or act out a similar situation using two children from the group. As in previous sessions, encourage the children to think of alternative solutions to the problem. Take one of the proffered solutions,

such as "push her out of the way", and ask the children what might happen next if this course of action was followed. Encourage the children to think of as many different consequences as they can. If they run out of ideas prompt them with further questions such as:

"What might the girl <u>do</u> if the boy pushes her?"
"What might the girl <u>say</u> if the boy pushes her?"
"How might the girl <u>feel</u> if the boy pushes her?"
"Will she be sad, happy or angy?"

Reiterate to the children all the alternatives they have thought of so far. When it becomes apparent that no further suggestions are forthcoming, ask the group if they think pushing is or is not a good idea and why. Then take one solution at a time and elicit all the consequences you can before going on to a different solution. Try to choose forceful as well as non-forceful solutions for the children to evaluate at each session. You may find it useful to record the solutions and consequences so that you can refer to them if need be.

Set out below are a number of problems which you might like to use in the sessions on alternative consequences. Remember to elicit a number of different solutions before examining them individually in terms of their consequences.

(i) A boy wants a girl to let him feed the animals.

(ii) A girl wants a boy to stop knocking down her building brick houses.

(iii) A boy on the slide wants a girl at the bottom to get off so that he can slide down.

(iv) A girl wants to be a nurse but someone else is already dressed up in the nurse's outfit.

(c) <u>Pairing Solutions and Consequences</u>
In these activities the children are given a problem, have to think of a solution and then think immediately of its consequence. Ultimately, it is hoped that the children will learn to think of solutions, evaluate them, and then decide which alternative is the most appropriate before taking action.

As in parts 'a' and 'b' explain the problem to the group and ask for solutions in the usual way. When one solution has been suggested ask immediately what might happen next as a consequence. You can use any of the following questions to elicit consequences:

"What might happen next if ....?"
"What might B <u>do</u> if A ....?"
"What might B <u>say</u> if A ....?"
"What might B <u>feel</u> if A ....?"

Ask only for one consequence per solution and then move onto a second solution and a second consequence, perhaps asking individual children for pairs of solution and consequence. Continue pairing solutions and consequences in this way until no new ones are offered. Occasionally follow up by asking a child if a particular solution is a good one and why.

Here are a few more suggestions for problem situations:

(i) A boy wants another child to stop scribbling on his picture.

(ii) A girl wants another child to stop chasing her.

(iii) A boy would like to play a game of lotto but all his friends are outside in the playground or in the Wendy House.

(iv) A girl on a bike wants a girl on a scooter to get out of her way.

Before going on to Part II which describes the informal use of the principles and techniques of the problem-solving approach throughout the day, some reference should be made to handling difficult behaviours which may occur in the group sessions.

Managing Difficult Behaviour in the Group Sessions

The Child who will not Respond

Since most of the activities require a response from the children in the group you will soon be aware of any child who is not participating. There may be many reasons why children do not respond : they may be too shy or hesitant to speak in front of even a small group; they mayprefer not to think about what is going on and are not listening; perhaps they are unsure of what is happening and hesitate to join in; or they may be temporarily upset and not in the mood to play games.

Children who consistently do not respond, and sit in the group day after day merely as onlookers, can sometimes be coaxed out of their passivity if you approach them warmly and with extreme patience. You could try phrasing the questions to them in such a way that they can respond with a nod or a shake of the head. Often a physical response may be easier for them than a verbal one. Similarly, in some of the games involving individual preferences, it is feasible to have shy children point to the object they would prefer, as even pointing is better than no participation at all. Any sign of a response, however minimal, should be praised but if, after gentle prodding, the child will not even respond with a nod of the head the matter should be dropped for a while. Too much pushing may upset the child and too much time taken with one child may cause the rest of the group to become restless and lose interest.

Shy children should not be further isolated by being allowed to sit at the back apart from the rest of the group. Have them sit near to you so that they can be encouraged to whisper in your ear when a verbal response is called for. Once shy children have been prompted to make a physical response, the next stage is often to parrot the responses of others in the group. They should be praised for this as such participation can be a stepping stone to thinking for themselves. Only after they have been allowed to parrot for several days should you ask them to think of a different idea of their own. Given simple choices, the opportunity to respond minimally at the beginning, and praise for even tentative signs of involvement, the shy child may blossom.

Sometimes children who normally join in may be temporarily upset or in an obstinate mood and refuse to participate. If this is the case, a useful way of gaining their attention is to engage the rest of the group in thinking about what they are doing and treating such behaviour as a problem to be solved. You could say, "Is Judith feeling happy or is she feeling sad? Yes, she is feeling sad. Judith, why are you feeling sad?" If the child does not respond, the rest of the group can be brought in - "Can anyone guess why Judith is feeling sad? Perhaps it is because ....?" or "Can anyone think of a way to help Judith feel happy again?" Often if children are only wanting attention then they can be supplied with it legitimately by using the techniques of this approach to 'solve' their problem.

Disruptive Behaviour

You may find you have a child in the group who cannot sit still, goes backwards and forwards from one side of the room to the other, fidgets with any object nearby and is generally a disruptive influence in the group. Obviously, it is best to position such children away from toys, bookshelves and distracting objects and to separate two such children who may happen to be friends.

If a child walks away from the group it is often more effective to ignore this than distract the others by calling the child back. Sometimes children like this will come back when they hear something that interests them. If they continue to be a nuisance you can call upon them for ideas or have them come to the front to be the leader. Another useful technique is to focus attention on the disruptive child by saying, for example, "George is doing something different. He is playing a different game. What is George doing?" Such attention is perfectly acceptable and far more effective than threatening that they will have to leave the group if they do not behave. Where the motive for disruptive behaviour is attention seeking, as with the obstinate child, they can learn through the games and activities that there are more efficient and satisfying ways of being noticed. Generally, such disruptive behaviour should not become contagious as children in the group receive plenty of attention whenever they respond and, as noted earlier, even when they do not.

Dominating Behaviour

Some children have long drawn-out stories to tell, or as soon as you ask a question they are the first to shout out an answer, oblivious to the fact that other children have not had a chance to participate.

Without meaning to, such a child can easily dominate the whole group with the result that the others lose interest and become restless.

You will have to handle dominant children with care, for if you stop them or discourage them they may also lose interest and become disruptive. An effective ploy is to let them tell their story on the understanding that afterwards it will be someone else's turn, perhaps allowing them to nominate the next child. Again, focussing on dominant children by allowing them to be leaders for some of the time can be helpful. The key to managing this kind of behaviour is to be firm but friendly, allowing such children to be the centre of attention within acceptable limits.

'Silly' Behaviour

Occasionally a child will respond with irrelevant or opposite answers, will laugh or make faces or funny gestures. If you are reasonably certain that the child understands the question being asked and is merely being silly to attract attention, then it is best to say, "Oh, you're just teasing me", and ignore any further outbursts. If a child carries on being silly and parrots another child just to be annoying, continue to ignore the behaviour and only give attention and praise for normal responses. Especially in the later games children may be silly because they have nothing to contribute. Try to focus their attention on the game, rather than reinforcing their silly behaviour, as only by developing their thinking skills, so that they have more to offer, will their silliness diminish.

2. ADOPTING THE PROBLEM-SOLVING STYLE

The games and activities are designed to increase a child's chances of success in dealing with real life problems but you will have to try and ensure that the skills learned in the group do generalise to the remainder of the child's day. Now that you are familiar with the basic principles of the approach, you should be able to incorporate them into conversations over difficulties which arise between children in the nursery and prompt them to work out a solution for themselves. By consistently applying the techniques of guiding children through problems as they arise during the day you will be helping them to handle similar situations with more success in the future.

Special Help in the Classroom

Outlined below are some examples of problems that commonly arise between young children and how the problem-solving style can be used to bring about a successful resolution.

Hitting and Grabbing

Hitting, grabbing, pushing and kicking can be started by a child but are often a response to having been attacked or mistreated in some way. Examples of both situations will be given.

Example 1

David was seen, by a member of staff, to push John off a scooter and she goes over to investigate.

Adult: David, why did you push John off the scooter?
David: I want a go on it.
Adult: What <u>might</u> happen if you push like that?
David: He might fight.
Adult: So is pushing a good idea?
David: (defiantly) Yes!
Adult: Why?
David: He won't let me have a go.
Adult: Pushing is <u>one</u> way to get the scooter, but can you think of a <u>different</u> way to get him to give you a turn?
David: (Shouts to John) Can I have it when you're done?
John nods his head.

Although this conversation was carefully guided by the adult she did not tell David what to do, but helped him to think through the problem and arrive at his own solution. When it was obvious that David was more interested in getting the scooter than the fact that John might fight, she accepted that 'pushing' was one way of getting what he wanted, but rather than condemn this tactic outright she prompted him to think of an alternative.

Example 2

A member of staff sees Susan hit Joanne, who then retaliates.

Adult: Joanne, why did you hit Susan?
Joanne: She hit me first.
Adult: Susan, why did you hit Joanne?
Susan: (Pouts and refuses to answer)

Adult: What did Joanne do when you hit her?
Susan: (Still sulking)
Adult: Did she go away or did she hit back? (a child is much more likely to answer if given a choice of two simple statements than if questioned directly)
Susan: Hit back.
Adult: Susan, how do you feel now? Are you happy or sad?
Susan: Sad.
Adult: How do you feel, Joanne?
Joanne: Sad.
Adult: Well, you don't feel happy Susan, and neither does Joanne. Can one of you think of a way to make you feel happy again?
Joanne: Play house with Susan.
Adult: Why is that a good idea?
Joanne: We'll be friends.
Adult: You'd better ask Susan if she wants to play with you.
Joanne: Do you want to play?
Susan: Yes.
(both children go off, chanting "We're friends", into the Wendy House)

In this situation the teacher does not simply remonstrate with the children about their behaviour but brings both together and guides them through thinking about the conflict themselves. Rather than make an issue out of who hit first she tries to restore positive feelings by using the problem-solving style. Direct questioning may meet with little response if the children are upset (as in this case), whereas the techniques of offering two alternative answers will often prove successful.

<u>Example 3</u>
Sometimes the problems that have been dealt with in the group sessions may actually arise in the nursery, and the strategies used then can be brought into play.
During story time Tracey cannot see because Andrew is kneeling up and she pushes him out of the way.

Adult: Tracey, pushing is one way to get Andrew to sit down but what might happen if you push him?
Tracey: He might push me back, but I can't see!
Adult: Can you think of a different way to get him to sit down?

Tracey: (Crossly) No!
Adult: Do you remember the picture I showed you of children at story time? One of those children wanted someone to sit down.
Tracey: Yes.
Adult: We thought of lots of things the boy could do. Can you remember one of them?
Tracey: (To Andrew) Please sit down.
Andrew: (Sits down)
Adult: There you are, that was a different idea and Andrew sat down.

It sometimes happens that a disagreement between two children gets out of hand before anyone notices, and you are faced with either two weeping or two angry children. If both of them are too emotional to respond it often helps to bring over a third child (or several) and encourage them to offer ideas and try out ways of making the unhappy pair feel better. Sometimes children respond to another child more readily than to an adult.

There may also be times when children will not respond at all to your attempts at involving them in the kind of problem-solving dialogues described so far. If this is the case you must decide whether to pursue the questioning or to drop it, as in the following illustration:

> Jane was hitting Sarah because Sarah wanted to share her plasticine. Jane grabbed all the plasticine and shouted, "You go away. I'm making a model on my own and I'm not playing with you!" The adult decided not to use the problem-solving approach for two reasons: Jane usually did share her possessions, and there are times when a child should have the right to play alone; and Jane was far too emotional to think clearly anyway. In this instance the adult simply interested Sarah in doing something else and left Jane to play on her own.

Avoiding Potential Problems and Accidents

As well as resolving actual difficulties, the problem-solving style can be used to avoid problems and accidents. Typical incidents when such techniques can be applied are, for example, a child standing in front of a moving swing, running around wildly inside, using scissors dangerously, or jumping off the top of a climbing frame without looking to see who was underneath. Rather than saying, "Don't do that" or "If you do that you'll hurt yourself" you can encourage the children to think of the consequences of their actions for themselves.

You can use the following dialogue in all potentially hazardous situations:

Adult: Is ...... a good idea?
Child: ....
Adult: How might you feel if you (fall, hurt yourself, land on Steven, etc.)?
Child ....
Adult: Can you think of a different (place to stand, way to use scissors, way to jump)?

Unless children have to be physically stopped because danger is imminent, they should be guided in thinking about the situation just as in handling problem behaviour. You help children to focus on the presence of a danger by means of its consequences.

A point which must be emphasised, when using the problem-solving style in real life, is that you should follow through each episode to ensure that the solutions arrived at are in fact carried out. If, for example, two children agree to share a book rather than squabbling over it, you should stay long enough to make sure they do. Although young children are usually responsive to the guidance given, initially they may be unable to carry through solutions of their own.

Conclusion

It is hoped that by using the techniques outlined above you will be able to improve the personal adjustment of children in your care by developing their ability to see a human problem, their appreciation of different ways of handling it and their sensitivity to the potential consequences of what they do.

Remember not to expect too much too soon, as a young child will not turn into a logical, reasonable being overnight. However, practice in the group sessions and a consistent application of the problem-solving approach in the nursery group should help in laying the foundations of more logical thought processes.

REFERENCE

Spivack, G. and Shure, M.B. (1974) Social Adjustment of Young Children. San Fransisco : Jossey-Bass.

Chapter 6

MAKING A PLAN OF ACTION

In this section we will try to offer you some guidelines to help you plan a programme of action to help a child with difficulties. You will need to:

1. collate all the available information about the child;
2. make further observations or obtain additional information if necessary;
3. examine the resources, support and time available.
4. draw up a plan of action;
5. write down a detailed plan;
6. try some pilot runs if appropriate;
7. implement the programme;
8. monitor progress;
9. decide when to stop the programme or take further action.

We will look at each of these points in turn and then describe in detail some case studies which were carried out by nursery staff in different schools, using a pilot version of this handbook.

1. Collating the Information

Assuming that the initial assessment and information gathering stage has been completed, this information should be summarised in Section I of the record booklet. Thus you should have details of

(i) the Behaviour Checklist (Schedule 1)
(ii) the Behaviour Assessment Schedule (Schedule 2)
(iii) the General Assessment Schedule (Schedule 3)
(iv) Talking to Parents (Schedule 4)
(v) Help from Others (Schedule 5)

Making a Plan of Action

A good starting point would be to read and thoroughly familiarise yourself with the details of Section I of the record book, and then go through all the assessment schedules in turn to obtain a general overview. Look also at all the notes you have made since the beginning - whether these are in rough form or not - in case you have missed some small point that could be of significance. Very often, details may not appear to be important until you have reviewed the whole problem.

Having thoroughly immersed yourself in the available information, take some time off to allow the whole thing to be digested, and then quickly review it again. It would be very useful if you could then discuss possible courses of action with your colleagues, who should be kept in touch with the whole procedure. Ensure that your colleagues have also seen the material and are familiar with it. You will then have a basis for discussion which could well lead to your gaining fresh perspectives on the problem and some concrete suggestions for tackling the difficulties.

2. Making further Observations and Obtaining more Information

When you have digested the information and discussed it all with your colleagues, you may decide that you need to know more about how the child behaves in certain situations, or that there is a need for observations of a particular activity which may be highly relevant to the problem. For example, a child may have a much wider repertoire of behaviour than you had originally thought. Remember the example of James (p. 33). His teacher, Mrs. S., after a period of observing him closely found that, ..." contrary to her immediate impressions he did, in fact, show interest in a wide variety of activities and was observed participating in almost the entire range provided by the nursery! His social contacts were much broader than at first thought."

We recommend in the Behaviour Assessment Schedule (2) that you observe the child closely for at least a week, but you may wish to extend that period in order to cover further situations or to look at more specific aspects of the problem behaviour in question. In the case of behaviour modification, a period of specialised observation to obtain a baseline of certain behaviour is essential. So if you are contemplating using a behaviour modification approach, you should ensure that you have sufficient information on which to base this extended observation. Is the behaviour sufficiently clearly defined? Have you covered adequately the most important situations in which the behaviour is likely to arise? Will the method of observing adopted be suitable to obtain a representative sample of the problem behaviour? These and other questions that occur to you should be considered carefully before you embark on further observation. Again, having examined all your notes, you may decide that you do not have sufficient information about the family or that you are unclear about how an outside agency is involved. You should try to decide now whether or not it is necessary for you to know more. If you conclude that you need more information, then now is the time to try to get it. For instance, you might have felt too inhibited on a previous occasion to ask the parents about a child's attitude to his brother or sister, but having observed that a lot of his behaviour shows evidence of being over-competitive and domineering, you might wish to find out if he behaves similarly at home. This could have an important bearing on how you plan the programme; for example, whether you include a routine specifically designed to counteract 'jealous' behaviour and provide insight for the child into how to deal reasonably with others.

There must come a point, though, when you have to decide to suspend the gathering of more information and to take action. It would be unwise to delay taking action once you have a reasonably sound background of information, as there will be further opportunities to gain relevant information as you proceed and continue to monitor the programme.

3. Examining the Resources, Support and Time Available

It would be of little use to plan a very detailed and beautifully designed programme of action if you were to find subsequently that you had neither the resources nor the time available to implement it. The action that you take must be based on a realistic assessment of your own situation.

(i) Resources

By 'resources' we mean all the available materials, activities and services that your nursery group has to offer. Thus, you should be sure that you have suitable toys, games and materials with which to implement a programme of play activities or take steps to obtain these.

Again, the amount of space and availability of additional rooms can be considered as a resource. In some open-plan nurseries it may prove difficult to find a quiet corner into which to take a child so that he can receive some individual attention and be afforded the opportunity to concentrate on a task. It may be possible to screen off part of the nursery or use another room for this purpose. Try to anticipate any difficulties and think of ways of overcoming them; nursery teachers and playgroup leaders, in our experience, have proved to be very ingenious with very limited resources.

(ii) Support in the group

A very important consideration will be the number of adults that you have to help you. In some cases you may have only limited support but you should consider carefully what is the best use of the resources available to you.

(iii) Time

The time available to you will, of course, depend to some extent on the support which you have, but it might be useful for you to look more closely at how you actually spend your time, to see if you can save a few minutes here and there that can then be used to deal with a difficult child. As we have said previously, a few minutes each day may be all that is needed to begin to change a problem behaviour, and this may lead to your saving time that would otherwise be spent admonishing or trying to control the child in question.

Of central importance is the question of how much time you should spend each day or every week on a special programme and how long the whole programme should last. Unfortunately, it is impossible to give very precise answers to these questions as they depend on many considerations such as the type and severity of a problem, the child's co-operativeness and ability to learn, and the type or number of approaches that you adopt. Some approaches, such as play or language activities, can readily be fitted into the ongoing routine of the nursery, whilst others, like some behaviour modification techniques, require specialised procedures for which extra time must be found. The best advice that we can offer is that you try out the procedures that you would like to use, and time these. You can then decide whether or not it will be feasible to start a programme using those techniques or whether you will have to cut them down in some way. As you become more skilled in their use, of course, you will reduce considerably the amount of time spent in initiating and carrying through those procedures, which is why trying pilot runs will prove useful, as we shall see a little later on.

4. <u>Drawing up the Plan</u>

To draw up a plan of action you will need to:

(a) note the most worrying aspects of the child's behaviour in the order of priority in which they will be tackled;

(b) write down the changes you hope to achieve;

(c) detail the approaches you intend to use, together with how and when they are to be implemented.

Section II of the record book provides space for a summary of these details, but you will probably need to have a fuller and more detailed account, written down separately, that will serve as a guide to direct your actions in implementing the programme.

(a) <u>List the Difficulties in Order of Priority</u>

You should now review thoroughly again all the information from the assessment schedules and elsewhere that relate to the child, and then write down a full list of the child's problems giving details, where appropriate, of how often they occur, how long they last, what seems to trigger them off and in what situations they occur.

Looking at the schedules and notes relating to <u>Brian</u> (whom we met at the beginning of Section IV) we might draw up a preliminary list of difficulties somewhat as follows:

(i) Brian seems to lack adequate stimulation at home - he is rarely given interesting or attractive activities to indulge in and his parents do not seem to take a great deal of interest in him;

(ii) his behaviour at home is similar to his behaviour at school, but he seems to have more temper tantrums at home where his parents fail to understand his requests;

(iii) he plays rather aimlessly on his own for long periods;

(iv) Brian's language is very poor and has not progressed much beyond the one-word stage - he frequently uses gestures and grunts to communicate his needs;

(v) his scores on the initial behaviour checklist reveal 2 'c's:
Item 9 - "Has seldom been known to talk to anyone at all"
Item 10- "Frequently 'clings' to adult for assurance and does not attempt to attend to his own needs"
On the Behaviour Assessment Schedule he obtained a 'c' on item H - "Plays mainly alongside other children rarely with them";

(vi) new situations or changes in routine prompt him to seek adult help - explanations and instructions have to be simplified to help him;

(vii) a sample of observations of Brian's behaviour in the nursery group :

Outside Play (10 a.m.)

Brian and three boys are outside on tricycles. Brian follows Peter around and gently crashes into him. He smiles all the time but there is no verbal communication. Stops crashing immediately when reprimanded by an adult. Continues to cycle aimlessly but happily.

Jigsaw Table (10.30 a.m.)
Brian and Julie. He is attempting to do a jigsaw - still with his outside coat on

as he cannot remove it and has not asked an adult to do so. Julie is being very 'bossy' and domineering about Brian's choice of puzzles - he is totally acquiescent.

Car Table (11 a.m.)

Brian and four other boys. Brian lies prone alongside the car table moving a car along a road mat. Is oblivious of the other children and makes no sounds or attempts to communicate.

Number Corner (11.30 a.m.)

Brian and small group and teacher. Brian sits on his own, matching Lotto cards slowly and silently.

Centre of Nursery (1.30 p.m.)

Brian and four boys. Brian is wearing a Batman cape and running around behind the other boys, who are shouting "Pow!" "Batman!" "Zap!" etc. Brian struggles with "Ba!" but is making an attempt to copy the others.

(viii) Outside Agencies

Because it has been suspected that Brian might be deaf, a number of outside agencies have been contacted, including the local clinic, Brian's family doctor and health visitor. Finally he has been referred to the Hearing Clinic at the nearby hospital as tests done locally proved inconclusive, but no report is available from them as yet.

(ix) Health problems prior to nursery enrolment

Brian had no real health problems prior to nursery enrolment apart from chronic nasal congestion. He was picked up at the Child Welfare Clinic during routine examinations, as he failed to score on the language section of the Denver Test. He was tested by an educational psychologist in January 1980 who recommended placement in a nursery school. His progress is to be reviewed at regular intervals.

It is clear from this preliminary list that Brian's problems are numerous and varied, but we now have to try to summarise these difficulties and arrange them in order of importance. So, ask yourself the question, 'Is there any one problem that occurs more <u>frequently</u> than others, or appears to be the cause of some of the other difficulties?' Looking again at the list it seems pretty clear that poor language development is a major problem because it is mentioned frequently, is a major area of development where he lags behind, and seems to underlie many of the other difficulties. Thus Brian is unable to follow instructions and cannot play cooperatively with other children largely because he cannot communicate with them. You will note that he does not shrink from contact with other children and plays happily alongside them, but he is unable to interact socially with the other children by word and deed. It would appear then that poor speech development and an inability to indulge in social play or learning situations are two major areas of concern.

In addition to these difficulties, however, Brian seems to lack the ability to concentrate or follow through any constructive activity, is subject to temper tantrums when frustrated and lacks some fundamental self-help skills such as being able to dress and undress himself properly.

The list of difficulties in order of priority might now be:

1. poor speech development;
2. poor social interaction;
3. lack of concentration and persistence;
4. tendency to have temper tantrums;
5. lack of self-help skills.

Having drawn up this list you should check back through the information on Brian once more to satisfy yourself that you have assessed the difficulties properly.

As well as noting a child's difficulties, you should always try to pinpoint the positive aspects of his or her behaviour, however few and far between these may be. It is highly unlikely that you will come across a child who has no good points, and once these good points have been noticed you will probably have a much more balanced picture of the behaviour as a whole.

Looking again at the observations of Brian's behaviour, we might list the following as being his good points or assets:

1. he is often cheerful and happy, and enjoys rumbustious activity;
2. he is prepared to ask for help when he does not understand something;
3. he does attempt to do things that he finds difficult, e.g. doing a jigsaw, and copying the other boys when they are playing at Batman.

When these assets are noted down separately they seem to highlight the fact that Brian's case is far from being a hopeless one. He does not descend into sullen and uncooperative withdrawal but tries his best and soldiers cheerfully on despite his difficulties. These are excellent qualities that can be built upon, and your programme of activities should make use of them whenever possible.

(b) Changes it is Hoped to Achieve

At this point you should try to detail the changes that you hope to bring about in the child's behaviour. As suggested in the previous section, you might decide to use a number of approaches simultaneously to bring about improvements in several areas of Brian's behaviour over the same period of time, but it would, perhaps, be wiser to set yourself a limited goal in the early stages. Of course, if a child exhibits several minor yet irritating difficulties that can be tackled by methods requiring little time or commitment, you might decide to try and bring about several changes at once. As a general rule, though, you would be wise to concentrate initially on one or maybe two major difficulties and worry about the others later.

So in Brian's case, you might decide that you want to:

1. improve his use of language and try to improve his ability to comprehend instructions;
2. encourage him to play with and interact more meaningfully with other children.

These aims are still couched in very general terms, however, so the next step is to work out, wherever possible, the details of what changes you would like to achieve by a certain date or point in the programme. To do that, you will need to have a clear grasp of the techniques or approach that you will be using and the time that will be involved in the different stages of applying that approach. You should now, therefore, go through the techniques that you are likely to use and try to assess which are appropriate and feasible.

(c) <u>Choosing the Approach(es) and Working out Details of the Programme</u>

You have now decided to try to improve Brian's use and comprehension of language and to encourage him to play and interact more with other children, so it seems logical that the next stage is to examine more closely what you normally do in the nursery group to stimulate these activities. It would be advisable also for you to read the sections on Language Activities (pp. 67-80) and Play Activities (pp. 92-128). You may recall, also, that we discussed some basic techniques in the Behaviour Modification section(pp.146-148)that might prove useful in improving speech and social play, so you might decide to have a closer look at the appropriate parts of that section as well.

Having read this material once more you should have picked up at least some techniques that you feel you could apply,so it is now a question of working out a programme in more detail. Before you proceed to work out these details, though, it would be useful for you to summarise the general points that this programme should encompass.

In Brian's case, these might be as follows:

(i) from your notes you recall that he has been assessed by an education psychologist, been referred for speech therapy and is currently receiving one therapy session a week. So you may decide to contact the speech therapist with a view to having the number of sessions per week increased, if possible; discuss the feasibility of the speech therapist designing a home-based programme (e.g. selected parts of the Portage Scheme) for the parents to use with Brian; and discuss with the speech therapist your own intended methods of encouraging language development, especially any new technique that you would like to try out;

(ii) your own programme might aim to:

(a) improve speech production and pronunciation initially by the use of simple programmes incorporating the techniques of shaping and positive reinforcement (pp.145-146);

(b) widen Brian's vocabulary and develop his ability to use sentences of increasing complexity by direct instruction, using selected parts of a structured language programme such as G.O.A.L. (p.75);

(c) increase Brian's involvement with other children by arranging situations so that he finds it difficult to avoid contact, and by using positive reinforcement to strengthen this contact. Also, introduce role playing games such as 'Who am I?' to improve Brian's social skills;

(d) develop social play further by the introduction of more structured group games such as 'Acting out Stories' (pp. 118-119).

Your choice of techniques will depend on several factors, such as:

1. you feel confident that you have understood the method and feel able to carry it out;
2. you have sufficient backing from others to carry the programme out properly;
3. you have sufficient help from other staff where this is essential;
4. you feel confident the technique will work;
5. the technique is appropriate to deal with the difficulty being tackled.

Your final choice of techniques, then, depends on your judgement of what is suitable for the particular situation you have to deal with and your personal preference for one method rather than another. Remember, also, that problem behaviour can often be tackled from several angles, so that if one method proves unsuitable in your case you might try another in its place.

5. <u>Writing Down the Detailed Plans</u>
You should write down a comprehensive plan of the action that you intend to take, giving details of how a particular technique will be applied, how much time you will spend on it each day and what situations you are most likely to find suitable to introduce it. Draw up a timetable to indicate when various stages should be reached.

It is not possible to give precise guidelines for you to follow, as individual programmes will vary considerably, depending on the type of approach adopted and the amount of time which that approach demands. However, you should aim to include as much detail as is necessary for the particular programme you have in mind. With an approach such as problem-solving, many of the stages are worked out for you in detail and you will not need to list each step in minute detail, and similarly many of the structured play activities have been clearly outlined already. However, individually designed activities or procedures will have to be worked out thoroughly.

Perhaps a good starting point would be to decide how long the total programme should last. In the case of certain behaviour modification techniques, for instance, you may decide that an initial period of twenty to twenty-five days will be long enough to try out the method on a specific problem - including both the baseline and intervention stages. However, no hard and fast rules apply here, and you should always aim to give a technique a fair chance of succeeding once you have made the decision to try it out.

Where you are attempting to deal with several problems at the same time or using techniques that require quite a long time to work out,or where changes in the behaviour may only emerge gradually, an extended programme may be necessary.

A fairly extensive programme would probably be required in the case of Brian, where improvements in the use of language and the level of social interaction may take some time to appear. His teacher might decide that the specialised programme of activities will take about three months to complete, and that she will spend one or two weeks on each of the various stages depending on how much material there is to cover in each. Of course, language difficulties and poor social skills are problems that are likely to require continuing help, and this might be offered as an ongoing feature of the nursery routine or by a further special programme to be commenced at a later date. However, this first programme of intervention might be outlined as follows:

Stage 1. Improving Speech Production by Shaping and Positive Reinforcement (one week)

Time: 20 minutes per day, Monday to Friday.
Situation: Nursery teacher (or N.N.E.B.if appropriate) in one-to-one situation with Brian.

N.T. to name objects laid out on table or in picture book; asks Brian to repeat word after her; N.T. will repeat words several times if necessary; Brian's responses rewarded if good approximations to correct pronunciation (i.e. shaped).
Repeat as necessary.
Make out list of objects e.g. cup, saucer, beaker, pencil, rubber, scissors etc. Note down improvements, difficulties - any ideas of how to tackle these.
Rewards to be used: simply praise and occasional hug e.g. 'good boy, you got it right that time' etc. Specify any other rewards.

Stage 2. Improving Vocabulary and Comprehension (two weeks)

Conditions: As in Stage 1 : 20 minutes per day: NT/NNEB
Ensure that Brian can pronounce the words and then proceed to describe how the words are used.

(i) Naming Words (nouns): words met in stories; naming classroom materials; specialised materials or objects; words denoting collection of things.

(ii) Words used to describe: colour, size, shape and function of objects, e.g. "a scissors is used to cut paper" etc.

(iii) Words denoting position: above, below, under, first, last etc. Arrange objects and describe their positions etc.

(iv) Words used in questions: Who? Why? When? How? etc.

Stage 3. Beginning of G.O.A.L. Programme (two weeks)

Conditions: As before.
Use of structured programmes

'What is my name?' (use of mirror)
'Where is my nose?' (parts of the body)
'What is this?' (pointing to hand etc.)

Specify further activities.

Stage 4. Extension of G.O.A.L. Programme (two weeks)

Conditions: As before.

(i) Use G.O.A.L. VOCABULARY CARDS - e.g. 'The Family'; 'Things we see around the house'etc.

(ii) Use of more complex sentences.

Stage 5. Initiating Social Contact (one week initially and then ongoing)

Time: Unspecified - as opportunities present themselves (when Brian is near to other children, etc.). If little contact, try to form a small group. This will be done at least twice during the morning session; only two or three in group initially.

Each time Brian approaches other children, he will be rewarded - e.g. smile, word of approval.
Any attempt at verbal contact will be specially praised. If little contact, then call Brian over to another child (someone he seems to find acceptable, preferably) saying, 'Come and see what David is doing, Brian' etc.
Attempt to keep Brian there and try to involve him in an activity, e.g. helping David fill a bucket with sand at the sand tray.
Specify other similar situations.
Try to create two or three such contacts in a session (morning or afternoon).

Stage 6. Role-playing Games (two weeks)

Time: 20 minutes per day.
Situation: One-to-one initially, Brian and N.T. (or N.N.E.B.). Later with group.

1. To improve Brian's chances of succeeding in a game and being accepted by a group, some of the following games will be played with him:

(a) Who am I?
e.g. mime a policeman directing traffic; a postman delivering letters.
Brian to imitate the teacher making sure he understands what is going on.

(b) What am I doing?
e.g. mime eating, washing-up, driving a car.
Brian to imitate the teacher.

(c) Bag of Hats
Use (e.g.) nurse's hat and soldier's helmet.
As above, get Brian to imitate and coach him as necessary.

2. Role-playing with a small group (e.g. three other children)

Use (a) Who am I?

(b) What am I doing?

(c) Bag of Hats

as before, only this time Brian is part of a group. If he gives the correct answer and offers to mime, encourage and praise him. If there is no response, ask him "Do you know, Brian; remember what we did before?" (i.e. try to coax him to respond in the group situation and mime for the other children).

Stage 7. More Structured Group Activities (two weeks)

Time: 20 minutes per day.
Situation: Group of children (not more than six)

Making a Plan of Action

1. <u>Language games for group</u>

   Use G.O.A.L. cards "Facial Expression" "Active Picture" etc., e.g. picture of child climbing.
   Get each member of the group to describe the picture in a sentence. Encourage and praise Brian especially (but not to the exclusion of other children).

2. <u>Active group games</u>

(a) <u>Nurse's hat</u> : Brian to play role of nurse. One child pretends to be ill, nurse (Brian) has to look at his tongue, feel pulse, take temperature etc.

(b) <u>Fireman's hat</u>
Brian to play key role.
Allow other children the key role as well, but try to involve Brian more - though as unobtrusively as possible.

(c) <u>Acting out stories</u>
E.g. 'The Three Billy Goats Gruff' and 'The Three Bears' etc.

<u>Home-based Programme</u>
To avoid over-taxing Brian with too much activity of the same type, it should be arranged that the parents will begin a home-based language programme once the school programme has progressed to dealing with social interaction in the nursery group.

Note: Brian's parents and the teachers to meet to discuss what is to be done before the programme is started, and dates for further meetings to be fixed to liaise on Brian's progress in the nursery and in the home.

<u>Planned Observations and Assessment of Progress</u>

(i) General observation will be continued as before on a day-to-day basis or as convenient during the whole of the programme.

(ii) Some simple tests of vocabulary and use of sentences will be devised.

(iii) A full re-assessment using Schedules 1 to 5 will be made two weeks after the programme has ended.

(iv) A decision will be taken after this re-assessment whether to carry out a further specialised programme with Brian.

(v) A final full re-assessment will be made ten weeks after the first re-assessment.

In your plan, you can include as many details as you wish; for instance, make little notes or highlight key words to prompt you at a later date when you come to utilize the programme. The important thing is that the plan should be down on paper and not just in your head, and it should help to order your thoughts and guide you through the successive stages that you have mapped out.

6. Trying Some Pilot Runs

You will be familiar with some of the activities that you wish to use in your programme but you may need to practise some of the less familiar procedures. Though you may grasp what is involved fairly easily it would be wise to run through the procedure to see how it operates in practice. Thus you might go through the various stages involved in 'sit and watch' using a different child from the one that you will be aiming to help, just to get familiar with the practical steps involved.

Again, certain approaches such as problem-solving require some rehearsal before you will be able to run through the whole programme smoothly.

Have a good look at your intended programme and try out some of the less familiar procedures that it involves. Make sure that any helpers fully understand their role and are able to carry out the procedures satisfactorily.

Trying out a pilot run will also highlight any problems that might be caused to the routine of the nursery or group, and it is better that you find out about these beforehand rather than when you have already started a programme of help.

7. Implementing the Programme

If you are satisfied that you are now ready to start the programme, you should go ahead and do so as soon as it is convenient. Try to avoid the programme overlapping with long holidays, and check that the behaviour achieved by a certain time is still being maintained if a break in the programme has been unavoidable due to illness or vacation. If problem behaviour has reappeared or improvement has not been maintained at the level it reached just before a break then try to regain that level either by introducing a crash revision course (i.e. going quickly through the previous stages again) or by modifying the remainder of the programme to incorporate some of the earlier procedures and allowing for more time to complete all the stages involved

8. <u>Monitoring Progress</u>

You should monitor the progress of the programme for the whole period of the intervention.

(i) With a behaviour modification programme, you should continue to repeat the specialised observations that you used during the baseline phase, but wherever possible these should be backed up by more generalised observations of the child at work on some task or at play. These broad observations might indicate changes in behaviour that might not be apparent from the more specific observations being made concurrently.

(ii) Where there is no specialised observation involved, continue to make sample observations of the child's behaviour as you did in Section II of the Behaviour Assessment Schedule (Schedule 2).

(iii) Where appropriate, devise some simple tests to try to assess whether any improvement is being shown. For example, in Brian's case you might draw up some simple tests of vocabulary or use of sentences to try to give some indication of the progress achieved.

(iv) Discuss your plan of action with other members of the staff from time to time, and especially those who come into contact with the child. An improvement might show itself in a change in attitude or generally more positive approach to life which may become evident in the child's behaviour in the playground, at dinner-time or at home.

(v) Keep the parents in touch with what you are doing and ask them to note any changes in the child's behaviour which become evident during and following the programme.

(vi) Rearrange the programme on the basis of your experience. Though you should not depart too much from the original timetable, you might decide to balance out the different activities involved to meet some contingency. Thus, if Brian becomes very tired of some of the language procedures you might consider alternating these with some group play activity or give him a rest from the specialised attention that he has been receiving. Follow your plan as much as possible, but be prepared to be flexible in handling certain difficulties as these arise.

9. Deciding when to Stop the Programme or Take Further Action

As we have said previously, you should give the programme a fair chance of succeeding by persevering with it, even if it has to be modified slightly to suit the nursery routine or a change in the behaviour of the child. If you find that the programme is taking much more time or requires a greater commitment than at first thought you should modify it to meet these needs, though without changing its essential character. Again, a child might begin to exhibit difficult behaviour that the programme is not designed to meet, so you might have to adjust it temporarily to cope with such a change.

Having said this, however, you should be certain in your own mind that the programme does need to be changed in the short-term and that you are not merely being discouraged by the fact that it is a little more difficult to carry through than you had originally thought. As time goes on you will find that you will become much more skilled in using the various techniques and will carry out a programme smoothly to its completion.

Assuming that you have carried out the original programme as planned, you will then have to decide whether to take more action or not. You should look closely at the assessments and observations that you have carried out during and immediately after the intervention and base your decision on these. Thus, if a child has improved markedly you may decide to suspend further action for the time being, to review behaviour in a few weeks time, and then to re-introduce the same or a slightly modified programme to boost this improvement if that is necessary.

Again, you may be satisfied that the difficulties that the programme was designed to help have largely disappeared but that there are other problems that need attention. You should design a further programme to tackle these. If you were Brian's teacher you might find, after completion of the programme, that his language skills and social behaviour were much improved and that the improvement could be maintained by ensuring his continuing involvement in the nursery routine. So, you decide now to tackle some of his other problems and, specifically, his lack of self-help skills and proneness to temper tantrums. You might decide to plan a programme involving Task Analysis to help to train him to be able to dress and undress himself properly and use a behaviour modification routine to tackle his temper tantrums. It is a question of priorities, and if your original programme has led to a change in the priority of the difficulties, you will want to design a fresh programme to meet this change.

APPENDIX TO CHAPTER 6 : CASE STUDIES

We will describe three case studies carried out by the staffs of different nursery groups, using a pilot version of the present handbook. The information given is taken almost verbatim from the record books kept by the nursery staff and the studies concern actual children, but the names of all children and staff have been changed to preserve confidentiality. Each case report is followed by some of our own comments on the study.

It should be made clear at the outset that these studies were carried out over two school terms, apart from a few weeks during which the nursery staff read and familiarised themselves with the material. For many of the nursery staff involved, the handbook contained much that was new and required them to use methods with which they had had no previous contact. It is a tribute to all concerned that they were able to achieve so much in a comparatively short time, and encouraging to those who intend to use the handbook in the future.

CASE STUDY 1

JANE (aged 4) an example of a withdrawn, dependent child.

Behaviour Checklist Ratings

2(b) Will cooperate with other children in some situations (e.g. adult directed activities) but not others (e.g. where turn taking is involved).

4(b) Occasionally can be a disturbing influence in a group.

5(b) May complete an activity once started but is not immune to distractions.

6(b) Has looked tense or upset on occasions.

7(c) Wanders around aimlessly or stares into space.

8(c) Watches others play but makes no attempt to join in. Will not be coaxed to take part in group activities.

9(b) Rarely initiates a conversation with an adult, but will respond appropriately and will talk to other children.

10(c) Frequently 'clings' to adult for assurance and does not attempt to attend to his/her own needs.

Behaviour Observation

1. Avoids contact and play with other children - this behaviour occurs in many settings.
2. Jane displays withdrawn, dreamy behaviour which prevents her making good use of materials, toys and apparatus provided.

Behaviour Assessment

2(d) Concentration - rarely makes use of materials in an appropriate way.
6(c) Social withdrawal - withdrawn and dreamy - difficult to make contact with.
7(d) Reaction to strangers - shrinks back even before approach is made.
8(d) Participation in play - no interest in play with other children.
9(c) Physical contact - withdraws from physical contact, reluctant to take hand, sit on knee, be lifted or helped physically.

Emotional Adjustment

(c) Over-anxious, timid, fearful
(d) Fussy, complaining, whining
(i) Listless, finds everything a great effort.

General Assessment - Her Behaviour at School

Areas where the child functions well
Jane has good mobility and hand-eye co-ordination, and is adequately self-sufficient for her age. Her expressive language is good in that she has clear speech and good vocabulary. Her receptive language is also good, although she is slow to respond to instructions, more out of lethargy rather than poor understanding.

Areas where child under-functioning
Jane displays poor quality of play, i.e. lack of concentration and imagination. She is

under-functioning in her response to learning and displays a slow response to new materials, approaches, requests, changes in routine, etc.

Family Background

Jane belongs to a loving, caring family and is used to a great deal of adult attention. She is particularly attached to mother, who being partially sighted has tended to keep Jane close to her both for Jane's safety and to be mother's eyes as she became more self-sufficient. She is her father's only child and spoilt by him and the half brothers and sisters who are so much older. The only other child she had regular contact with before coming to nursery is her mother's oldest grandchild, of whom she shows marked jealousy.

Her Behaviour at Home

Jane displays behaviour quite normal for her age at home, where she appears to be happy and outgoing. Mother describes her as being a "bit dreamy" but she is healthy, physically active and self-sufficient for her age. Her speech and vocabularly are good and she is an incessant talker both with the family and other adults who are known to her. The only behaviour her mother objects to is her unwillingness to share material possessions and adult attention with visiting children - particulary the grandchild - who is the most frequent child visitor.

Her mother does also show a slight concern for the fact that Jane does not - indeed never has - slept on her own. She always sleeps with mother and will not go to bed until mother does.

Teacher's Conclusions

Jane presents a picture of a healthy, happy little girl at home, but she resents attending nursery since it means parting from "Mum". Apart from a few tears the first week, she has shown no outward emotional signs of this, but her reaction has taken the form of avoidance behaviour in that she avoids any contact with the other children and physical contact with adults, though she does offer conversation frequently to adults and her apparent aimless wandering around the nursery does take her in the direction of an adult, e.g. she frequently follows me at a distance but if I notice her, will turn away.

This behaviour is not disruptive at all to the other children or to the calm, happy atmosphere I encourage in the nursery, but it has a marked effect on Jane since she is obtaining absolutely no benefit from the nursery environment. Her avoidance of contact with other children means that she is not concentrating long enough in any one setting to finish a task or game (other than painting which can be done without contact), or to obtain any enjoyment from the materials provided.

Action to be taken

(a) I would hope to change Jane's behaviour with regard to the other children. I would like her to begin by tolerating the presence of other children near her, so that she is in a situation of "playing alongside" another child. I hope that, following on from this, she will progress to participating in play and interacting with another child in play situations. This hopefully will progress still further into co-operation with other children in the use of space, furniture, toys, apparatus and materials and to the development of an attitude of sharing and an understanding that the facilities in the nursery are for the use and enjoyment of all the children.

I also hope to increase Jane's powers of concentration and encourage perseverance with regard to the use of puzzles, instructional toys, modelling materials etc. I hope to instil enough confidence and sense of security in Jane that she will be able to accept adult visitors in the nursery.

(b) I intend to use a Behaviour Modification approach, firstly to encourage Jane to accept and tolerate the presence of other children alongside her, secondly, to encourage social interaction.

I will begin with a time-sample recording with observation periods of 30 minutes between 1.15 - 1.45 p.m. each day. (Thus allowing children to settle into afternoon session and allowing time for latecomers - not allowing children to get tired or interference from time-tabled activities, i.e. use of hall and T.V.)

I will continue time-sample recording for a period of six days - data to be graphed.

(c) I intend to use simple contingent reinforcement procedures. Firstly, by means of intervention encourage Jane to remain at an activity when another child approaches and becomes involved. Every time Jane remains to play alongside a child she will be rewarded with a smile and verbal praise - "Good girl Jane, you are playing with the children." Every time Jane approaches another child she will be rewarded with this reinforcement plus the reward of giving the hamster a nut (Jane is very fond of animals) with the other child. This will be varied with holding Hammy, finding him dandelion leaves in the garden, cleaning his cage, changing his water etc. As soon as Jane begins to approach play situations and join in by self-motivation, prompts will be gradually faded out. This method will be implemented throughout the nursery session when necessary. Should this prove successful when the child is re-assessed at Easter, I will introduce a programme of play to encourage social interaction using suggestions from the section on 'Play Activities' (pp.123-127).

<u>Time-Sample Recording 23.2.81. : Base-Line Period</u>
<u>Recording Social Interaction</u> - defined as remaining at an activity when another child approaches, talking to or playing with another child.

Time of day - 1.15 - 1.45 p.m. daily
5 minute intervals.

	5	10	15	20	25	30
23.2.81	-	-	-	+	-	+
24.2.81	+	-	-	+	-	-
25.2.81	-	-	-	-	-	-
26.2.81	-	-	-	+	+	-
2.3.81	-	+	+	-	-	+
3.3.81	-	+	+	-	-	-

<u>4.3.81</u> Intervention programme begun. Every time Jane remained at an activity when another child approached she was rewarded with verbal praise varied with tasks related to hamster (see above). There has been very little initiation of desired behaviour by Jane during the first two days, so prompts to be introduced - Jane

to be led to a child, group or activity by staff and encouraged to participate with staff remaining with her.

Programme has been continued for next ten days - there was a noticeable improvement in Jane's behaviour after four days and prompts were gradually dropped.

4.3.81. Time-Sample Recordings (Time as previously recorded) Intervention Period.

	5	10	15	20	25	30
5.3.81	-	+	+	-	+	+
6.3.81	-	+	+	-	-	+
9.3.81	-	-	+	+	-	-
10.3.81	+	+	+	-	+	-
11.3.81	+	-	+	+	+	+
12.3.81	-	+	-	+	+	+
13.3.81	+	-	+	-	+	+
16.3.81	+	-	+	+	+	+
17.3.81	+	+	+	+	-	+
18.3.81	Child absent					

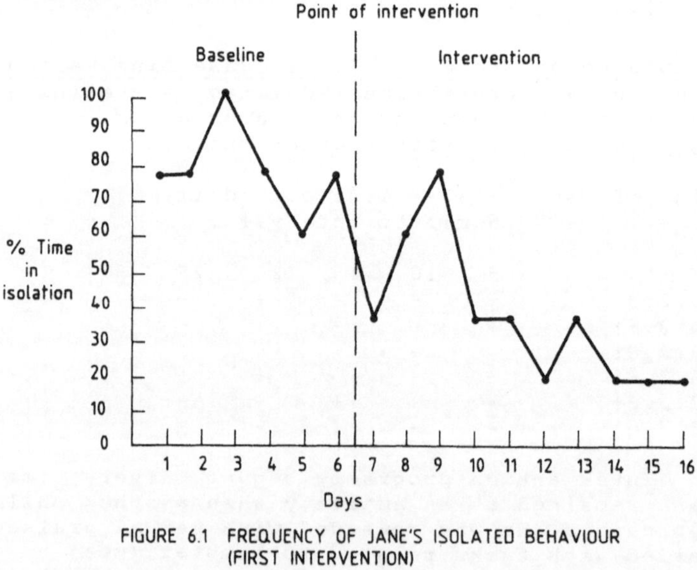

FIGURE 6.1 FREQUENCY OF JANE'S ISOLATED BEHAVIOUR (FIRST INTERVENTION)

Continuing Record

7.4.81 Jane has been absent from school since 27.3.81. She has a virus infection. I have completed first re-assessment.

27.4.81 Returned to school after Easter break - Jane extremely withdrawn - not participating at all in activities.

28.4.81 Jane again displaying isolated behaviour and resisted attempts to encourage any play or interaction with children.

29.4.81 Jane absent from school - mother came to tell me she has measles after just recovering from a virus infection which persisted over the Easter holidays. Mother also informed me that Grandpa had died a few days earlier and that Jane was extremly upset because the family dog (aged 15 years) had died. All this can explain the child's behaviour on returning to school. I have informed mother that, when Jane is better, she will be joining the morning session with the older children, as she will be attending the reception class in September.

11.5.81 Jane returned to school.

12.5.81 Jane distressed on returning to school and for the first time was crying not to stay. She was difficult to pacify since she showed no interest in toys or materials. She exhibited extreme isolated behaviour but stayed fairly close to me although resisting my attempts to involve her in conversation or in any activity.

13.5.81 Jane did not cry today but was very withdrawn. She did ask to paint but chose the painting easel on its own away from the others and would not be persuaded to join the other children. At squash time she carried her own chair but carefully placed it about a metre away from the other children. Jimmy put his chair next to hers - she pushed him off his chair and said, "You're not sitting by me." This behaviour was unusual - Jane does not normally display aggressive behaviour but is rather timid of any physical contact. When I sat by her at the table she moved her chair away slightly but did not go. The following conversation ensued:

Mrs. T. "Can you find me the red lego bricks, Jane?"

Jane "My Mammy will buy me these for my house."

Mrs. T. "You can sort them for Mummy then, Jane."

Jane "My Mammy is going to buy me all these toys."

Mrs. T. "You will have a lot to play with, Jane."

Jane "My Mammy is going to buy me a whole nursery all to myself."

Mrs. T. "We all enjoy sharing this nursery don't we, Jane?"

Jane "My Mammy will buy me a Mrs. T. all for myself."

15.5.81 In view of this regression in Jane's behaviour I decided to begin again with another Time-Sample Recording - Time of day 9.30 - 10.00 a.m. daily 5 minute intervals for a period of eight days beginning 18.5.81. Nursery nurse to record Jane's behaviour.

Intervention was begun 1.6.81. and continued for a further eight days.(See Graph 6.2).

10.6.81 Jane has been slower to respond to this intervention - prompts were not begun to be faded out until the sixth day after the intervention, so Jane was monitored for a further two days. Jane's isolated behaviour decreased from around 70% at time of intervention to under 20% after ten days.

15.6.81 Contingent reinforcement procedures are no longer necessary. I intend now to encourage Jane to interact with a larger group of children to cooperate in group games and activities and encourage confidence when involved in activities with the infants school. I intend to do this by using the following:

1. Jane to participate in group art work rather than her own which she likes to take home.
2. Use of snap games, lotto, matching and pairing games.
3. Cooperation in physical activities - throwing and catching in groups - using see-saw and wheeled toys which need two or more children to help each other - climbing tasks involving cooperation of a group of children.
4. Jane to do "errands" to infant school and headmistress.
5. Jane to be "helper" in nursery along with other children - a rota for a day helper. Helper to wear badge and feed animals - give children squash, take register etc. Two children at a time.
6. Introduce for 5 - 10 minutes daily dancing and singing games which involve all 25 children, e.g. Looby Loo, Farmer in his Den, On the Mountain, Duke of York, etc.

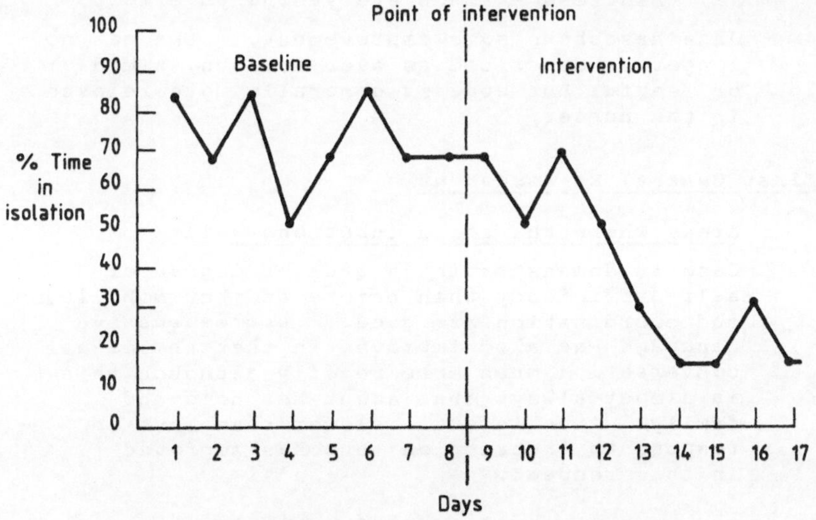

FIGURE 6.2 FREQUENCY OF JANE'S ISOLATED BEHAVIOUR (SECOND INTERVENTION)

First Behaviour Observation

1. Jane still tends to be listless and dreamy which impairs her use of toys and activities, e.g. will sit and day dream at puzzle table if not constantly encouraged.
2. Jane still withdraws from contact with strangers or even other adults she knows from the infants school.

Behaviour Re-assessment

6(c) Social withdrawal - still tends to be with-withdrawn and dreamy.
7(d) Reaction to strangers - child shrinks from contact with visitors.

Jane now has only two "c" and "d" scores - she has improved greatly in ability to concentrate and particularly in her interaction with other children.

Emotional Adjustment

(d) Fussy, complaining, whining.
(i) Listless - finds everything an effort.

Jane has shown some improvement. She can no longer be described as over-anxious, timid or fearful but appears generally more relaxed in the nursery.

First General Re-assesment

Areas where the child functions well

Jane is demonstrating a greater degree of self-sufficiency than before and her mobility and coordination are good. Her expressive language has also improved in that she offers conversation much more readily although this is almost always chat about her home and family. She is still slower than most to respond to instruction, but has improved in this respect.

Areas where child under-functioning

Her quality of play is much improved in that she will concentrate and persevere at an activity for longer but her imagination is poor, and she still does not like to participate in imaginative play. She does show a more enthusiastic approach to new materials and more interest in activities generally.

Second Behaviour Observation

1. Jane is still lethargic and dreamy and will sit doing nothing for long periods unless constantly encouraged.
2. Jane still withdraws from contact with strangers, indeed, she moves quickly as far from the door as possible when a visitor enters.

Behaviour Re-assessment

6(c) Social withdrawal - tends to be withdrawn and dreamy still.
7(d) Reaction to strangers - shrinks back even before an approach is made.
8(c) Play activities - mainly plays alongside children.

Emotional Adjustment

Jane still tends to be fussy, complaining and whining, and is listless, finding everything an effort and needs constant encouragement to participate in activities.

Second General Re-assessment

Areas where child functions well

Jane's mobility and coordination are good and hearing and eyesight normal. She has mastered a good degree of self-help skills and has good receptive and expressive language.

Areas where child is under-functioning

Jane is still under-functioning in play which is still moderate to poor in quality and has shown very little improvement in her response to learning and adaptability.

Progress Report

The graph of the first intervention which demonstrates the frequency of Jane's isolated behaviour shows a marked decrease in this behaviour from 70%

until the point of intervention to 20% after 9 days of the simple contingent reinforcement procedure. Time-sample recordings were discontinued and contingent reinforcement procedures gradually became no longer necessary. Jane appears to be more relaxed generally and happier than she has been in the past. I feel that my personal relationship with her has improved a great deal, and she no longer avoids physical contact but will approach me for comfort and reassurance. She is now seeking the company of two little girls, particularly that of another shy, quiet little girl who is new to nursery, and although she is not eager to partake in group activities, she does show more willingness. I am very pleased with these improvements to date and would tentatively assume they show some degree of success with the approaches used so far. Should this success continue when we return to school after the Easter break, I intend to introduce play activities to encourage greater participation in group activities and more social interaction with a greater number of children. I will also introduce activities which encompass the infant school to overcome Jane's apprehension of older children and adults she does not know well.

After the Easter break Jane's behaviour has regressed and the incidence of isolated behaviour was again around 70% of the time that Jane was observed. Time-sample recordings were again taken (this time by the nursery nurse) following the same criteria. Jane's isolated behaviour again decreased after intervention to 20% although she was a little slower to respond to contingent reinforcement procedures. These are now no longer necessary and Jane is interacting well with the other children. She is happier and more relaxed than when returning from the Easter break and is making good use of materials and toys available. She does need encouragement still, since she is generally a lethargic child; this probably has much to do with the fact that she still sleeps with her mother and does not go to bed until mother does. Jane still lacks enthusiasm even for activities I know she enjoys, but I feel this must be accepted as part of her character. She offers conversation frequently to adults but is more reticent with children. Her conversation continues to be mostly about her home and family. I will continue to encourage greater social interaction with the introduction of more group activities.

1.7.81 Jane has made little progress in interaction with other children since the above comments, but despite this I feel some measure of success has been achieved. Jane will be in a reception class in September and I feel this might suit her better since she will be required to work alone to a great extent and will be guided more rigidly in activities with the introduction of more formal "work".

Comments

The nursery teacher, Mrs. T., achieved considerable success with Jane in a comparatively short period of time using a simple contingent reinforcement procedure. There was quite a dramatic drop in the amount of time that Jane spent in isolated activity following intervention on both occasions.

It is a pity that Jane's illness and the Easter break disrupted the ongoing programme, and likely that a more permanent change in behaviour would have been achieved if the contingent reinforcement procedure had been backed up immediately by an extensive series of play activities. Such an extended programme might well have built on the progress already attained and established a solid foundation for Jane's social behaviour, but unfortunately it was not to be.

Jane's behaviour in the nursery group reverted after the break to being withdrawn and isolated, and the decision to re-introduce the contingent reinforcement programme was a perfectly correct and appropriate one, and once more achieved its purpose. The follow-up programme of play activities meant to encourage social interaction achieved only partial success, though, in Mrs. T's estimation.

It became clear that only limited success could be achieved by the help given in the nursery school. Jane was still very tied to home and to her mother. It would have been useful to approach the mother with a view to weakening the over-dependence exhibited by both mother and child. Of course, this is a very delicate matter and would require a considerable amount of time in order to build up the mother's trust and confidence, and was not feasible in the present study because of the limited time-scale. It is to be hoped that, as Jane is required to spend more time in formal schooling, the problem will gradually diminish and that a more balanced relationship will develop between her and her mother.

CASE STUDY 2

ERIC (aged 4), an example of an aggressive, disobedient child, who is subject to temper tantrums.

Behaviour Checklist

- 1(b) Can be destructive and has to be watched more carefully than some children.
- 2(c) Demands his own way in all situations and cannot 'take turns'. Often takes toys from children whilst refusing to share his own.
- 3(c) Screams, bangs objects, has a tantrum whenever provoked; inhibited or frustrated, however minor the incident.
- 4(b) Occasionally can be a disturbing influence in a group.
- 5(b) May complete an activity once started but is not immune to distractions.
- 6(b) Has looked tense or upset on occasions.
- 8(b) Usually found in the company of one or two particular children. Takes part reluctantly in group activities.

Behaviour Assessment

- 4(c) Aggressive behaviour - frequently rude, offers verbal aggression if thwarted or frustrated.
- 5(c) Demanding behaviour - demands own way frequently and over-reacts (crying tantrums) if demands not met.
- 9(c) Physical contact - tends to withdraw from physical contact; reluctant to take hand, sit on knee, be lifted or helped physically.

Emotional Adjustment

- (b) Over-excitable.
- (e) Prone to temper tantrums.
- (f) Disobedient.
- (g) Seeks to be the centre of attention.
- (h) Tearful - when having a tantrum.

Making a Plan of Action : Case Studies

General Assessment - His Behaviour at School

Areas where child functions well

1. Good mobility.
2. Good co-ordination.
3. Vision apparently normal.
4. Good hearing.
5. Good self-help skills.
6. Good expressive language.
7. Good receptive language.
8. Good response to learning.

Areas where child under-functioning

8. Moderate quality of play - hampered by anti-social behaviour - unable to share toys - results in tantrums.

Family Background

Eric now finds himself the middle child - he has an older brother (6 years old) and a new baby sister. This could result in aggravating his already obvious behaviour problem. He lives in the same street as his maternal grandmother and his aunts, of whom some are still of school age. They all play an active part in disciplining him - an unavoidable problem for him, I should say. I believe his father is unemployed - this more often than not creates tension in the home - this again is unavoidable.

His Behaviour at Home

Mother has admitted giving in to his tantrums for "peace" as she said. She also said he listens better to his 'Gran'. I did mention to her that it is causing problems in school for him and that I cannot "give in" to his demands - it is bound to impair his learning - I suggested that she might have a word with him.

Help from Others

Nature of Problem	Agencies contacted	Information received/action taken
Possibility of child not having enough sleep	School nurse and Health Visitor	Not yet received

Teacher's Conclusions
It would be interesting to know when, during Eric's pre-school years, did he realise that by having a tantrum he could succeed in getting what he wanted - this habit had become quite a strong part of his behaviour before he came to school.

I feel it will take quite a while to break' him of it in school - he may still be allowed to have his tantrums at home - thereby making my task even harder.

His redeeming qualities are such that his tantrums do not last for very long and he can be eventually brought out of them by his observing an activity which interests him.

But I have failed to get his immediate interest in another activity - he still decides himself when he feels like picking himself up and joining in - as if nothing unsociable has occurred. I do not show too much concern for his tantrums. This I feel is the right attitude in that the more I take notice of them, the more demanding he will get. The other children are obviously aware of his unacceptable behaviour and do not bother him when he has his tantrum.

Action to be Taken

(a) For Eric to become more sociable - for him eventually to realise that my N.N.E.B. and I will see to it that he does have his share of the toys which attract him, just by waiting for his turn - he will be emphatically praised for his successful achievements and encouraged to help other less able children. He will be encouraged to lead "play" in an imaginative game - so becoming so pre-occupied with the activity that he might refrain from having a tantrum.

(b) Approaches I intend using with the help of my N.N.E.B.
1. Social Play: The first simple dice game I teach them involving four children - THE FLOWER GAME - a coloured die is used and petal shapes are given out to the children when their colour comes up on the dice. The first to complete a flower is the winner.
2. Rocking Boats: Having to co-operate with another child to "rock" successfully.

3. Steps and Slide: Having to wait one's turn to have a go - emphasising the danger of accidents if one does not wait.
4. Play People: Plastic Road Mat; Collection of Vehicles : A group activity - encourage children to speak for one particular "play" person.
5. A large piece of paper - a group of children will draw a picture of a farm, for example.
6. Faces: I'll use a collection of cardboard figures of the Seven Dwarfs. We'll discuss their names and their facial expressions - I shall encourage children to try making similar faces.
7. The Mouse and Clock - Dice Game: 4 or 2 players.
8. Flying Ball: throwing a ball between 2/3 players.
9. Puppets and "Guess Who I Am" games (see pp.117-119).

(c) These games will be implemented during the "Activities Session" - 9.30 a.m. - 10.15 a.m. Eric's reactions to them will be observed and noted.

Observations during Particular Activities

Dressing-Up Games: He was very difficult - he still wanted what others had. Could not be pacified. There was a selection of different shaped "guns" - I have decided to remove them and replace them with some wooden ones - all the same shape.

Climbing Frame: He did co-operate for about 5 minutes then cheated his turn - when told to wait he refused to continue to play.

Flower Game: He did not want to be leader and give out the 'petal' shapes - he became disinterested before the end of the game on the first occasion he played it, but stayed to the end during the second time.

Boats: He was happy to be with his cousin, Tom, but refused to go with another child. On another occasion when Tom was purposely given a task to do, he did consent to going with another child, Peter, who also lives near him.

Construction Toys: Fit-links, large lego and building blocks - he shows good powers of concentration to create things.

16.3.81 A Monday morning - he had a bad morning - he seems obviously tired, irritable, nothing was right for him. Baby sister has arrived.

17.3.81 Dressing-up game - an unpleasant incident - he hit another child. He had a little accident - tore his finger nail. He let me nurse him - he has refused before. Formal work - behaviour very good and painting, sticking pictures, sand and water play - no incidents. Mother brought his new baby sister for us to see - mother very rarely comes for him. It is usually another child's parent who takes Eric home for his mother.

23.3.81 One incident - when he was in the yard for a P.E. lesson - he would not allow another child to play with him and Tom - when I said that Peter was to play he immediately refused to join in the game and grizzled.

1.4.81 Still refuses to play unless Tom is in the group. Social play is improving, we have had a few days with no incidents! N.N.E.B. has observed that in the playground situation he continues to be aggressive and irritable if Tom does not always want his company. He needs to make other friendships.

2.4.81 We visited the Rural Studies Department in the Senior School to see the chickens, rabbits and bees etc., yesterday. Eric's comments while counting and colouring his chickens in his work book - "I'll stick a pin in the chicken." When I asked him, "Wouldn't it hurt the chicken?" he said, "No." But I explained that pins were sharp - he said, "Mammy sticks them in Gaynor's napkin."

6.4.81 He started off the morning session by crying for a cushion - not the same one as before. I told him to stop crying as he had not hurt himself - only babies cry for nothing.

He soon stopped. This comment I may use again to reduce the length of his tantrum.

7.4.81 He observed Tom (his cousin) having a see-saw game with another child. He started grizzling. We ignored his behaviour. When the time came for Tom to get off we asked Eric if he would like to help Peter to make the see-saw go. He accepted and appeared to enjoy the activity. He is improving.

8.4.81 Our Annual Easter Parade through the village - girls in home-made Easter bonnets - boys dress up in whatever outfit they have or can borrow from our collection. Eric refused to dress up and did not seem bothered. He walked quite happily and had his photograph taken without any trouble.

His favourite colour is black - whatever the picture is about his choice is invariably black. Can this be related to his mood? His particular "off" days are Monday, I have noticed, he appears more tired and irritable - quite a number of children are not as receptive to teaching on a Monday as they are on the other days of the week, I have found. They are also noisier and more irritable - could this be due to there being less restriction on volume of sound they make and hours of sleep are not quite the same as on week days?

9.4.81 He continues to create an incident over which cushion he is going to sit on - I have decided to remove boys from cushioned storage boxes to chairs and let the nursery girls sit on the cushions - their turn to have them. This will stop Eric's performance. These cushioned storage boxes make up the nursery 'train'.

He seemed to be more tired than normal today. He lay down in the T.V. room and objected to anyone talking or touching him. He could be sickening for something. He refused to go with the N.N.E.B. and the nursery class for toileting - I insisted that he went and observed the school "pets" en route. He has to respond to teacher's instructions - other children could begin to copy him, if I continually provide an alternative course for him. We are continually over-compensating with praise for good work and good behaviour.

Next term we hope to be more out of doors with large toys - cars, tricycles etc. - it will be interesting to observe whether Eric's behaviour problems will be more or less. He did seem to be happier on the few occasions when we have been out in the playground for P.E. during the past few months - having more space to move about in might suit him better.

Behaviour Assessment Checklist

4(c) Aggressive behaviour - less frequent lately.
5(c) Demanding behaviour - again less frequent.
9(c) Physical contact - refuses any physical contact other than being helped with shoe lacing or having plasters on cuts.

Emotional Adjustment

(b) Still quite excitable at times.
(e) Fewer temper tantrums than the original assessment.
(f) Disobedient - at times - according to his mood at the time.
(g) Still likes to seek to be centre of attention at times.
(h) Still tearful when having a tantrum.
(i) Sometimes shows signs of listlessness - these are times when I feel that he is obviously not 100% fit and he should not be in school.

First Re-assessment - General Assessment

Areas where child functions well

1. Mobility - good.
2. Good coordination.
3. Vision - apparently normal.
4. Hearing - apparently normal.
5. Good self-help skills.
6. Good expressive language.
7. Good response to learning.

Areas where child under-functioning

8. Moderate quality of play - tantrums are becoming less frequent in group games.

12.5.81 Eric has been absent for a few days - returned today - very fractious from the time he came in. He became more and more difficult and obviously upset as the morning went on. His older brother has chicken pox - perhaps he could be sickening for it? When mother was told of his behaviour she replied that that is how he was at home - not very sympathetic towards him. This may be the reason why he will not respond to affection from my N.N.E.B. or me when we try to console him. He has become so used to having tantrums and having to get over them in his own time - a very sad situation for a child so young.

8.6.81 Eric has returned after being off for two weeks with chicken pox. He appears to be happy to be back - no tantrums today.

9.6.81 He came into school at 9.25 accompanied by his aunt who is 11 years old. He was obviously in a tantrum over how he was to spend his lunch money. He had been to a local shop and had not had his own way. I ignored his crying and went on to discuss our hymn about holidays by the sea - not an easy task but it succeeded - he stopped crying and then joined in the activities for the rest of the morning without an incident.

10.6.81 No incident today. Eric took the lead in a group activity - he was the "engine" driver.

11.6.81 Again he joined in amicably in a group game - "The Flower Game" as previously described.

12.6.81 Eric is enjoying out of door activities - use of large toys - tricycles,cars, barrows etc. I explained that they would have turns on everything - he is accepting my word and there are no tantrums - so far!

Behaviour Observation

The home situation remains the same for him - father unemployed, mother has even less time for him with another child to see to. He still lives in the same street as his grandparents and young aunties, who are too young to take charge of him or to show responsible control of his demands or needs. Full-time education from September should result in a more stable and amenable environment for him but his programme of activities must still be especially chosen to help him with his problems.

Second Re-assessment - Behaviour Assessment Checklist

4(c) Aggressive Behaviour - offers verbal aggression if he has a tantrum, though tantrums are now less frequent.

5(c) Demanding Behaviour - less frequent than previous assessment but will still over-react if demands not met on some occasions.

9(d) Physical Contact - still tends to withdraw from physical contact; cannot be comforted when he over-reacts and becomes distressed - my guess is that he is not used to being comforted at home.

Emotional Adjustment

(a) His behaviour is noticeably better when he appears to be physically fit.
(b) He is obviously excitable. This is shown when he is chatting about his experiences.
(e) Less prone to tantrums now.
(f) Disobedient - can be when in a tantrum.
(g) This is shown especially in news chats.
(h) Tearful - when in distress.
(i) Listless - at times - I have queried this with the health visitor, have not yet heard her report on a home visit.

Second Re-assessment - General Assessment

Areas where child functions well

1. Good mobility - he enjoys being out of doors with large toys and P.E. equipment. He needs space around him but with no hall and our annual average rainfall at 100" approx., this is not possible for most of the year.
2. Hand-eye coordination good.
3. Vision - good.
4. Hearing - normal.
5. Good self-help skills.
6. Expressive language - good.
7. Receptive language - good.
8. Play - is beginning to obviously enjoy play in a group and has recently taken the lead.
9. Response to learning - good.

Areas where child is under-functioning

8. Tantrums are becoming less frequent and he is beginning to make new friendships as he is getting more involved with social play.

> I trust this will continue so that wanting to be involved will deter his reaction to unsociable behaviour should he disagree with other children's ideas.

Progress Report

By taking particular notice of things which can create problems for Eric, e.g. cushions with a variety of appliqued pictures on them; a collection of various types of toy guns; it has proved successful to remove these things from his use for the time being in order to help him behave more socially. I am hoping that as he makes friendships with other children and gets to enjoy social 'play' activities he might eventually take less notice of the 'props' and more of the verbal response of other children.

I shall, as a matter of interest, present him (later on this term) with these things, which have proved to arouse unsociable behaviour.

I believe he is responding to our praise - emphasising what a big boy he is - in helping to carry apparatus and being able to do things babies cannot do. I have already mentioned that by saying that "only babies cry for nothing" stopped Eric crying. He obviously wants to be considered as a "big" boy not a baby. Having an older brother is a reason for this perhaps. My N.N.E.B. and I have to consciously try to give him as much attention as possible because he obviously needs it, being the middle child.

He obviously likes talking and I often purposely call upon him to tell us something about a topic we are discussing - this obviously gives him pleasure by the expression on his face - this I feel will help him to gain self-confidence and it involves his co-operation. He comes into school quite cheerful and usually has something to tell me or to show me - this is a sign that our relationship is good. He comes willingly to me for more formal tuition and his progress is average for his age.

Comments

This study reveals a picture of a child who is aggressive and prone to temper tantrums when frustrated and who is quite often disobedient. These difficulties are gradually reduced by the efforts of the nursery teacher and assistant, who praise his achievements, play down the temper tantrums and seek to involve him much more in play situations involving cooperation with other children. There is no sudden or dramatic change but rather a gradual and general improvement in his behaviour.

It is not entirely clear whether the nursery staff had previously tried to control Eric's temper tantrums by means other than ignoring them, and whether the approach described would be a fundamental departure from what was commonly done. Again, it is not stated categorically that each and every temper tantrum was ignored, so how consistently this was done is a little uncertain. Perhaps it would have been better to make these points clear and to draw up the plan accordingly at the outset.

Further, though it is obviously desirable that Eric's social interaction be encouraged, and though the use of play activities is appropriate, it might have been advantageous to have included a procedure designed specifically to reduce the incidence of temper tantrums. This might have been the introduction of a consistent regime of ignoring such outbursts, and reinforcing behaviour that made them less likely to occur. The programme carried out by Mrs. T. contained elements of these procedures - but perhaps an initial period involving a more specific focus on temper tantrums would have been useful.

The nursery staff are to be admired for their persistence in giving Eric the special attention that he needed. His difficulties seemed to disappear for a while only to re-emerge again at a later date, either because of stress at home or some other reason not known to the nursery staff.

The situation in the home would appear to be far from satisfactory. Eric seemed to be largely ignored by his mother and he often seemed tired in the nursery, perhaps because of lack of adequate routine and rest at home. Though Mrs. T. approached the mother about this she had little success, seemingly, in bringing about any change in attitude that would benefit Eric. Again, the school nurse and health visitor would appear to have been rather slow in providing information and guidance to the nursery staff. This is not necessarily meant as a criticism of the individuals involved, since there are often very complex reasons why information is slow in coming, but it does highlight the need for information to be exchanged fairly quickly if suitable action is to be taken in the home to coincide with the ongoing programme in the nursery group.

CASE STUDY 3

NICOLA (aged 4) an example of a child who is restless, lacks concentration and can be destructive.

Behaviour Checklist

1(c) Deliberately destroys her own and other children's property.
2(b) Will cooperate in some situations but not others.
4(b) Occasionally can be a disturbing influence in a group.
5(c) Is unable to sit still, runs about, jumps up and down and is easily distracted.
10(b) Needs adult support when tackling something new.

Behaviour Observation

Lacks concentration and is overactive and restless.
This leads her into all kinds of difficulties. Set out below are a few examples of Nicola's behaviour taken from observations:

20.1.81 Free play - 10.45 a.m.
Nicola was outside playing and threw her scarf down on the ground. She was asked to pick it up by Mrs. S. Nicola ran inside, took off her scarf and coat, dropped them where she stood and two minutes later was back outdoors.

11.15 a.m.
Within the space of a few minutes she went from pushing the pram to the sand tray, back to the pram, into the music corner, then the home corner where she finally settled.

26.1.81 Chalk board 1.45 p.m.
A new chalk board was brought out. Whilst the other children used it properly, Nicola broke the chalk, spat on the board and managed to cover most of the front of herself with multi-coloured chalk dust.

Behaviour Assessment

1(c) Nearly always on the move, boisterous active play, very wearing to others.
2(d) Constantly 'flits' from activity to

activity; rarely making use of materials in an appropriate way.

3(c) Has no understanding of need to be careful with breakables, tends to suck and chew toys baby fashion.

8(c) Plays mainly alongside other children, rarely with them.

Emotional Adjustment

Normal happy relaxed child.

General Assessment - her behaviour at school

Areas where child functions well

Mobility is good. Shows this in her enjoyment of outside activities. Her span of concentration improves during these sessions.

Areas where child under-functioning

Tends to make more mess than most children when using paint, water etc. Cannot concentrate and sit still for any length of time.

Family Background

Nicola is youngest of a second family, and both families are closely knit, although the eldest daughter has left the home to live with her natural father because of a discipline problem with mother. This elder sister has a big influence on Nicola and she does miss her. Mother seems a strong person and is ready to seek advice from agencies outside the home. Since the departure of her eldest sister Nicola has directed most of her affection towards her brother, who is 15 years old. She sometimes sleeps with him.

Her Behaviour at Home

Nicola has been difficult about her mother working. She cries when it is time for her to go to work, although father and others are at hand. Mother works three evenings per week. She generally has to be kept occupied and can be strongwilled about things she wants to do. Nicola often takes part in verbal quarrels with mother but shows remorse later. Sometimes when disciplined she is sent to bed.

Help from Others

It is felt that because behaviour problem is not an extreme case no outside agency will be involved.

Teacher's Conclusions

Generally, Nicola is a happy, carefree child, but we feel that she shows signs of insecurity, i.e. still tends to put things into her mouth and sometimes has a dummy; she also enjoys covering herself with bed-clothes and layers herself with dressing-up garments. Mother works part-time which takes her out part of the night and Nicola will demand to sleep with another member of the family during this time, again this shows her insecurity

Nicola seems to enjoy being in a mess. She is well dressed and seems to have a variety of fashionable clothes, but within a few minutes she is covered in paint, milk, water or clay.

Action to be Taken

Play activity approaches will be used because they will most easily fit into our nursery routine and we hope they will help Nicola apply herself in various situations and to prolong her periods of concentration. Two sessions of 15 minutes each day will be carried out. The group will consist of 6 children taken in rotation from the nursery class register. The two teachers concerned will take the group on alternate days. The work will take place in the Story Room, which can be closed off from the main body of the nursery. Morning session at 11.00 a.m. Afternoon session at 1.45 p.m.

Plan of Activities

A typical week's plan of activities, as follows:

Monday a.m.

Large toys will be used to promote cooperative and imaginative play. Children will be encouraged to use these to go on a journey to the shops and supermarket. Bags and other props will be provided. A group discussion together with large pictures will help to encourage their ideas.

Monday p.m

Bead threading, large jigsaws and sorting trays to be provided - again to encourage cooperative play. Two children will be assigned to each activity and it will be pointed out to them that they are helping each other in their work. A record will be kept of each child's activity and they will be encouraged to change their activity the next time they attend.

Tuesday a.m.

Large drawings to be provided for each pair of children for them to fill in with coloured felt pens.

Tuesday p.m.

Imaginative play - a trip to the seaside. Using large pictures to stimulate discussion beforehand, the children will be encouraged to play out a trip on a bus, building sand castles, paddling, having a picnic etc.

Wednesday a.m.

Action songs and rhymes. The children will be encouraged to participate as fully as possible in singing and carrying out the actions of these songs.

Wednesday p.m.

Games with rules. Each child to be given a card for a simple racing game using a die and counters, e.g. spiders up drainpipes, cars along a race track etc.

Thursday a.m.

Each pair of children to be given a set of picture dominoes and taught how to play, with encouragement to help each other to complete each game.

Thursday p.m.

Role play to be encouraged by providing a bag of hats and a bag of animal masks (made by the children themselves) for the children to assume a new identity, e.g. nurse, king, postman, cat, dog, mouse etc. Each child to pick out a hat or mask and act out a situation involving his chosen character and the other children. Help and encouragement from teacher.

Friday a.m.

Imaginative/dramatic play - acting out familiar nursery rhymes and simple stories. Each rhyme or story to be recited/told beforehand and the actions discussed.

Friday p.m.

'Planting the Flower' game. This is a simple

game which involves no competition between children but is dependent on the children helping one another.

We plan to repeat this weekly programme with variations, throughout the Easter Term.

Week ending 13th March

Nicola has not shown any change at all. She has been away from School for 2 days this week; therefore, has not had enough work done with her. It must be emphasised though, that during the sessions she has concentrated for short periods and has cooperated well.

Week ending 20th March

Nicola is beginning to show some signs of improvement. She has been seen to sit quietly for several minutes with a table top activity and does not seem to be quite so accident prone.

Week ending 3rd April

There has been a slight improvement in skills but she still tends to put toys and materials into her mouth.

Week ending 1st May

Nicola absent all week.

Behaviour Observation

Still lacks concentration, but we feel there is slight improvement in as much as she will sit at a table and concentrate for short periods.

Behaviour Assessment

2(c) Concentration: rarely perseveres long enough to make the most of a chosen activity.

Emotional Adjustment

Usually a happy relaxed child but has been sometimes tearful on arrival; we feel that because she does not attend regularly, she finds it difficult to re-adjust to the school routine.

First Re-Assessment - 1.5.81

Areas where child functions well

Nicola functions well during role play situations. Still favours outside activities. Has become most attentive during story periods.

Areas where child under-functioning

She is unable to conform to a more restricted pattern of activities throughout the day. She still enjoys the more 'free play' situation because she still tends to flit from activity to activity. Has become less messy when using paint, clay etc.

Progress Report

In the small group sessions we feel that she can now concentrate more fully and start and finish a task. Nicola enjoys all drama sessions but because she has been absent frequently this term there appears to have been little improvement in her general behaviour.

Week ending 8th May

Again absent.

Monday, 11th May

Nicola returned to school today. Her mother and father have separated, hence her two week absence.

Week ending 22nd May

Mother informs us that Nicola has become unruly at home. On one occasion she threw £15 into the fire and on another tipped over a tin of paint in a shop. If mother corrects her she tends to retaliate by saying that she is going to tell her teacher. I feel that she is missing her father and the split has obviously affected her, although her mother denies this.

Nicola does not, however show this kind of behaviour at school and in fact, she has been very attentive during group sessions (i.e. story time discussion etc.)

During a tape recording session, she showed signs of obvious embarrassment when hearing her own voice, but on another occasion she went off singing alone making up the words as she went along, demonstrating her vivid imagination.

Week ending 12th June

Nicola is beginning to show signs of unruly behaviour at school. She has to be corrected repeatedly and will pretend that she has not heard an instruction. Since introduction of more structured work in preparation for entry to infant school in September she has to be brought in from outside continually throughout the day. She does not seem to be able to cope with this more directed approach to the nursery day.

Week ending 26th June

Again this week Nicola has shown that she cannot conform to a more restricted situation, she has to be continually brought in from outside. She does not listen when asked to do, or not to do something.

Week ending 3rd July

General improvement in behaviour. During a dominoes matching session she concentrated sufficiently to complete the game.

Behaviour Observation

No remaining problems other than above.

Behaviour Assessment

2(c) Concentration:rarely perseveres long enough to make the most of a chosen activity.

Emotional Adjustment

Usually happy relaxed child but can be disobedient, not always responding to instructions. This has been more noticeable since the split-up of her parents.

Second Re-Assessment -17.7.81.

Areas where child functions well

As first re-assessment.
No improvement.

Areas where child is under-functioning

Still unable to concentrate. Her attendance is irregular, she often arrives late and this seems to put her on a bad footing for the rest of the day.

Comments

The staff of this nursery worked out a comprehensive programme of play activities both to help Nicola and another child who was experiencing difficulties. Initially it was felt that Nicola was making some progress, for instance, her attention during story time improved greatly. But a series of absences interrupted the continuity of the daily activities and hoped for improvements in other areas of her behaviour failed to materialise.

Nicola was included in the special activities whenever she attended nursery, although she continued to show signs of insecurity and her 'flitting' remained a problem. The programme had been in effect for a term when a major setback occurred; Nicola's parents separated and naturally this had an unsettling effect upon her. At around the same time the nursery introduced a more structured timetable to prepare the children for the kind of day they would shortly be experiencing on entry to Infant Schol. This added to Nicola's disorientation, as within a short space of time she had lost her regular routine both at home and school. The staff realised she was not finding it easy to cope with these new situations and maintained a firm but warm approach when dealing with her more exasperating behaviour.

An additional complicating factor arising during the course of the year was the series of staff changes this nursery suffered, and it is to the staff's credit that they managed to plan, maintain and monitor the programme for two terms. Although the staff felt they had only achieved partial success with Nicola, it is probably true to say that the events of the year could have had a much more adverse effect upon her had it not been for the extra attention she received whilst participating in the programme.

APPENDICES

A. The Schedules
   (1) Behaviour Checklist
   (2) Behaviour Assessment
   (3) General Assessment
   (4) Talking to Parents
   (5) Help from Others

B. Record Booklet

C. Explanatory Notes

D. Guide to Case Studies

Appendices : Schedule 1

APPENDIX A:

SWANSEA ASSESSMENT SCHEDULES

SCHEDULE 1

SWANSEA BEHAVIOUR CHECKLIST

Child's name ....

Sex .... D.O.B. ....

Name of school/Group ....

Date completed ....

Completed by ....

Schedule 1

Read all the descriptions carefully. Put a tick alongside the description (either a, b or c) which most closely approximates to the child's current behaviour. Do not omit any of the ten categories and check that you have exactly ten ticks when you have finished.

1. (a) Takes care of his/her belongings and those of the nursery, although like most children is occasionally destructive.
   (b) Can be destructive and has to be watched more carefully than some children.
   (c) Deliberately destroys his/her own and other children's property.

2. (a) Will play co-operatively in group situations and is prepared to share and 'take turns'.
   (b) Will cooperate with other children in some situations (e.g. adult-directed activities) but not others (e.g. where turn taking is involved).
   (c) Demands his/her own way in all situations and cannot 'take turns'. Often takes toys from children whilst refusing to share his/her own.

3. (a) Temper rarely seen at all, remains self composed unless the provocation is very great.
   (b) May become irritable or show temper under considerable provocation but can be steadied by adult.
   (c) Screams, bangs objects, has a tantrum whenever provoked; inhibited or frustrated, however minor the incident.

4. (a) Plays amicably and shows consideration of other children's needs.
   (b) Occasionally can be a disturbing influence in a group.
   (c) Disruptive, tends to annoy and may attack other children.

5. (a) Is able to work towards a definite goal and is usually capable of ignoring distractions to achieve it.

(b) May complete an activity once started but is not immune to distractions.

(c) Is unable to sit still, runs about, jumps up and down and is easily distracted from anything he/she is doing.

6. (a) Never looks bothered by things, a happy child.

(b) Has looked tense or upset on occasions.

(c) Appears miserable, unhappy or tearful most of the time.

7. (a) Makes enthusiastic use of the range of activities offered by the nursery. Is rarely unoccupied.

(b) May need help in choosing an activity but sometimes manages on his/her own.

(c) Wanders around aimlessly or stares into space.

8. (a) Joins in happily with other children and enjoys group activities.

(b) Usually found in the company of one or two particular children. Takes part reluctantly in group activities.

(c) Watches others play but makes no attempt to join in. Will not be coaxed or take part in group activities.

9. (a) Often initiates and can conduct extended conversations with adults and children.

(b) Rarely initiates a conversation with an adult, but will respond appropriately and will talk to other children.

(c) Has seldom been known to talk to anyone at all.

10. (a) Faces new tasks and experiences with confidence. Is self-sufficient in meeting his/her ordinary needs.

(b) Needs adult support when tackling something new.

(c) Frequently 'clings' to adult for assurance and does not attempt to attend to his/her own needs.

<u>Behaviour Profile</u>

Put a cross in the appropriate box, a, b or c, according to how the child was scored for each of the ten categories

	1	2	3	4	5	6	7	8	9	10
a										
b										
c										

<u>Key</u> 'b' and 'c' scores indicate a degree of difficulty in the following categories:

1, 2, 3, 4 - aggressive behaviour

5 - overactivity

6, 7, 8, 9 - withdrawn behaviour

10 - 'clinging' dependent behaviour

Please answer these two questions briefly (continue on separate sheet if necessary).

1. Does the child exhibit any other problem behaviour not covered by this checklist?

2. What is the child good at?

Next Step
If the child has scored 2 or more 'c's or 6 or more 'b's, go on to the next stage, ASSESSMENT.

Consider also whether there are any other children who might require further assessment, e.g. those who score 4 'b's in the aggressive or withdrawn categories.

Bear in mind the child's age.

SWANSEA ASSESSMENT SCHEDULES

SCHEDULE 2

BEHAVIOUR ASSESSMENT

This schedule is in two parts:

PART I consists of a series of recording sheets on which to note down your observations of the child's behaviour over a period of time.

PART II is a checklist which describes in more detail the kind of problem behaviour which may be shown by a particular child.

Please read the instructions accompanying each part before you begin.

Child's name ....

Sex ...................D.O.B. ....

Name of school/group ....

Date(s) completed ....

Completed by ....

Appendices : Schedule 2

PART I

Behaviour Recording Sheets

In order to assess the degree of a child's difficulty and the extent of the problem for both yourself and the child, you will need to gather as much information about the child's behaviour as possible. To do this you will need to:

1. observe the child systematically for at least a week using these recording sheets, which allow for ten observations daily (five in the morning and five in the afternoon);

2. note down the time and date of each observation as well as the setting (e.g. play house, sand tray) and the names of other adults and children in the vicinity;

3. describe the behaviour as exactly as you can. It is important to be accurate, saying, for example, "Sid snatched a spade from Bert and hit him over the head with it" rather than "Sid was aggressive at the sand tray";

4. include examples of the child's positive behaviour as you will need to know what he/she is good at and what interests him/her when you are planning a programme for him/her later on;

5. observe the child in a variety of different settings and on several occasions in each setting.

Appendices : Schedule 2

BEHAVIOUR RECORDING SHEET

NAME: DATE: MONDAY A.M.

TIME	SETTING	ADULTS/ CHILDREN PRESENT	DESCRIPTION OF BEHAVIOUR
			MONDAY P.M.

PART II

Behaviour Assessment Checklist

Read the descriptions (a-d) in each of the categories 1-12. Tick the description (either a, b, c or d) which most closely resembles the child's current behaviour.

1. Restlessness

(a) Normally active child

(b) Often does not settle down in any one place for long.

(c) Nearly always on the move; engages in boisterous active play, very wearing to others.

(d) Very highly over-active child; never stops for a moment.

2. Concentration

(a) Capable of total absorption in one activity for a reasonably long period.

(b) Can concentrate quite intently on one or two favourite activities (such as sand or water play).

(c) Rarely perseveres long enough to make the most of a chosen activity.

(d) Constantly 'flits' from activity to activity; rarely making use of materials in an appropriate way.

3. Destructive Behaviour

(a) Careful with toys and possessions.

(b) Can be careless with toys; sometimes breaks things; tears books etc.

(c) Has no understanding of need to be careful with breakables or the need to preserve material objects; tends to suck and chew toys baby-fashion.

(d) Extremely destructive child; dismantles and damages everything encountered.

4. Aggressive Behaviour

(a) No more aggressive than most children of his age.

(b) Bossy; attempts to control other children forcefully.

(c) Frequently rude; offers verbal aggression if thwarted or frustrated.

(d) Predominantly aggressive style of play; frequently offers physical aggression to others (including adults).

5. Demanding Behaviour

(a) Makes no more demands than most children.

(b) Demands own way more often than others of same age but responds reasonably well to firm handling.

(c) Demands own way frequently and over-reacts, (tantrums)if demands not met.

(d) Very demanding in nearly all situations. Often persists despite adult intervention; defiantly refuses to accept situation and becomes very worked up.

6. Social Withdrawal

(a) Outgoing and relates well to all others.

(b) Shy; speaks in a low voice; averts eyes, even with people he/she knows well.

(c) Tends to be withdrawn and dreamy; occasionally difficult to make contact with.

(d) Extremely withdrawn; lives in own world; deliberately avoids or shuns contact with other adults and children.

7. Reaction to Strangers/Visitors

(a) Child carries on normally when visitors present.

(b) Tends to over-react - rushes up to visitor; acts in a silly or giddy way.

(c) Definitely disturbed by visitors; suspicious and wary; very excitable.

(d) Child will in some way withdraw or shrink back even before an approach is made.

8. Participation in Play Activities

(a) Participates actively in play in a group of children.

(b) Plays mainly with one or two particular friends.

(c) Plays mainly <u>alongside</u> other children rarely <u>with</u> them.

(d) No interest in play with other children; prefers solitary pursuits; wanders about aimlessly.

9. Physical Contact

(a) Readily accepts physical demonstrations of friendliness from staff and children.

(b) Accepts such contact when appropriate (e.g. comforting after a fall).

(c) Tends to withdraw from physical contact; reluctant to take hand, sit on knee, be lifted or helped physically.

(d) Shrinks away from physical contact, stiffens, refuses, cries.

10. Attitude to Nursery

(a) Always likes coming to nursery.

(b) Sometimes does not want to come to nursery/school and makes a fuss on arrival; usually settles in after 15 - 30 minutes.

(c) Always makes a fuss on arrival; takes a very long time to settle in, often tearful.

(d) Does not like nursery/school at all (cries, screams etc.); constantly asked to go home; tried to escape from buildings or playground.

11. Dependent Behaviour

(a) Fairly independent in group situations; can stand up for self.

(b) Gives in unnecessarily to other children; looks for adult support if things go wrong in play with other children.

(c) Tends to be more clinging then most and/or not very happy about being left by mother for any length of time.

(d) Great difficulty in separating from mother; will not leave the side of a familiar adult.

12. Popularity

(a) Popular; generally well regarded; often chosen by others to join in their activities.

(b) Has one or two particular friends who seek him/her out.

(c) Tries unsuccessfully to latch on to the most popular children of the group.

(d) Unpopular, generally shunned and disliked by others.

Additional information:-

Emotional Adjustment (Tick any of the following which apply to the child. More than one item may be ticked).

(a) Over-excitable.

(b) Over-anxious, timid, fearful.

(c) Fussy, complaining, whining.

(d) Prone to temper tantrums.

(e) Disobedient.

(f) Seeks to be the centre of attention.

(g) Tearful.

(h) Listless, finds everything a great effort.

(i) Habits, tics, obsessional behaviour.

Please note any further information not covered by the above.

Appendices : Schedule 3

SWANSEA ASSESSMENT SCHEDULES

SCHEDULE 3

GENERAL ASSESSMENT

This checklist is designed to give you an overall impression of a child's general level of development. Before you begin please read the accompanying instructions with care.

Child's name ....

Sex .... D.O.B. ....

Name of school/group ....

Date completed ....

Completed by ....

Read all the descriptions in categories 1 - 9. Based on your observations of the child over the past few weeks <u>underline</u> any of the descriptions within each of the categories which best fit his/her functioning at the moment.

1. MOBILITY

A. Good Mobility
Hops on one foot / jumps forward with both feet / walks up and downstairs with alternating feet / climbs up and slides down a slide / pedals a tricycle / runs easily / kicks a large ball when rolled to him/her.

B. Moderate Mobility
Walks without difficulty but runs unsteadily; awkwardly / bumps into things / cannot use a climbing frame; slide without assistance / falls down more than most children.

C. Poor Mobility
Walks a little unsteadily / has difficulty with stairs / has difficulty going up or down or two steps / finds slopes; slippery surfaces a problem / cannot step over objects / balance poor.

2. HAND EYE COORDINATION

A. Good Coordination
Uses both hands singly or together as appropriate / manipulates small objects easily / uses pencil or crayon purposefully / can catch a ball with both hands / uses scissors fairly accurately / can build a tower with 10 or more bricks / can thread large wooden beads / turns pages of a book one by one / unscrews lids / folds paper / shows a preference for one hand.

B. Moderate Coordination
Is slightly clumsy with hands / often drops things / manipulates small objects with some difficulty / holds pencil correctly but poor control / has begun to paint / tries to unscrew lids.

C. Poor Coordination
Holds pencil or crayon in fist / has definite

difficulty in using hands / has poor grip / uncontrolled jerky movements / lack of coordination of two hands / very poor at form boards ; building with toy bricks; modelling sand or clay.

3. <u>VISION</u> (If the child has a visual defect which is corrected by the use of glasses then please tick the most appropriate statement when glasses are worn.)

A. <u>Good Eyesight</u>
Vision apparently normal / adequately corrected by glasses.

B. <u>Moderate Eyesight</u>
Has no real problem in moving around but has some difficulty in judging distances / has difficulty in seeing small objects, pictures at a distance / seems to have difficulty with a 'lazy eye' or squint.

C. <u>Poor Eyesight</u>
Poor visual recognition of a person more than 10 feet away / has poor orientation to objects more than 10 feet away / has occasional collisions with furniture / often 'loses' objects close to hand / poor vision is definitely hampering movement.

4. <u>HEARING</u> (If child has hearing aid please tick the most appropriate statement when aid is being worn.)

A. <u>Good Hearing</u>
Hearing apparently normal / adequately corrected by hearing aid.

B. <u>Moderate Hearing</u>
Does not hear quite as well as normal / statements often have to be repeated / sometimes does not hear speech unless directly facing the speaker / speech has to be louder than normal for adequate comprehension.

C. <u>Poor Hearing</u>
Speech must be much louder than normal even when child facing the speaker / perception of speech presents difficulties in all circumstances

/ does not always respond to loud voices or noises.

5. SELF-HELP SKILLS

A. Good Self-Help Skills
Beginning to use knife and fork well / attends to toilet needs without assistance / washes and dries hands and face / dresses without help except for shoe laces and difficult fastenings/ copes well with taps; switches; drawers; lids; door handles etc./ avoids common dangers such as broken glass.

B. Moderate Self-Help Skills
Uses spoon instead of knife and fork / usually indicates need to use toilet / attends to toilet needs with some assistance / has occasional accidents / needs help in getting on coats and pullovers / finds dressing a struggle / has to be assisted with taps; switches; drawers etc / avoids hazards such as sharp furniture corners; open stairs.

C. Poor Self-Help Skills
Uses fingers in preference for spoon / sometimes indicates wet and/or dirty / does not indicate need to use the toilet / has to be toileted at regular intervals if to remain clean and dry / assists with dressing by holding out hands and feet in anticipation / has to be dressed entirely / no co-operation at all when being dressed / cannot cope with taps; drawers; door handles etc. / very little sense of danger / covers self and clothes with paint; mud; water etc. much more than most children.

6. EXPRESSIVE LANGUAGE

A. Good Expressive Language
Speaks clearly / vocabulary well developed for age / uses complex sentences ('I didn't come to school yesterday because I was poorly') / describes past events in a fairly well organised manner.

B. Moderate Expressive Language
Speech a little unclear but no specific defect/ has a slight stammer / has mild speech defect

(not stammer and not baby speech) / knows names of most objects / language and vocabulary rather poor for age / uses simple sentences / uses 'babyisms' ('me want dat').

C. <u>Poor Expressive Language</u>
Speech very unclear but no specific defect / bad stammer / moderate to severe speech defect (not stammer and not baby speech) / language and vocabulary very poorly developed for age / unable to describe / sentences usually incomplete / uses mainly nouns / tends to use gesture to obtain needs.

7. <u>RECEPTIVE LANGUAGE</u>

A. <u>Good Receptive Language</u>
Understanding entirely normal for age / can follow a series of three instructions well / is attentive to quite long stories / is able to recall the sequence of events in a story / will answer questions about a story correctly / responds to humour.

B. <u>Moderate Receptive Language</u>
Understands most of what is directly said to him but is less able than most to understand conversations when not directly involved / follows simple instructions only if given slowly with repetition / will follow a short story if encouraged / tends to jumble sequence of story.

C. <u>Poor Receptive Language</u>
Understanding of what people say is very limited / has great difficulty in following a simple instruction / does not seem to understand questions put in the normal course of day / rarely listens to stories / listens only for a short period of time / shows no interest in stories at all / has no concept of what a story is.

8. <u>PLAY</u>

A. <u>Good Quality of Play</u>
Very good at making things with plasticine; sand; clay; wooden or plastic constructional toys / plays a lot with toys and creates very

realistic games using cars or dolls etc. / inventive and realistic in playing other roles (e.g. in play house) / uses props to maximum advantage / paints and draws often and produces imaginative or realistic pictures / normally agile and energetic in active games both inside and outside / enjoys group games and can relate his/her actions to others.

B. <u>Moderate Quality of Play</u>
Constructions; models never look much like the object they are supposed to represent / plays with toys and creates fairly realistic situations and games / does take on other roles in play but limited repertoire and imagination / likes to paint and draw but often loses direction and ends up with scribble or coloured mess / occasionally plays active games but not very keen on them / not physically agile / will join a group game but is often with the group but not part of it.

C. <u>Poor Quality of Play</u>
Likes to handle plasticene; sand; clay; constructional toys but never achieves an end product / manipulates toys but little idea of how to use them realistically / never adopts another role is always himself/herself / rarely paints or draws and only produces unrecognisable scribble or daubs / seldom takes part in active games / physically very awkward / unable or unwilling to take part in any group game.

9. <u>RESPONSE TO LEARNING/ADAPTABILITY</u>

A. <u>Good Response</u>
Is quick at doing things / responds quickly to new materials; teaching approaches; requests; changes in routine / seeks and enjoys most new experiences provided they are not frightening.

B. <u>Moderate Response</u>
Tends to be rather slower than most / often has to be hurried up / always last or behind / slow to respond to new materials; teaching approaches; requests; changes in routine etc. / tends to prefer familiar routine and is a little disturbed by change / over reacts to new experiences.

C. Poor Response

Extremely slow in every way / never seems to complete anything / takes a very long time to do even the simplest task / functioning appears at 'half speed' or slower / adheres to routine whenever possible / rigid adherence to routine regardless of what is going on in environment.

Any Additional Information you Care to Record

Note

The individual items in each section are organised in such a way that the first item in each section denotes a higher developmental level than the last. You must remember, however, that individual children may vary markedly in the order in which they achieve certain skills and the stages presented in the schedules should be regarded merely as guidelines.

If the majority of your underlinings fall in the first section of any of the categories 1-9.e.g.

2. Hand-eye Coordination

A. Good Coordination

Uses both hands singly or together as appropriate / manipulates small objects easily / uses pencil or crayon purposefully / can catch a ball with both hands/ uses scissors fairly accurately / can build a tower with 10 or more bricks / can thread large wooden beads / turns pages of a book one by one / unscrews lids / folds paper / shows a preference for one hand.

this will give you an indication of what the child is particularly good at. Now that you are aware of the child's strong points it may be possible to use them as a basis for tackling his/her problem behaviours. You should always bear a child's positive qualities in mind when devising strategies to overcome his/her difficulties. Also, take into consideration that a marked weakness in a particular area may be due to an additional handicap, e.g. deafness could be affecting both expressive and receptive language. The schedule may in such cases indicate areas where the child may require extra help.

What to do Next

When you have completed this schedule transfer the information to the relevant section of the Record Book (pp.290-302) where you should be building up a clearer picture of the child's strengths and weaknesses across a broad front.

Having come so far in your assessment of a child and his/her difficulties you may feel that now is the time to approach his/her parents, with a view to gathering information about home background factors and possibly enlisting their support in your plan of action to help the child. See the chapter 'Talking to Parents' (pp.39-49) and associated schedule.

SWANSEA ASSESSMENT SCHEDULES

SCHEDULE 4

TALKING TO PARENTS

Child's name ....

Sex .... D.O.B. ....

Name of school/group ....

Date completed ....

Completed by ....

Appendices : Schedule 4

The Swansea Assessment Schedule No. 4 : Talking to Parents (or other caretakers)

Introduction

This schedule is in three parts, I, II and III; it has been drawn up to help you obtain relevant information from parents about the child's family background and behaviour in the home.

PART I consists of some general areas and a list of items of a reasonably routine nature that you may feel free to approach the parents with directly, i.e. ask a direct question about the child's behaviour. Note that this is a list of items, and that the way you ask the questions has been left to you. Take into consideration what has been said (pp.42-47) about how to phrase a question so as to avoid biasing the answer.

PART II consists of items of a more personal and delicate nature which will have to be broached very carefully. Here, the onus is very much on you as the interviewer and practitioner to probe these. These Part II items are merely 'starters' to guide you into talking with the parents. Many other items or areas of significance will occur to you and should be entered and reported as attached information to Part II.

PART III is simply a series of blank pages on which you are required to give a description of the child's family background. It may repeat much of the information already given in Parts I and II, but this does not matter. It will be very useful to have a brief total picture of the family, and this may, of course, contain some information obtained from sources other than the parents. Whenever possible try to quote the source of your information, and state how reliable you feel this is.

Recording

In this particular situation when you are talking confidentially with the parents (and it is emphasised that you should ease the parents' minds on the confidential nature of your discussions), you will wish to keep them relaxed and create an easy atmosphere, so it would be very unwise to make notes or tick off items on a sheet whilst asking the questions.

What we suggest as the best course is to tick off the items and make notes in Part I and II as soon as possible after talking to the parents. By doing this you will ensure that you have the most accurate recall of the information possible. A considerable amount of evidence exists that recall, even after a matter of hours, is subject to wide distortion and you would wish to avoid this source of error.

Do not feel bound to the format of Parts I and II; they are merely some suggested items that you may want to know about. You will almost certainly think of more questions to ask and have to make notes at your convenience; do this and worry about collating the information later.

Again, a number of items, in both Schedules, may be covered by a single general question (e.g. What is X like at home? Is there anything that you would like to tell me about the family? Is X in good health?), but if you feel that the information given is incomplete or inaccurate pursue the matter with more specific questions.

PART I

Direct Items of Information from Parents

Listed below are some general areas of the child's behaviour in the home with examples of specific items that you may feel free to ask the parents about directly. You might open the conversation by asking a general question and then go on to ask about individual items one by one. Ensure that you have asked about the individual items listed and any others that might occur to you (note these down). Try to give a description or example of the behaviour in question and remember that this is information about how children behave at home and should not be coloured by your knowledge of how they behave in the nursery group.

You may wish to ask about:

1. The family background

   (a) How many children in the family?
   (b) Position in the family (1st, 2nd, 3rd etc., child)?
   (c) The other children's ages?

(d) The sex of the other children?

2. General activity and self-help in the house

Does he/she
(a) help mother and father and join in activities in the home?
(b) show interest in his/her surroundings and is normally active rather than lethargic?
(c) have any special interests or abilities?
(d) dress and feed himself/herself?

3. Physical attributes and health

Does he/she
(a) have normal vision and hearing?
(b) eat and sleep well?
(c) have any special physical defect or attribute?
(d) see a doctor and dentist regularly?
(e) have any health problem for which he/she is currently receiving treatment or which has required specialised help in the past?

4. Intellectual and lingusitic performance in the home

Does he/she
(a) recognise and name familiar objects or sounds?
(b) respond to simple instructions?
(c) have a good memory and show curiosity about his/her surroundings?
(d) talk freely to other children and adults?
(e) express himself/herself clearly?
(f) like listening to stories?
(g) ask questions and listen to the answers?
(h) repeat words not normally heard in the home?

5. Emotional characteristics of the child at home

Is he/she
(a) well-adjusted to (i) adults?
(ii) children?
(b) well-adjusted emotionally (i) as an individual?
(ii) in a group?
(c) shy or timid when in someone else's house?
(d) subject to temper tantrums when corrected or frustrated?

(e) happy and contented in general?
(f) very variable in mood during the day?
(g) stable in temperament on the whole?
(h) upset by anything in particular?
(i) especially happy with anything in particular?

6. <u>Play, co-operativeness and social functioning</u>

Does he/she
(a) regularly become absorbed in play situations of all kinds?
(b) have many friends?
(c) have a lot of children of his/her own age range in the immediate vicinity?
(d) have a favourite pastime?
(e) have a pet hate - something he/she dislikes doing intensely?
(f) prefer outdoors to indoors or vice-versa?
(g) take his/her turn with other children?
(h) take good care of things he/she uses?
(i) which of the following best describe him/her

(i) is fairly obedient on the whole;
(ii) will eventually listen to appeals before sterner measures have to be invoked;
(iii) often has to be restrained physically in order to achieve the desired behaviour.

PART II

Indirect Items of Information from Parents

The format here is 'open-ended'; thus more space is provided for your written comments and observations.

1. The Child

(a) Lives with his/her natural parents.

(b) Both parents are alive and living together.

(c) Is adopted/fostered.

(d) Has another adult (e.g. grandparent, relation or friend of the family) who exerts a particular influence on him/her.

(e) Is from a single-parent home.

(f) Has a family background which is not typical.

(g) Anything special to note about any other member of the family?

2. <u>The Family</u>

(a) Tend to do things together (are closely knit).

(b) Individual members tend to go their own way (loosely knit).

(c) Father has a particular problem/worry.

(d) Mother has a particular problem/worry.

(e) Family as a whole has a particular problem/worry.

(f) Father/mother/other is head of and strongest influence in family.

(g) Child pays most attention to...

PART III

Write a brief description of the child's family background; include information that may have been obtained from sources other than the parents. Give more details about those aspects of the family that you feel are particularly relevant to the child's difficulties. Do not worry if you repeat information given elsewhere.

SWANSEA ASSESSMENT SCHEDULES

SCHEDULE 5

HELP FROM OTHERS

Child's name ....

Sex ....   D.O.B. ....

Name of school/group ....

Date completed ....

Completed by ....

Appendices : Schedule 5

Place a tick in the appropriate box. If no action has been taken yet, you should consider whether it would be useful to contact someone knowing what you do about the child. If in doubt, it is better to make contact and be safe rather than sorry. Discuss the matter with your Headteacher/Principal.

	Agency already involved	Contact pending HT has asked for help	No action taken yet
A. School based behaviour problem			
Advisory teacher			
School doctor			
Peripatetic specialist teacher (e.g. of the deaf)			
Educational/school psychologist			
Child psychiatrist			
Social worker			
School nurse/health visitor			
Educational home visitor			
Other			
B. Speech problem			
Speech therapist			
Peripatetic specialist (e.g. of the deaf)			
School Doctor			
Educational school psychologist			
Child psychiatrist			
School nurse/health visitor			
Educational home visitor			
Other			

	Agency already in- volved	Contact pending HT has asked for help	No action taken yet
C. <u>Home-based behaviour problem</u> Advisory teacher			
Educational home visitor			
Educational/ school psychologist			
School doctor			
Social worker			
School nurse/health visitor			
Other			
Local community organisation			
Appropriate voluntary organisation (e.g. Association for all Speech Impaired Children; Dyslexia Institute; Toy Libraries Association)			
N.B. With some children it may be necessary to complete more than one section.			

Appendices : Schedule 5

If the child has been seen by anyone, summarise any information received;

Has the child already been seen or is he or she currently being seen by any specialist in either a hospital or a clinic? If so, indicate for what purpose, how often, and, if possible, the name of the person(s) concerned. Is there to be any follow up?

If the child has been referred to anyone, what action has been taken following that referral?

Underline as necessary

school visited and head/principal seen by

....

school visited and teacher seen by ......

....

arrangements made for child to attend

clinic (specify which) ....

....

arrangements made for child to be seen in

school by ....

home visited by ....

case conference called by ....

....

school has received a report from ....

....

school has been asked to submit a report to

....

regular review advised by ....

on-going treatment being undertaken (specify)

....

....

....

....

no action as far as known (follow-up required)

any other action taken (specify) ....

any other action contemplated (specify) ...

APPENDIX B

RECORD BOOKLET

Child's name ....

Sex .... D.O.B. ....

Name of school/group ....

RECORD BOOK

(see pages 29-31)

The record book is in four sections:

Section I	-	a summary of information from the assessment schedules
Section II	-	a detailed plan of the approaches to be used
Section III	-	a weekly progress report
Section IV	-	a record of termly re-assessments using schedules 1 and 2

SECTION I

Summary of Information from the Assessment Schedules

(a) Behaviour Checklist Date completed ....

Note down in the appropriate category any 'b' and 'c' scores the child obtained.

aggressive behaviour	1	2	3	4
over-activity	5			
withdrawn behaviour	6	7	8	9
dependent behaviour	10			

(b) Behaviour Assessment Part II

Date completed ....

Make a note of any of the 'c' or 'd' behaviour descriptions which were ticked for the child.

e.g. 1. Restlessness (d) Very high overactive child, never stops for a moment.

Note also any descriptions ticked under the heading Emotional Adjustment.

(c) <u>General Assessment</u>   <u>Date completed</u> ....

Make a note below of any categories in which the child functions well.

e.g. 1.A Good Mobility. 5.A. Good self help skills etc.

Make a note below of any categories where the child is experiencing difficulty, e.g. 6.C Poor expressive language. 7.C Poor receptive language etc.

Note any particular difficulties related to <u>VISION</u> or <u>HEARING</u>

(d) <u>Talking with Parents</u>   <u>Date completed</u> ....

Please summarise below any information concerning <u>Family Background</u>:

also the <u>Child's Behaviour at Home.</u>

(e) Help from Others   Date completed ....

Summary of child's health problems prior to a nursery enrolment and treatment received.

Summary of treatment/therapy child is currently receiving, if any.

Nature of current difficulty

Agencies contacted

Information received/action taken

Appendices : Record Book

Write down your conclusions about the child and his/ her difficulties based on the knowledge you have gained so far.

SECTION II

Planning your Approach
(see pages 203-222)

(a) Note the most worrying aspects of the child's behaviour in the order of priority in which they will be tackled.

(b) Write down the changes you hope to achieve.

(c) Detail the approaches you intend to use together with how and when they are to be implemented.

SECTION II

Planning your Approach (cont'd)

SECTION III

Weekly Progress Report

At the end of every week note down how the approach is working in practice, how it is being received and what effect it is having upon the child etc. If you decide to modify your original plan in any way please record the changes you make.

SECTION IV

Re-Assessments

At the end of each term, re-assess the child using Part II of the Behaviour Assessment Schedule (Schedule 2) and the General Assessment Schedule (Schedule 3). On each occasion mark the schedules with different coloured pens so that you can see at a glance any improvements that have been made by the child. Record your findings in the appropriate spaces below. Finally, write down your comments about the progress made during the term.

First Re-assessment

(a) Behaviour Assessment Part II

Date completed ....

Make a note of any 'c' or 'd' behaviour descriptions ticked for the child.

Emotional Adjustment

(b) <u>General Assessment</u>   <u>Date completed</u> ....

Make a note of any categories showing improvement. e.g. 5. Self-help skills.

Any categories showing deterioration?

<u>Termly Progress Report</u>

Carry out the 2nd and 3rd re-assessments in the same way as you have done for the first.

APPENDIX C

EXPLANATORY NOTES

The Handbook was devised in the United Kingdom and tried out in pre-school facilities there. It, therefore, reflects current practice in nursery schools and playgroups in that country, practice which may show differences from that in other countries. It is felt, however, that the basic principles in the Handbook have universal application and that the approaches advocated can inform and extend methods of working with young children wherever they may be.

There are, however, references to people or procedures which are typically British. The following notes may help to explain these as it was felt that it would not be appropriate either to remove the references or pause to explain them in the text itself.

Advisory teachers. Advisory teachers have special responsibility for various aspects of education. As well as an advisory teacher for children in early education, there is usually in each district an advisory teacher whose concern is special education and who has working with him/her a number of organising teachers, for example, for the deaf or partially hearing, the visually impaired or the physically handicapped.

Court Report. This was drawn up in the U.K. in 1976 by the Committee on Child Health Services under the title of 'Fit for the Future'. It recommended among other things that there should be general practitioners with a special interest in young children. This, however, has not been supported by the medical profession who prefer to increase the paediatric component in the doctor's general training. The report also urged the setting up of 'handicap teams' of various professionals to discuss children with special needs.

Education Welfare Officers. It is envisaged that education welfare officers will have a role not unlike that of social workers. They have close links with specific schools and are well placed to be the main point of referral for teachers and head teachers concerned about a child's development or progress. How far they can take up the social worker role depends on their training and on local policy, but it has been shown that it is to them that headteachers are most likely to turn. Although not attached to pre-school provision, they can often provide valuable information if contacted through the local primary school as their work with families extends beyond problems of non-attendance.

Educational psychologists. Educational psychologists have a contribution to make to the comprehensive assessment of young children in each district although, in recent years, the emphasis on formal testing for placement has declined in importance. Educational psychologists, who in the U.K. normally have had teaching experience, are now more concerned with programme planning, discussion and monitoring of children's progress and development. They have, in fact, the responsibility for dealing with any child from the age of two years, although some psychologists with a special interest in young children will be involved with them from birth.

Health Visitors. Since 1956, health visitors have been seen as being primarily concerned with health education and social advice. As part of this function, they visit all homes in which there is a new baby and should continue to give advice and guidance at least until the child is five years of age. The number of visits made is left to their discretion so that they can accommodate to differences and fluctuations in need. The health visitor, therefore, is unique among other professionals in having access to every home with a young child in it, whether or not that child or home has a problem. The health visitor will be qualified in nursing and have taken a subsequent course in health visiting. On her routine visits, the health visitor normally carries out a series of screening tests as well as her usual advisory commitments, and these tests are especially important in picking out children with problems of vision, hearing or speech. Any child suspected of having difficulties, particularly in these aspects, is referred for further investigation and treatment.

Medical examination. All pupils should have a routine medical examination on entry to school carried out by the school doctor. Subsequent examinations are made when the need arises. These may be carried out by the doctor, the school nurse or nursing auxiliaries depending on the nature of the inspection. If difficulties arise, children can be examined medically at times other than those normal for their age group on the special request of the headteacher.

Nursery classes/schools. A nursery class is attached to a school for older children and children move from it into that school. A nursery school usually consists of several classes and is in a separate building which may or may not be near the school the children will go on to. Children, usually aged 3-5 years, attend part-time (morning or afternoon sessions) or, in special circumstances, full-time. No payment is made for this provision.

Nursery nurses. These are non-teaching assistants who receive a two-year training in the care and and stimulation of young children. They are examined by the N.N.E.B. (Nursery Nurses Examination Board) and are sometimes referred to by these initials.

Playgroups. Playgroups, which have flourished in the U.K. since the 1960s, are registered with and supervised by the Social Services Departments if they run for more than two hours a day. Premises must be suitable for young children and there are restrictions on the number who can attend in relation to the number of adult staff available. A small payment is made by parents unless they are financially unable to do so.

In a number of areas, courses aimed at training playgroup leaders and helpers are run and those who are trained supervise the mothers who have volunteered to help. Playgroups have done invaluable service in offering nursery-type experience to young children in areas of the country where such experience would otherwise be unavailable. There is also considerable interest in setting up 'mother and toddler' groups for children below the age of three years.

<u>School Nurses</u>. It is desirable but not necessary for school nurses to have had additional health visitor training. Some school nurses may be without such a training but, if this is so, they will work closely with qualified health visitors and have access to their expertise. The health visitor/school nurse is the key person for advice on health problems in young children.

<u>School Psychological Service</u>. Educational/school psychologists staff this service along with other professionals such as social workers and remedial teachers. The extent of the service obviously varies with the size of the area covered, so that large urban centres will have several psychologists and perhaps separate special and remedial education organisations. Some rural areas may have a single psychologist who directs other services and may operate from a school psychological centre situated in a convenient place. The service usually offers help and guidance to schools, sees individual children and their family and organises workshops, lectures or other training session for teachers.

<u>Speech Therapists</u>. Before 1974, speech therapists might work under either the health or the education authorities. Since 1974, however, they have moved over completely to the District Health Authority where they are organised under a District Speech Therapist. It has been estimated that there ought to be 6 speech therapists for every 100,000 of the total population but many areas do not have their full complement. In addition, many speech therapists are part-time, which may give rise to problems of continuity.

<u>The Warnock Report</u>. The full title of this report, drawn up in 1978 for the Department of Education and Science, is 'Children with Special Needs'. It suggests that schools should tackle the question of how much help a child needs through a series of discussion with various personnel, the parents also being actively involved. It provided the basis for consultation leading to the drawing up of the 1981 Education Act with reference to special education.

GENERAL INDEX

advisory teachers/school
advisers 53,56,285,
286,303
Ainscow, M. 176
Archer, H. 72,73
Argyle, M. 49
arts and crafts 63-4
Axelrod, S. 175
Aronson, E. 49
assessment (behaviour
difficulties) 16-57,
137-44, 218-9
see also behaviour
assessment (Schedule 2)
autistic children 11

Barlow, D.H. 176
Behaviour Assessment
(Schedule 2) 4, 33-7,
52, 204-5, 220, 224, 232,
236, 242, 247-8, 251-2,
253-4, 262-8
Behaviour Checklist
(Schedule 1) 4, 14-5,
223-4, 236, 242, 244, 247,
257-61
behaviour modification
4, 128-76
assessment 137-44
desensitisation 152
extinction 136, 149-50,
157-8
modelling 147-8
Premack principle 135
principles 132-7
prompting and fading
146-7
recording 140-44
restraining 150-1,159
shaping 145-6, 161-2,
173, 215
'sit and watch' 151-2
Bereiter, C.E. 74, 78
Blackham, G.T. 176
Blank, M. 76, 78
Bower, E.M. 31
Brown, T.W. 176
Bryant, B. 57
Burland, J.R. 176

Cambrill, E.D. 176
Cannell, C.F. 49
Carr, J. 165, 176
Categories (behaviour
difficulties)
aggressive/anti-social/
destructive 10, 13-4,
26, 41, 94, 96, 98-103,
122-3, 161-2, 196,
198-200, 236-46
immature/dependent 10,
12, 27, 95, 106-7,
156-8, 223-35
restless/overactive
10, 12-3, 28, 103-4,
123, 128-31, 159-60,
170-3, 177-81, 247-54
shy/withdrawn/timid 10-1,
61, 104-6, 113-4, 121-2,
154-6, 168-70, 195-6

Causative factors
(behaviour difficulties) 17-29
developmental delay 19-20
home 22-9
nursery group 20-2
physical 19
temperament 18-9
Cazden, C.B. 78
Chazan, M. 31, 57, 67
classroom management 87-90, 113-5, 205-8
Cohen, L. 49
Conger, J.J. 31
Court Report 51, 303
creative activities, 4, 60-71, see also arts and crafts, music, movement

Davie, R. 57
Dixon, D. 127
doctors
family doctor 50, 53, 55
school doctor 53, 55, 285, 286, 305, see also Court Report, paediatrician, psychiatrist
Downes, G. 71, 76, 77, 78
Dunn, L.M. 74, 78

educational home visitor 285, 286
educational/school psychologist 51, 53, 56-7, 285, 286, 304, 306
educational welfare officer 53, 56, 304
Eliason, C.F. 67
emotional development
normal 8-10
and language 68-70
Engelmann, S. 74, 78, 79
Engelmann, T. 79

Family Welfare Association 57
Fitzherbert, K. 49, 57
Freyburg, J. 127

Gagné 165, 176
Gahagan, D.M. 75, 79
Gahagan, G.A. 75, 79
Gardner, J. 166, 176
Garvey, D. 127
General Assessment (Schedule 3) 4, 37-9, 224-5, 232-3, 237, 244-5, 248, 269-76
Giles, D. 176
Graham, P.J. 32
Garland, C. 57
Gillham, B. 77, 79
Gould, R. 127

Hahn, S. 127
Hall, V. 130, 175
Halsey, A.H. 79
Hancock, L.E. 57
Hare, B.A. 92
Hare, J. 92
Harris, M. 57
Harvey, D. 78
Harvey, S. 73, 79
health visitor/school nurse 49, 50, 53, 55, 304, 306
Help from Others (Schedule 5) 4, 49-57, 237, 248, 284-9
Herbert, M. 176
Herbert-Jackson, E. 175
Hemsley, R. 165, 176
Herriot, P. 79
Hersen, M. 176
Hewson, S. 92, 127
Humphrey, G. 49
Hudson, M. 74,79

identification (behaviour difficulties) 8-15
see also Behaviour Checklist (Schedule 1)

Jeffree, D.M. 77,79,92,127
Jenkins, L.T. 67
Johnson, J. 127
Jones, G. 57

Kagan, J. 31
Kahn, R.L. 49
Kamii, C. 74, 79

Karnes, M. 75, 79

Laing, A.F. 57
language activities 4, 67-80, 213-6, 218
  direct instruction 74-6
  informal approaches 72-3
  instructional dialogue 76-7
  programmes 72-80
  role of adults 70-1, 78
  problem-solving 185-7
language difficulties (severe) 77
Lee, C. 31
Lee, T.R. 73, 79
Lewis, M.M. 79
Lindsey, G. 49

McConkey, R. 77, 79, 92, 127
Manning, M. 95, 127, 128
Marshall, H. 127
Mendham, R.P. 176
Merritt, H. 67
movement 66-7
music 64-6
  percussion 65-6
Mussen, P.H. 31
Myklebust, H.R. 79

National Council of Social Services 57
Newton, D. 57
nursery nurses 36, 88, 234, 238, 241, 305

occupational therapists 53
O'Leary, K.D. 176
Osborn, J. 79

paediatricians 53
Painter, M. 80, 121, 127
parents 4, 39-49, 218 and passim
  attitudes 25-8
  illness 25
  see also Talking to Parents
Parry, M. 72, 73
Philps, J. 80, 92
physiotherapists 53
Piaget, J. 73
Pickering, D. and M. 67
play activities 4, 92-128, 217-8, 238-40
  imaginative 108-13, 115-20
  principles 93-6
  role of adult 96-7, 110-3
  social 120-7
playgroups 206, 305
Plewis, I. 80, 92
Porterfield, J.K. 151, 175
Price Williams, P.R. 49
Pringle, M.L.K. 57
problem-solving approaches 4, 177-202
  awareness of others 187-90
  group activities 181-97
  language activities 185-7
programme planning
  behaviour difficulties 90-1, 225-7, 238-9, 249-51, 252-3
  language 72-80
psychiatrist 285
punishment 136-7

Quigley, H. 74,79

Radin, N. 74, 79
Record Booklet 4, 30-1, 207, 290-302
record keeping 4, 29-31, 207, 220-2, 227-35, 240-2, 242-3, see also Record Booklet
reinforcement 132-6, 145, 155-6, 159-60, 161-2, 215
Richman, N. 32
Risley, T.R. 175
Reynell, J.K. 79
Riddick, B. 128
Roy, C. 80, 121, 127
Rutter, M. 32

Sainsbury, E. 57
Saltz, E. 127

Sarason, I.G. 133, 175
selecting approaches 203-23
separation from mother 24
Shackleton Bailey, M. 57
Sharp, A. 127, 128
Shea, T.M. 138, 175, 176
Shiach, G.M. 75, 80
Shure, M.B. 182, 202
sibling rivalry 28
Silberman, A. 176
Singer, D.G. 127, 128
Singer, J.L. 127, 128
Smilansky, S. 127
Smith, L.O. 74, 78
social workers 50, 53, 55, 285, 286
speech therapists 53, 81-2, 212, 285, 306
Spivack, G. 182, 202
Stevenson, J. 32
Stroud, J. 57
Swansea Assessment Schedules
see
Behaviour Checklist,
Behaviour Assessment,
General Assessment,
Talking to Parents,
Help from Others
Sylva, K. 70, 71, 80, 121, 127

Talking to Parents (Schedule 4) 4, 39-49, 225, 237, 248, 277-83
task analysis 163-77
chaining 164-6, 173
temper tantrums 47, 81, 82, 86, 87, 98, 122, 210, 222, 236, 244, 245, 246
Thomas, V. 70, 80, 89, 92
Tizard, B. 70, 80, 89, 92
Tough, J. 76-7, 80
Tsoi, M. 176
Tweddle, D.A. 166, 176

Vargas, J.S. 176

Walker, J.E. 138, 175, 176
Warnock Report 16, 20, 306
Webb, L. 92
White, S. 57
Willis, J. 176
Wilson, G.T. 176
Woodhead, M. 80

Yardley, A. 67
Yule, W. 176

CHILD STUDIES INDEX

*Alec 95-6
*Andrew 199-200
*Anna 154-6

Brian 20, 81-3, 208-22

*Christoper 65

*David 178, 179-80, 191,198

Eric 13, 26, 81, 98-101, 109, 236-46

*Frank 161-2

*Gareth 191

Howard 27, 34-7, 61-2, 66-7

Ian 28, 41-2

James 33-4, 204
Jane 200, 223-35
*Jenny 151-2
*Jimmy 168-70
*Joanne 198-9
*John 198
Jonathan 12, 22-3, 24, 25, 81, 106, 122

Karen 86-7

*Lucy 159-60

*Malcolm 156-8
Margaret 64-5
*Mark 128-30

Nicola 24-5, 61, 103, 108, 247-54

Philip 177-8, 179-81

Rachel 62
Richard 11, 81, 95, 96-7, 104, 108, 109, 113-4

*Sally 170-3
*Sarah 200
*Susan 198-9

Tom 239-41
*Tracey 199-200

William 12, 23, 24, 25, 81, 94-5, 103, 108, 123

* denotes imaginery child